W9-BXV-899

BOEING

IN

PEACE AND WAR

BOEING
IN
PEACE AND WAR

Eugene E. Bauer

TABA Publishing
Enumclaw, Washington

Copyright © 1990 by Eugene E. Bauer

Published by TABA Publishing
24103 S.E. 384th St.
Enumclaw, Washington 98022

All rights reserved. No part of this publication may
be reproduced or transmitted in any form or by any
means electronic or mechanical, including
photocopy, recording, or any information storage or
retrieval system, without permission in writing from
the publisher.

ISBN 1-879242-05-2 (hardcover)
ISBN 1-879242-04-4 (softcover)

Library of Congress Catalog Card No. 90-92124

Cover: Concept—Courtesy of Malcolm T.
         Stamper, Seattle, Washington

         Design—Bridget Culligan Design, Seattle,
         Washington

Photos: Courtesy of The Boeing Company
         Historical Archives

Book design, typesetting and production by
Media Weavers, Hillsboro, Oregon

Printed in the United states of America at Gilliland
Printing, Inc., Arkansas City, Kansas

To Lori

for
enduring faith,
infinite patience,
and helpful suggestions

ACKNOWLEDGMENTS

The author is indebted to the late Harold Mansfield, who graciously consented to the use of numerous quotes from two of his books, *Vision*, and *Billion Dollar Battle*.

Special thanks are extended to The Boeing Company Historical Archives staff, including Tom Lubbesmeyer, Dave Olson, Marilyn Phipps, Paul Spitzer, and Leone Vangelder, who enthusiastically searched out historical information and provided thousands of photos from which to choose.

Special thanks are also extended to Malcolm T. "Mal" Stamper, retired vice-chairman of The Boeing Company, for his helpful advice.

Above all, the author salutes the employees of The Boeing Company, past and present, who in the final analysis, by their devotion to excellence, made such a book possible.

Grateful acknowledgment is given for use of short quotes from a number of publications.

An American Saga, by Robert Daley. Copyright © 1980 by Riviera Productions Ltd. Reprinted by permission of Random House, Inc.

An Analysis of Labor Relations News Coverage in the Boeing Company Paper and the Union Paper During the Strike of 1948, by K. L. Calkins, University of Washington Master's Thesis, TH 17015. All rights reserved. Reprinted by permission.

Aviation Week & Space Technology, Copyright © August 4, 1980. All rights reserved. Reprinted by permission.

Business Week, Copyright © December 18, 1989. All rights reserved. Reprinted by permission.

Boeing News, multiple issues. Reprinted by special permission.

Clipped Wings, by Mel Horwitch, MIT Press, Copyright © 1982. All rights reserved. Reprinted by permission.

Forbes, Copyright © November 26, 1979. All rights reserved. Reprinted by permission.

Fortune, Copyright © September 25, 1978, and September 28, 1987. All rights reserved. Reprinted by permission.

Industry in the Pacific Northwest and the Location Theory, by E. J. Cohn, Jr., King's Crown Press, Copyright © 1954. All rights reserved. Reprinted by permission.

International Herald Tribune, Copyright © February 27–28, 1982, and September 12, 1985. All rights reserved. Reprinted by permission.

New York Times, Copyright © February 16, 1976, February 23, 1977, and February 15, 1979. All rights reserved. Reprinted by permission.

Ready All!, by Gordon Newell, University of Washington Press. Copyright © 1987. All rights reserved. Reprinted by permission.

Seattle's Economic Development 1880–1910, by A. N. MacDonald, University of Washington Ph.D. Thesis, TH 10395. All rights reserved. Reprinted by permission.

Seattle Post Intelligencer, Copyright © January 1, 1980. All rights reserved. Reprinted by permission.

Seattle Times, Copyright © March 20, 1984, June 3, 1984, and October 24, 1989. All rights reserved. Reprinted by permission.

Sky Master, by Frank Cunningham, Dorrance & Company, Copyright © 1943. All rights reserved. Reprinted by permission.

Technology and Change, by Donald A. Schon, Delacorte Press, Copyright © 1967. All rights reserved. Reprinted by permission.

The Grease Machine, by David Boulton, Harper & Row. Copyright © 1978. All rights reserved. Reprinted by permission.

Time, Copyright © April 7, 1980. All rights reserved. Reprinted by permission.

Wall Street Journal, Copyright © December 4, 1975, May 7, 1976, February 20, 1979 and October 9, 1980, Dow Jones & Company Inc. All rights reserved worldwide. Reprinted by permission.

Washington, Copyright © November, 1988. All rights reserved. Reprinted by permission.

William E. Boeing 1882–1956

Founder, Pacific Aero Products Company, becoming The Boeing Airplane
Company in 1917, and The Boeing Company in 1961. First president, elected
to chairman in 1922, continued as chairman until divesting in 1934.

PREFACE

Generations come and go, fading into the shrouds of history. Centuries live on, and are remembered fondly—or tragically—for all time. The twentieth century had its share of both euphoria and calamity. It will be remembered for its terrible wars and periods of uneasy peace—but more importantly, for its awesome strides in technology.

It was the century of antibiotics, atomic energy, automobiles, powered flight, radar, television, transistors, and xerography. It witnessed an explosion in electronics, spawning computers that exhibited the speed and adroitness to nearly challenge the human brain. Man rocketed himself to the moon and returned safely, sent obedient satellites to the planets and the vicinity of the sun—indeed, dispatched a lonely robot that escaped the solar system itself—entering the vast, unexplored reaches of the space beyond.

In 1900—as the century opened—with a mixture of fear and hope, President McKinley sent American troops to China to quell the Boxer Rebellion, while the British dispatched Lord Roberts to South Africa to shore up their forces, bogged down in their fight against the Boers. The world wars to come were destined to leave their indelible scars.

Some fifty companies, most of them in Detroit, were experimenting with combustion-engine-powered automobiles. Henry

Ford, in February, took a reporter from the *Detroit News Tribune* for a ride at the phenomenal speed of twenty-five miles per hour. The reporter was certain he was witnessing the dawn of a new era, and indeed he was. It had been more than 100 years since the first automobile—a single cylinder, steam-powered de Dion Bouton— appeared on the streets of Paris in 1769.

Still another new era, the age of manned flight—with more profound promise than the automobile—was growing on the horizon.

The automobile promoted an insular climate of narrow nationalism, focusing on materialistic motives—a divisive international economic force. On the other hand, airplanes began to bring people together—from all nations and from all walks of life—and before the end of the century, became a predominant factor in shaping their lives. For the first time in history, the world was beginning to be linked and bonded as had been visualized by Wendell Willkie in his *One World* in 1943. At last, the focus was on a common thread—the reality that the fragile Earth is surrounded by a hostile universe.

From the time of the mythical, wax-winged Icarus, the lure of the skies had captivated man's imagination. Leonardo da Vinci, the first pioneer in the science of flight, who lived centuries before the days of mechanical power, was limited in his experiments to contrivances attached to the human body. Four hundred years later— after the invention of steam and gasoline engines—government incentives for a practical flying machine were offered. In 1894, Senator Lodge introduced a bill in the U.S. Congress to award $100,000 to the inventor of a machine capable of carrying 400 pounds of passengers and freight.

Noted scientist, Samuel P. Langley designed, built and flew a model with a twelve-foot span and weighing thirty pounds, powered by a small steam engine. It flew two-thirds of a mile and achieved twenty-five miles per hour before running out of steam. The Wright brothers had begun experimenting on a machine for powered flight in their bicycle repair shop in Dayton, Ohio. They built their own air-cooled, internal-combustion engine—developing twelve horsepower.

There were many who were certain that flying machines could never be successful, and in 1903, a respected American scientist, Simon Newcomb, published proof that powered flight was impossible.

In Germany, Count Ferdinand von Zeppelin was pursuing lighter-than-air vehicles. In 1900—after working with balloons since 1891—he flew his first hydrogen-filled airship near Friedrichshafen. Its two sixteen-horsepower engines gave it a speed of fourteen miles an hour. Zeppelins were destined to play a strategic role in World War I. When the Belgians entrenched themselves in the impregnable fortress of Antwerp, zeppelins soon appeared in the skies—dropping bombs. Hydrogen-filled airships continued to be employed, until in 1937, the Hindenburg—after ten successful crossings of the Atlantic—was consumed in a ball of fire as it attempted to land at Lakehurst, New Jersey. Dirigibles were dead.

On December 17, 1903, the Wright brothers proved Newcomb wrong, when they maintained their manned craft aloft for twelve seconds, covering 120 feet of North Carolina beach at Kitty Hawk. Their success was more than a mere invention—rather the result of meticulous research and attention to detail in many disciplines, even employing a crude wind tunnel for testing scale models.

Persistence and determination counted heavily in this new field. Nevertheless, after the Wright brothers laid all skeptic notions to rest in subsequent flights, the U.S. Army remained unconvinced that airplanes could ever be put to military use.

Everywhere, it seemed new feats of flying were being announced, and improved craft were appearing. The fever had seized tinkerers, mechanics, engineers and scientists alike.

Glenn Curtiss, another American air pioneer—motorcycle builder and specialist in lightweight power plants—provided the engines for many of the early airplanes, including the first to thrill crowds at the 1904 St. Louis World's Fair, and the U.S. Army's first military aircraft, tested at Fort Meyer in 1905.

Curtiss went on to design and manufacture his own airplanes, and on the 4th of July, 1908, his *June Bug* won the *Scientific American* prize by staying in the air one minute and forty-three seconds. A year later, the first Curtiss *Pusher* appeared, again winning the *Scientific American* trophy, and leading to a successful series of patrol airplanes for the U.S. Navy.

On July 19, 1909, Hubert Latham headed his fragile plane from the coast of France toward the white cliffs of Dover. After seven miles, with the motor failing, he landed in the English Channel and was rescued by a torpedo boat. Louis Bleriot, survivor of fifty crashes, had crawled out of bed a half hour earlier than Latham—at 2:30 a.m.—limped to his plane, and thirty-seven minutes later, landed at Dover—first to cross.

Champion kite flyer of the Kansas prairies at age six, Glenn Martin made his first flight in a homemade plane on August 1, 1909. In 1909, too, the world's first great aeronautical meet took place at Reims, France. Thirty-eight planes were entered, and Curtiss won the Gordon Bennett trophy—two laps at 47.8 miles per hour. Hubert Latham set a new altitude record—powering up to 508.5 feet.

The same year that the Wright brothers first flew at Kitty Hawk, a young engineer with no knowledge of airplanes, came west to Seattle, Washington, to acquire new timber holdings, an ambition to build a yacht of his own, and an attraction to the vast, mysterious territory of Alaska. His name was William E. "Bill" Boeing.

Bill Boeing was not an inventor in the strict sense, but rather a master at innovation—and an uncompromising perfectionist—

establishing himself as one of the principal pioneers of the aviation industry.

Beginning in a primitive, isolated corner of the United States, how did Boeing manage to build the largest and most respected aircraft company in the world? It is the purpose of this book to provide the answers.

No attempt is made to discuss all the Boeing products, locations, or people. Such an undertaking would require several volumes.

CONTENTS

1

An Era Dawns

Observers on the seventy-sixth floor of the Columbia Building in downtown Seattle, Washington, on the morning of September 30, 1988, barely needed to lift their gaze to witness the unfolding of a once-in-a-century panorama. Two giant airplanes were flying in formation at 1,000 feet above the waterfront.

Both were Boeing 747s—old *Number One*, which opened a new dimension in air transportation exactly twenty years earlier—and the *Dash 400*, culmination of advances in design and production over a series of twelve commercial versions.

With no increase in body length, and only sixteen feet added to the span, the majestic new flying machine carried 400 passengers, twenty-seven more than the original—while increasing the range from 4,600 to 8,470 statute miles. New technology—much of it

The Giants—1988

The original 747-100 leads the newest derivative, the -400 in the skies over Seattle, capping a twenty year domination of the world's international skies.

developed in Boeing laboratories—allowed a reduction in crew size from three to two. Advances in avionics alone—changing from analog to digital instrumentation—cut the number of gauges and switches in the cockpit from nearly 1,000, to less than 400.

On the day of the flyby, Boeing had delivered 705 of a total of 877 on the order books, and the program had achieved that golden financial pinnacle referred to in the industry as a "cash cow."

Perhaps predictably, the 747 had run the course from unbridled optimism in 1968, to the brink of despair only three years later, before steadily climbing back out of the red.

When Presidents William M. Allen of Boeing and Juan Trippe of Pan American agreed by a simple handshake to a go-ahead on December 22, 1965, they put the corporate existence of both companies on the line. Boeing agreed to build the 747 and Pan Am agreed to buy twenty-five of them. There were no other orders. Even though universally pessimistic about the 747, the world's airlines hedged their bets—rushing to secure delivery positions—and within five months, fourteen carriers had pushed the firm order total to ninety-three. Almost overnight, Boeing had a $1.8 billion production backlog, an airplane on the drawing boards, and no plant suitable to fabricate the giant machine.

After clearing 250 acres of forest near Seattle, and constructing the largest building in the world, 5,000 employees were on the job by May 1967. Vice-President Malcolm "Mal" Stamper, a mid-century visionary in charge of the 747, named them *The Incredibles*. Caught up in the mystique of their fascinating new adventure, they wore Paul Bunyan stickers on their hard hats and lunch pails, and most refused to go home at the end of the shift.

Juan Trippe had prophesied that the 747 would be racing the intercontinental missile for man's destiny—as a powerful weapon for peace—as it transported millions of curious tourists to foreign lands. Mal Stamper confidently predicted sales of 600 airplanes by 1980.

The road to those achievements proved to be strewn with obstacles. In the fall of 1967, Lockheed had offered the L-1011, and two months later, McDonnell Douglas began taking orders for the DC-10—beginning a cutthroat competition for the long-range market.

Early in 1969, twenty-six airplanes, representing nearly the net worth of the company, were parked on the flight line—

undeliverable because of engine delays. For the first time in twenty-two years, Boeing recorded an operating loss.

With the U.S. economy heading for a recession in 1970, some U.S. carriers began putting their 747s up for sale, while others left them parked in the hangars. Continental Airlines sold their entire fleet of six. The program epitomized the feast or famine nature of the airplane industry.

Twenty years later, as The Boeing Company approached its seventy-fifth anniversary on July 15, 1991, the total backlog of orders stood at over $85 billion, including 1,800 commercial airplanes yet to be built. *Fortune* had named Boeing as the country's third most admired corporation, saying, "The company's managers, from top executives to the factory floor, are among the most skillful in the U.S."[1]

Earlier in the century, Boeing had been acclaimed as the premium builder of heavy bombers, from the B-17 Flying Fortress and the B-29 Superfortress of World War II fame, to the eight-engined giant B-52, mainstay of the Strategic Air Command since March 1954, and still its backbone into the nineties.

Still earlier, Boeing fighter planes dominated the skies of the Army Air Corps and the Navy. Other major ventures found the Boeing logo on many significant military and space programs, including the Minuteman missile, the Lunar Orbiter, the Saturn Apollo, and the Manned Space Station.

Bill Boeing, the company's founder, was brought up by his Viennese mother after his German-born father died when he was eight years old. The family was wealthy, with large holdings of timber and iron ore in Minnesota's fabulous Mesabi Range. He had the advantages of education both in Switzerland and in the United States, where he attended Yale in the Sheffield Scientific School in engineering. At age twenty-two, a year before he was scheduled to graduate, he headed west.

The scene had the stuff of legends. Coincidence, confidence, conquest, and courage merged to focus the talents and the vision of one man who attracted others of like minds. From the beginning, Bill Boeing laid down the exacting standards and the strict ethics that have pervaded the company throughout its life.

Seattle was an unlikely site for an airplane factory. Tucked away in the remote northwest corner of the country, the area was a vast ocean of timber, lakes, rivers, mountains, and islands. In 1880, then in its twenty-ninth year, it was still no more than a good-sized clearing in the heavy forests that covered the Puget Sound area. The main settlement along Elliott Bay was centered on a patch about a mile and a half long, which stretched three quarters of a mile back from its eastern edge. Some houses had been built as far north as Lake Union, and a few had reached Lake Washington, several miles to the east. MacDonald portrays the stark panorama—"The town's outer edges with its numerous ten foot diameter stumps, relics from the giant virgin Douglas fir forest; slashings from those newly felled, and the occasional forlorn tree which had been left standing among the debris, impressed the observer with the community's newness, rawness, and bleakness."[2]

The milestone that first set Seattle apart from the many small settlements in the Puget Sound area, was the discovery of coal at Newcastle, only ten miles away. The second significant factor—which began to ordain Seattle as the future heart of the Pacific Northwest—was the merchant fleet of steamships which had been attracted to its natural harbor.

During the next 30 years, the period from 1880 to 1910, Seattle took off—exploding from an isolated frontier town to a substantial city—with 237,194 inhabitants. No 30-year span in its history matches that period, which represented a sixty-sevenfold increase. In the nation at large, urban population had only tripled, and of the ten cities with similar populations in 1880, the highest—next to Seattle—was Los Angeles, with a twenty-sevenfold increase.

Land transportation evolved as the final key. In 1884, Seattle gained its connection to the east—via the Columbia River route, after the Northern Pacific Railroad completed its branch line north from Portland.

When the Great Northern Railroad reached Seattle nine years later, the city achieved terminus status for a major transcontinental connection, and in 1909, the Chicago, Milwaukee and St. Paul, the "Milwaukee Road," provided a fifth transcontinental route. Seattle was on the map—but lumber and coal made up 86 percent of all rail shipments.

By 1910, downtown Seattle appeared as a modern city, largely rebuilt after twenty-six city blocks had been destroyed by the great fire of 1889. A Seattle housewife could buy Campbell's tomato soup, Ivory Soap, or Post's cereal at the neighborhood store. Blatz's Milwaukee beer was available at the corner tavern.

However, in one major respect Seattle had not matured by 1910. In comparing it to ten similar-sized cities, only Washington, D.C. had a smaller number of people engaged in manufacturing.

In January 1910, America began to take its place in the new science of heavier-than-air flight, hosting its first international flying tournament in Los Angeles. The Europeans had forged ahead, and the achievements of the daring Frenchman, Louis Bleriot, were not lost on the adventuresome Americans.

At the air tournament, Boeing was among the spectators. None would have suspected the keen interest behind the thin-rimmed glasses of the tall, mustached man who appeared to be a college professor. His attention was riveted on a Farman biplane, a four-wheeled craft with two vertical tail surfaces and a wide cloth-covered horizontal surface installed considerably in front of the wings. The engine was attached behind the lower wing. As the aviator climbed from his seat on the wing and approached the crowd, Boeing led the excited group.

"Monsieur Paulhan, my name is Boeing," he announced. "I like the way you fly it." The Frenchman clicked his heels and did a quick bow. "Merci, Monsieur Boeing," he replied.[3]

Boeing inquired for details about the Farman airplane, and attempted to get permission for a ride on it. Paulhan was polite but evasive. The next afternoon, Paulhan completed forty-seven laps around the 1.6-mile course. The closest American, Charles Hamilton, had dropped out after twelve, and Glenn Curtis at ten. Boeing, again in the forefront of the spectator group, asked once more about a flight. Still polite, Paulhan suggested he would take him—a little later.

Time ran out after many dignitaries were taken up—Boeing eyeing each potential opportunity with anticipation. The next day was reserved for the cross-country event—to Lucky Baldwin's ranch, twenty-three miles away and back—for a prize of $10,000.

Stiff breezes were hazardous for the delicate craft, and when a gusty wind came up close to the starting time for the cross-country race, all the fliers balked—except the flamboyant Frenchman. The Farman lurched, lifted, and then steadied into the wind. The crowd shouted, some pursuing along the country roads on bicycles, motorcars, and even on horseback. In one of the motorcars, Madame Paulhan cried as she prayed aloud.

Paulhan held steady at an altitude of about 1,000 feet, made a successful turn over the Baldwin ranch and arrived back at the field in an elapsed time of one hour and two minutes. The crowd enveloped the triumphant aviator, two men hoisting him to their shoulders, as the yelling, pressing multitude surged around the airplane.

Boeing never saw Paulhan again. The inviting wings on which he had visualized himself were dismounted, crated, and hauled away for shipment back to France. The bitter disappointment which Boeing felt, though carefully concealed, became a further fire for his own ambitions.

In 1910 also, at lower New York Bay, a young boy of ten stood with his father, watching an air race. The Statue of Liberty was one of the turning pylons. The planes were open kites with pusher engines, and the boy could see the pilots manipulating the controls with feet and hands. He could see the propeller blades flailing. On each lap the planes flew close over the awed crowd, and one plane crashed. From that day on, Juan Trippe yearned to be an aviator.[4]

The Los Angeles meet was recreated later in the year at Belmont Park in New York. Americans like Glenn Curtiss, who was defending the Gordon Bennett trophy he had won at Reims the year before, were being followed with a national fervor.

In the crowd at Belmont, was a young navy lieutenant by the name of George Conrad Westervelt. As an engineer and junior officer with the Navy Construction Corps in New York, he had obtained permission to represent the Navy at the meet. Although Paulhan did not attend, French aviators dominated the event; with Leblanc and Hubert Latham winning ten of the speed events, flying Bleriot monoplanes. The Gordon Bennett trophy was won by Claude Grahame-White of England. Ralph Johnstone, who flew to an altitude of 9,714 feet in a thirty horsepower Wright Flyer, was the only American to set a world's record. The astounding progress in aviation surprised the young officer, and he noted with concern the quickening pace of the Europeans.

Westervelt's next assignment was out west at the Puget Sound Naval Yard in Bremerton, Washington, as assistant naval constructionist. Still later he moved to the Moran shipyard in Seattle. While there, he was introduced to Bill Boeing at Seattle's University Club.

Boeing purchased the Heath shipyard on Elliott Bay to build a personal yacht, and needing some nautical advice, invited Westervelt to visit his new enterprise. The two men, both bachelors, found many common interests. They cruised on Puget

Sound on weekends, played bridge, and talked about mechanical things. Westervelt, known as blustery and argumentative, easily penetrated the aura of aloofness attributed to the straightlaced Boeing.

Airplanes became a common topic of their conversation, and the restless vision of Boeing was peaked when a barnstorming flier named Terah Maroney brought a Curtiss-type seaplane to Seattle.

On Independence Day 1914, the two men arranged for a flight, the first for both, in Maroney's plane. Driving to Lake Washington, they found him waiting and ready to take them up. The plane sat facing a board ramp, its pusher propeller idling. The two straight wings were covered with muslin on both lower and upper surfaces. The plane was mounted on a sled-like float. The water-cooled engine was hung between the wings, its massive radiator forming a vertical backrest behind the pilot's seat.

Boeing, anxious for the adventure, flew first, climbing up beside Maroney on the front edge of the lower wing and steadying himself with his feet on an open footrest that resembled a shoeshine stand. A mechanic in overalls pushed the machine out into the water. Maroney gunned the engine in short bursts. Both men adjusted their goggles, and Boeing took a firm grip on the leading edge of the wing with both hands.

The plane taxied in jumps and spurts, the noise of the engine shutting out all other sounds as the struts vibrated in the wind with the increasing speed. The plane required a long takeoff run, and the water seemed to rush at them, with the wind beating on their bodies. Boeing gripped all the tighter. Abruptly, the ride became less violent. There was a bump and a jerk, a surge of power as Maroney poured on the gas, and the water dropped quickly away.

As the landscape tilted, Boeing realized they were banking and turning away from the lake. Looking down at the tiny buildings and the people who had been transformed to ant-like proportions, he marvelled at his feeling of detachment and freedom. Relaxing momentarily on his perch as the plane leveled off at about 1,000 feet, he felt a certain mastery over the land below. Perhaps that was the moment that Bill Boeing decided to learn to fly.

Westervelt, who had waited eagerly on the ground for his turn, seemed equally impressed in the air. In the days that followed, there were more flights with Maroney. Boeing examined every detail of the airplane. "I think it would be easy to build a better one," he said, finally confiding his thoughts to Westervelt. "Of course we could," the young naval engineer replied.[5]

Westervelt wrote to Jerome C. Hunsacker, professor of aeronautical engineering at the Massachusetts Institute of Technology (MIT), and designer of the first American wind tunnel, for information on the theory of stability and control, stresses, engines, and other technical criteria. He corresponded with experts in the embryonic field of flight, careful to glean the best from theoreticians and aeronautical engineers.

A local exhibition flyer, Herb Munter, came to Boeing's attention early, when in his careful, meticulous way of studying details, he was seeking the experiences of anyone he could find in the field. Thus, early in 1915, Boeing took Westervelt for a visit to Munter's shop on Harbor Island in the Duwamish River waterway. The shop consisted of a fifty-foot wide hangar of shiplap, built on sand that had been dredged up from the bay. Munter was working alone. Boeing inquired as to the type of craft Munter was building. "It's a Munter," he replied matter-of-factly.

In those days, each machine was a handcrafted article and no two were ever exactly alike. Boeing found that Munter was building his fourth airplane, the other three washed out in some stage of construction or testing. The first two had been built at home in the kitchen, based on a photograph of a Curtiss airplane in *Aerial Age*.

"Did you study engineering?" Boeing asked.

"No, I went to high school—nights."[6]

A plan was forming in Boeing's mind. The yacht he had commissioned Heath to build at the shipyard was a reality. Indeed, it was described as one of the finest and most technically advanced on the Pacific Coast. Now he thought about the possibility of building a pleasure airplane of his own—but only fleetingly.

The war in Europe, an area he had visited often, disturbed him. The possible role of the airplane as a decisive instrument was becoming sharply focused. In fact, aerial combat had already erupted, when on December 25, 1914, British residents of Southend-on-the-Sea were roused from their Christmas dinners by the sudden hum of airplanes.

Running, gawking into the streets, thousands looked skyward to see two German planes which had flown up the Thames River, being chased by two British aircraft. The first air battle of the war had been joined, 9,000 feet above the ground at the breathtaking speed of seventy miles an hour.

Soon after the meeting with Munter, Boeing and Westervelt invited him to lunch. "We're going to get a group together to build some airplanes," Boeing announced. "Will you join us?"[7]

No one was more pleased at Munter's acceptance than Bill Boeing—who recognized him as a visionary—cut from the same cloth.

1. Kenneth Labich, *Fortune*, 28 September 1987, 64.
2. A.N. MacDonald, *Seattle's Economic Development, 1880–1910*, (Seattle: University of Washington, Ph.D.. Thesis, 1959), 1.
3. Harold Mansfield, *Vision*, (New York: Popular Library, 1966), 8.
4. Robert Daley, *An American Saga*, (New York: Random House, 1980), 6.
5. Mansfield, *Vision*, 12.
6. Ibid., 13.
7. Ibid., 14.

Edgar N. Gott 1887–1947
President 1922–1926.

2

The Beginnings

With Herb Munter as the first employee of the yet-to-be-formed company, Boeing and Westervelt decided to build two airplanes, to be called the B&W. They would get engines from Hall-Scott in San Francisco, build the pontoons and wings at the Heath shipyard on the Duwamish River, and construct the fuselage at a rented hangar on Lake Union.

Meanwhile, in Los Angeles, the "Flying Duke," a young barnstormer by the name of Glenn Martin, was starting a new company to build the army's first training and bombing planes.

Introspective and reserved, Boeing did not always reveal his plans to those around him—but in his mind the next logical steps were forming—and sometimes he surprised his closest associates.

Meticulous and thorough, he was bent on understanding every aspect of this new science that had taken a consuming grip on his life.

After corresponding with Martin, one day he abruptly informed Westervelt—"I'm going down there to learn to fly."[1]

Learning to fly was only one of Boeing's purposes in going to Los Angeles to meet with Glenn Martin. He wanted to see the many new innovations that Martin was incorporating—the Day Tractor design with the engine and propeller in front; building a fuselage in place of the box-kite structure; and installing the vertical and horizontal control surfaces at the aft end—all forerunners of modern airplane design.

With aerodynamics still in the embryo stage, and with a paucity of wind tunnels, many of these innovations remained to be proved and refined in the air. Martin had only one trainer flying at the time, and when one of the five students crashed it, Boeing returned to Seattle, his training cut short.

Boeing had learned enough, and his creative mind was already racing ahead, contemplating improvements on the Martin plane. Thus, it was not too unexpected when he ordered a Martin T. A. Trainer.

Martin sent the crated parts to Seattle along with Floyd Smith, a pilot, who supervised the assembly of the airplane as well as topping off Boeing's instruction in the air.

The airplane and engine together cost more than $10,000, but Boeing had deep pockets—the result of his timber holdings. He also hired a mechanic, L.G. Stern, and seven men skilled in wood and fabric craftsmanship.

The Martin plane, referred to as a "gigantic bird" in Seattle newspapers, "making the other airplanes look like sparrows," was flown around the Puget Sound area by Boeing and Munter, who was himself still learning.

At about the same time, Boeing created a flying association, the Aero Club of the Northwest—a private club for friends. The B&W airplanes were to be built by Boeing to serve the club. The new hangar on Lake Union was part of the plan.

One day while Munter was flying with another member of the club, he banked too steeply, stalling the plane. Boeing, watching close by, groaned as the plane hit the water—disappeared—and quickly bobbed up, tail in the air and wings on the surface. Unhurt, the two men were brought ashore in a motorboat. Munter was apologetic, but Boeing told him to forget the airplane—the important thing was that they came through the accident safely.

The fuselage was retrieved for repair, but the pontoon had to be replaced. The Martin plane had been designed with a single pontoon in the center and sponsons near the outboard ends of the lower wing. Boeing quickly perceived the need for an improved landing platform and the B&W was designed with twin pontoons.

However, the immediate problem was to fabricate a new pontoon for the Martin. Thus, coincidentally, construction of the new airplanes started from the bottom up, based on the experience in woodworking gained on the Martin rehabilitation. Like everything associated with him, Boeing insisted that his pontoons be of the best quality. They were made of layered wood veneer, and riveted together, replacing the original plank construction. The Martin was soon back in the air.

When German submarines torpedoed the British luxury liner Lusitania in May 1915—with the loss of 124 Americans—concern about the war was brought to the dinner tables of the average American family.

Boeing, fearing that America was falling behind the Europeans, and the likelihood that we would be drawn in, began a campaign of his own to highlight the impending danger. In November, along with certain unidentified acquaintances, he took the Martin off from Lake Washington and flew a bombing run over Seattle.

Flying low over the downtown district, he dropped red cardboard bombshells. These cutouts were in the shape of artillery shells and carried a variety of warnings; America, citizens were warned, was unprepared to defend itself, and there was a critical lack of airplanes. "For national defense," one message urged, "encourage aviation...for our country needs more airplanes."[2]

The military had become the dominant force in aviation, and the German zeppelins, which had begun to bomb London in June, would soon bow to the sweep of the new technology.

Boeing, now with eight men in his employ, began construction of the B&W. Everything had to be started from scratch. After the pontoons, the wing ribs followed; however, shipyard techniques were woefully inadequate to build the fragile parts. Designed to saw timbers for ships, the yard did not even possess a jigsaw, so a subcontractor was brought in to make the lightening holes. The

B&W—First Boeing Airplane—1916
Gross Weight, 2800 lbs, top speed 75 mph, 125 horsepower.

first product was rejected. The second, although of improved quality, was also rejected. Boeing sent one of his own men to supervise the work. This emphasis on quality became the hallmark of Boeing products.

Charles "Charlie" Thompson, one of the early employees, who hired in as an electrician's helper at the age of fifteen, recalls that Bill Boeing was particularly interested in the wood shops. "Once he came through and noticed a workman cutting lightening holes in the wing ribs. These were three-ply wood, with several pieces put together and cut all at the same time. This workman made a few nicks, which immediately caught Boeing's attention. He said they were unsatisfactory. The workman said they were good enough. Without a word, Boeing picked up the ribs and ran them through the saw, throwing the pieces on the floor."[3]

Although Westervelt contributed strongly to the design of the B&W airplanes, working steadily while Boeing was in Los Angeles for flying lessons, he never designed another, and was gone before there was a company.

In January, 1916, Westervelt was assigned to navy fleet duties in the East. He resisted the move, attempting to resign, but in spite of appeals all the way up the command to the secretary of the navy, his resignation was denied.

Westervelt never drifted far from airplanes. Perhaps his most notable assignment was overseeing the construction of the first plane to fly across the Atlantic Ocean, the NC. Four of those flying boats were built, and on May 27, 1919, NC-4 landed at Lisbon, Portugal. He never returned to the West Coast, but lived long enough to see The Boeing Company lead America into the jet age.

During the first six months of 1916, Boeing's work force doubled in size, to twenty-three. With management duties increasing, Boeing brought in his cousin, Edgar Gott—with a degree in chemical engineering from the University of Michigan—as vice president. The hierarchy included superintendent, J.C. Foley; and foreman, L.G. Stern.

On the bright Thursday morning of June 15, 1916, Boeing realized the first major milestone in his airplane manufacturing efforts, as he proudly surveyed his new machine being readied for flight at the ramp on the tranquil waters of Lake Union, the fresh varnish of the spruce struts gleaming in the sunlight. Its 125 horsepower engine and its span of fifty-two feet were identical to the Martin trainer, but it was lighter, with an improved aerodynamic wing section.

Harold Mansfield describes the events that followed: Boeing kept looking at his watch. "Where is that Munter?" he inquired.

Superintendent Jim Foley said he was sure he would be along soon.

"I'll take it out myself," said Boeing.

He got in, taxied out to the middle of the lake, swung around to head north and gunned the Hall-Scott full out. The plane gathered speed. It skipped along for a time, throwing up a good deal of spray. Then Boeing lifted it into a quarter mile straightaway flight low over the water and set it down again. When he got back to the ramp, Munter had arrived. "Taxi it around and try out the controls," Boeing said, eyeing Munter. "That's all I want you to do. Don't fly it."

Munter taxied for several days, wondering if Boeing was afraid to let him fly. One day when he was practicing small hops off the water, he concluded it was time for action. He hauled back on the stick, roared into the air and winged across the city to Lake Washington. Boeing rushed over. "Don't ever do that again unless I authorize it," he ordered. Then he looked at the airplane with pride. "How was it?"

"Great."[4]

It would not be the last time a Boeing test pilot second-guessed the boss.

Boeing took the airplane to the Navy, and despite its approval, he was turned down for any orders. Disappointed but undaunted, he forged ahead—incorporating the Pacific Aero Products Company on July 15, 1916.

According to the articles of incorporation filed on that day, the new company would have ambitious objectives. It was to be "a general manufacturing business...to manufacture goods, wares, and merchandise of every kind, especially to manufacture aeroplanes and vehicles of aviation...." The articles would also allow Boeing to "...operate a flying school and act as a common carrier of passengers and freight by aerial navigation."

1. Harold Mansfield, *Vision*, (New York: Popular Library, 1966), 14.
2. *Boeing News*, 7 August 1987, 2.
3. Charlie Thompson, interview by Paul Spitzer, 28 August 1981, Boeing Archives.
4. Mansfield, *Vision*, 16.

3

The Crucible of War

The second decade of this century was one of the most significant periods in the history of American aviation. A number of farsighted, ambitious, and adventurous young visionaries were experimenting with various innovations.

Two of those early pioneers were named Loughhead. The name was soon changed to Lockheed, the way everyone misspelled it anyway. When the Wright brothers flew, the Lockheed brothers, Alan and Malcolm, were fascinated teenagers. After studying the new science of aerodynamics, and tinkering with different designs, they succeeded in building—and flying—a wood and fabric biplane called the Model G. That machine caught the imagination of the Bay area when it flew over San Francisco early in 1913. By a stroke of luck and his flair for showmanship, Alan Lockheed made a profit by charging $1.00 a head to fly daredevil passengers at the 1915 Panama-Pacific International exhibition. Those were heady times.

A year after the flight of the Model G, the Lockheed brothers joined up with another of the early pioneers, John Northrup, and they set up a business in an old garage in Santa Monica, California.

The Lockheed-Northrup team turned out hand made planes similar to the early Boeing models, but included a twin-engined, two-seat monster known as the F-1. On April 12, 1918, the F-1 flew from Santa Barbara to San Diego, a distance of 211 miles— quickly claimed as a new American endurance record.

Even before the B&Ws flew, Boeing decided that a plane could be built along their lines that would be suitable for navy training duties. Work was immediately begun on a new model, although the first dollar in profits was still to be made.

Bill Boeing, searching for additional engineering talent, hired Wong Tsoo, a young Chinese recently graduated from MIT, where he had studied under J. C. Hunsaker. Many new ideas were supplied through him from Hunsacker, who seemed to be actively interested in the new project. Wong designed the Model C, which flew on November 23, 1916.

Wong had incorporated some new innovations as a result of wind-tunnel testing. He put dihedral in the wing to improve stability, at the same time drastically cutting down the vertical fin, and eliminating the horizontal stabilizer—assigning its function to the placement of the wings—moving the upper wing to a position slightly forward of the lower wing. The elevator remained at the aft end with the tiny tail fin.

The new design troubled Munter, assigned to test the plane, and he was reluctant to fly it. The fin and rudder design didn't look right to him. With encouragement from Boeing, Munter took the plane off. Once airborne, he found difficulty in the turns.

Shaken, he landed on Lake Union, storming back to announce to designer Wong that he would not fly the airplane again until something was done about the small fin and rudder. The plane was altered and improved and finally accepted by the navy.

The war became a reality for America on April 6, 1917, after President Woodrow Wilson asked the Congress for a formal declaration. "The world must be made safe for democracy," he said. Less than two weeks later, on April 18, Pacific Aero Products was renamed—and the Boeing Airplane Company was born.

Soon Douglas Fairbanks and Mary Pickford were selling Liberty bonds, and school children were saving peach pits and dropping them in containers at grammar schools.

When the United States entered the war, the country was far down the list of air powers. The army had thirty-five pilots, six flying boats, forty-five seaplanes, three land planes, seven balloons, and one rigid airship.[1]

At the time, France had 1,200 military airplanes, and Germany 1,000 in addition to fourteen zeppelins.

The navy ordered fifty of the new Model C's. Boeing was determined to make the airplane better than anything flying for the navy, and he recognized the crucial importance of the pontoons in the performance of the final product. Their function as the launching mechanism for the plane was primary; however, weight was a major factor in the overall efficiency of the machine, and the pontoons represented a large fraction of the total airframe weight. He decided to concentrate on the pontoons, certain that the riveted design for the B&Ws—itself an improvement over the Martin—was already obsolete.

One day early in 1916, Dr. Henry Suzzallo, president of the University of Washington, came into the old Tokyo Tea Room to visit the young Pocock brothers, George and Dick, who were to become famous builders of racing shells. With him was a gentleman they didn't recognize. George recalls the meeting, which had a major impact on his career:

"These are the boys I was telling you about, Bill," he said. We had a newly finished "eight" in the shop awaiting shipment to the University of California. Bill whoever-he-was got under the boat and spent some time on his knees inspecting it with apparent interest. "This is the kind of work I want," he observed to Dr. Suzzallo, who by that time was at the door, tapping the floor with his cane and saying, "Come on Bill. I must go." Emerging from under the shell, Bill took out his card case, dropped a business card on the workbench, and said, "Come and see me as soon as you can." We looked at the card to see who Bill was. The card read *W. E. Boeing, Hoge Building, Seattle*.[2]

The Pocock brothers had commitments for some work in California, so it was near the end of the year before they returned to Seattle. With the war intensifying in Europe, many things had changed at the university, and the future of rowing seemed tentative. So, early in January 1917, as George recorded:

We went to see Mr. W. E. Boeing. He seemed glad to see us, and he said he would like us to build two sets of pontoons for his seaplanes. He said his plant manager, Jim Foley, would bring the plans and show us what he wanted. He did so, and it looked to be an interesting little job. After all, they were to be built of wood, and they weren't much different from small boats.

Foley asked what we thought they would weigh, since that was such a major factor. We told him "about 115 pounds each." He said, "If you can build them for that I'll buy you each a new hat." When we finished the first pair, one weighed 114 pounds; the other 116.[3]

Although the prototype for the "C" series did not receive rave reports after testing at Pensacola, the navy made a special comment on the "workmanlike job" on the pontoons. The fifty-plane order called for seventy-five pairs, including spares, and the Pocock brothers joined the Boeing work force. The old Tea Room

The Red Barn—1917

The Heath building, modified to house the workers and the manufacturing facilities for early airplanes, the Red Barn was one of the central buildings in the subsequent Plant I complex. The Red Barn has been moved to the new Museum of Flight near Boeing Field, and restored as a historical monument.

on the University campus was too small for a job of this magnitude, and the operation was moved to the Red Barn, Boeing's main building at the Duwamish plant.

George eventually became foreman of assembly while Dick took charge of pontoon construction, and with a dozen men, were soon turning out a pair of pontoons a day. The total order of 150 pontoons was completed before a single C Model airframe was assembled—passing a legacy of perfection in manufacturing processes to those who came after them.

After the departure of Westervelt, Bill Boeing sought to increase his engineering staff, which he viewed as the key to a strong company.

On May 2, 1917, Louis Marsh, having been told by a friend about the company, applied for a position, and was employed as a draftsman. Marsh had studied mechanical engineering at the University of Washington, and he was the first of a steady stream of talent that flowed to Boeing over the course of its corporate life. Indeed, the University of Washington was by far Boeing's largest single source for professionally trained people in the entire United States, and must be considered as a prime factor in Boeing's success.

Later in May of the same year, both Claire L. Egtvedt and Philip G. Johnson joined the company. Egtvedt, then a senior at the University of Washington, entered the engineering department to work on design and stress analysis. He was one of three students recommended by the dean of the school when W. E. Boeing asked for "the brightest students in the class."[4] Two months after hiring in, Egtvedt was appointed chief engineer, with Marsh as his assistant.

Johnson, a fellow student with Egtvedt in mechanical engineering, also entered the drafting department,[5] and soon became production manager. These key men were continuing champions of integrity of product—the heart that Boeing had brought to the company.

Notable also in 1917, was the hiring of a woman—a first for Boeing—and a first in the engineering department. Helen Holcombe was studying architecture at the University of Washington, and applied as a draftsman. John Foley responded in a positive manner. He sent a blueprint "to have duplicated and returned to us; and if same shows up favorably, we will be pleased to advise you further in the matter."[6]

Holcombe departed for a time to return to her studies, came back in 1922, when a second woman joined the company, and finally returned to architecture permanently. These women were the pioneers. By 1945, the 3,000-person engineering department included nearly 1,200 women.[7]

During the tenure of the Model C contract, Boeing made large additions to both the engineering and manufacturing departments. Mass production had begun, the plant spilling over with industry. Draftsmen worked from 7 A.M. to 11 P.M. The first plane was delivered in the spring of 1918, and the order was substantially complete by late summer. By the end of the contract, a new assembly building had been added to the expanding Boeing plant.

The mass production fever had not yet subsided when Boeing received a contract to build fifty HS-2L navy gunnery training planes. These were three-place flying boats, a Curtiss design that was in standard use by the navy, equipped with Liberty engines. This airplane was the ideal next step for the expertise learned in building pontoons. The navy commended Boeing for building the best HS-2 hulls at far less cost than at the other plants around the country. The giant Curtiss plant with over 14,000 employees required 2,400 man-hours to complete a plane. Boeing built them in 900.

The first American-built warplanes, Curtiss JN-4's, known as "Jennys," began to see action over France in May 1918. Two years earlier, American volunteers had flown British observation planes to locate the placement of men and artillery. At that time, there was still an air of camaraderie among the pilots on both sides, making a practice of waving a gloved hand and giving a nod as they swept by. The practice was short-lived. When a German pilot mounted a machine gun on a Fokker, the war moved to the air.

The ensuing fierce aerial battles became the center of attention around the world. This new dimension in warfare threatened to unhinge old concepts—it would not be long before the pilots dropped bombs—simply releasing them by hand over the side of their open cockpits. The era of flying aces dawned, as each side strove mightily to drive the other from the skies.

Most famous of the aces was Baron von Richthofen, the Red Baron, finally shot down at the battle of the Somme—in his

Fokker triplane—after destroying eighty Allied aircraft in the space of two years. America's leading ace, Captain Eddie Rickenbacker, accounted for twenty-two enemy aircraft and four observation balloons, returning from the war unscathed.

World War I proved to be the crucible for the airplane manufacturing industry in the United States. American enterprise had performed an awesome task to tool for the war, reaching a plant capacity for producing 21,000 flying machines a year when the war ended.

Among the builders were Aeromarine, Burgess, L-W-F, Sturtevant, Engel, Springfield, St. Louis, Standard, Dayton-Wright, Curtiss, Fisher Body, Thomas-Morse, and Boeing.

At the time of the Armistice, there were twenty-four companies, employing almost 200,000 workers. Curtiss predominated, turning out 10,000 airplanes—from the smallest to the largest—and 15,000 engines.

1. Frank Cunningham, *Sky Master*, (Philadelphia: Dorrance & Company, 1943), 75.
2. Gordon Newell, *Ready All!*, (Seattle: University of Washington Press, 1987), 52.
3. Ibid., 55.
4. *Annual Report*. The Boeing Airplane Company, 1957, 19.
5. For many decades, drafting and engineering were inseparable, with engineers doing their own drafting.
6. Boeing letter, J.C. Foley to Helen Holcombe, Boeing Archives.
7. *Boeing News*, 26 April 1945, 5.

4

Postwar
Depression

T he signing of the Armistice on No-
vember 11, 1918 signalled disaster. Within a few months, approximately ninety percent of the aviation companies had gone out of
business.

The poorly financed partnership of Lockheed-Northrup was
one of the casualties, missing the opportunities afforded by the
war. The sale of two seaplanes to the navy represented their total
contribution to the war effort. The young venture folded and the
Santa Barbara garage closed its doors. Malcolm Lockheed left the
aircraft business entirely, and for the next six years, Lockheed did
not exist as a company.

Boeing's superior performance in the manufacture of the HS-
2L gunnery training planes for the navy was not sufficient to avoid

the avalanche that overwhelmed the industry. At war's end the order was cut in half—to twenty-five planes.

Hopeful for the future, during the fat years of 1917 and 1918, Boeing engineers had been busy creating a new design, the B-1 flying boat. The B-1 was destined to make history—as a one-and-only—but could not fill the production gap.

In an attempt to hold the engineering force together, a modification of the B-1, the BB-1 was created. Postwar depression quickly settled into the plant.

However, even in periods of downturn, Boeing continued to seek outstanding people. One of these, hired as a draftsman in 1919, after completing his studies in engineering at the University of Washington, was Fred P. Laudan. As the work load in engineering also began to drop off precipitously, Laudan took on factory duties, and in later years was credited with fine tuning mass production in the Boeing plant, eventually rising to vice president of manufacturing.

Soon the engineering department was back down to two—Claire Egtvedt and Louis Marsh—who kept plugging along on new airplane designs. Faith in a future market flickered, but was kept alive.

Work for the factory was another matter. Crisis followed crisis. Employment dropped to thirty. There was talk about closing the plant. It would not be the last time.

Intent upon holding a nucleus of the manufacturing force together, Boeing officials decided to manufacture furniture. Phil Johnson was placed in charge of a production program. Chief among the new products were bedroom suites.

Another was the Speed Sea Sleds, a scow-bowed boat with an inverted V-bottom and remarkable power and speed for the period.

George Pocock wrote of this experimental effort:

Our first sea sled was a twenty-six-footer for Mr. Boeing's personal use. He was at that time courting his future wife, and we

Model B-1, One and Only—1919

Eddie Hubbard used this airplane to fly the nation's first privately contracted international mail route. Here, unidentified mermaids adorn the airship.

knew he was rather anxious to see this one completed so he could take her out joy riding. He used to come in quite often to the shop where we were building it and watch us work.

One afternoon he was sitting on a bench, and seemed to be in such good spirits that I thought I would ask him a question which was uppermost in the minds of everyone working for him. I said, "Mr. Boeing, it must be a problem to you to decide what to do with this plant. We know you are spending a great deal of money every week. The boys think every time you show up you have the key to lock this place up."

He replied, "No, it is no problem. I'm prepared to run it like this with the people I now have on the payroll as a nucleus, for another two years, *and after those two years, we will never look back.*"

How right he was in his faith and foresight. All his friends were imploring him to quit, lock the place up and cut his losses, but he refused to listen to the prophets of doom. It almost seems that some men are selected...divinely or not, who knows...to be leaders in their fields. William Boeing was one such man.[1]

In due course, the prototype sea sled was finished and ten were built. However, only three of them sold, the remaining seven sat, gathering dust until Prohibition took effect in January 1920. Fast rumrunners began bringing illicit cargoes from British Columbia, and the speed of the Boeing sea sleds—forty-five miles an hour—provided a vehicle capable of outrunning the Coast Guard. The seven sleds were sold immediately—for cash.[2]

The furniture business expanded from its mainstay, Queen Anne bedsteads, to include phonograph cabinets, showcases, booths, library tables, and stools. They even bid on interior design and renovation. A notable example was a $1,500 proposal to modify Mrs. Nettles Corset Shop.[3] At first, furniture and fixtures sold well. Then prices fell. Eastern manufacturers, closer to the market, were able to outbid Boeing. Soon, there were 720 bedroom sets on the factory floor and no takers. At one point, the factory manager reported a $100 cash balance after meeting the payroll. There was an outstanding note for $100,000 against the company.

The fall and winter of 1919 were grey indeed, as the fortunes of the company looked steadily worse. Bill Boeing was advancing money from his personal account almost weekly, and the specter of folding up the Boeing Airplane Company became his daily companion.

As historians reported later, there was no economic reason for Boeing to survive in the isolated Pacific Northwest.

1. Gordon Newell, *Ready All!*, (Seattle: University of Washington Press, 1987), 60.
2. Ibid., 61.
3. *Boeing News*, 11 August 1960, 4.

5

Postwar Progress

With thousands of hours of trial in the war, airplanes were ready to demonstrate their versatility and potential for peace.

In Europe, aviation history was made on February 9, 1919, when a commercial plane completed the first round-trip between Paris and London. The aircraft, named *The Goliath*, took off from England, and three hours and thirty minutes later, arrived at a French airport near Versailles. A twin-engined craft, *The Goliath* had a top speed of ninety-seven miles an hour. The pilot reported that the passengers did not complain about the long flight—they were busy smoking and playing bridge.

At home, on March 3, Bill Boeing and his hired pilot, Eddie Hubbard, completed the world's first international airmail flight from Vancouver, British Columbia, to Seattle. Flying a C-700

Model C—First Production Machine

Built for the Navy as trainers—1916–1918. Also established first regular airmail service between Seattle and Victoria, B.C. Eddie Hubbard and Bill Boeing with the first mail pouch.

seaplane, they carried a mail bag containing sixty letters. On the way to Vancouver, they encountered a snowstorm and were forced down, staying overnight in Anacortes. On the delivery flight back to Seattle, headwinds caused them to put down for gas twenty-five miles from their destination. Measured against the odds, the operation was a success.

On May 8, the U.S. Navy seaplane, NC-4, took off from Rockaway, New York, to begin the first successful transatlantic flight. The actual crossing was made in three hops: Trepassay Bay in Newfoundland to the Azores, across the Azores, and the final leg to Lisbon.

A new service—carrying the mail—was becoming popular all across the United States, and in June, daily flights were inaugurated between Chicago and New York.

Before the year was out, Captain Ross Smith, in a series of planned hops, flew from England all the way to Australia.

The following year, Eddie Hubbard, who had left Boeing and purchased the one-and-only B-1, was awarded the nation's first international airmail contract, flying between Seattle and Victoria, British Columbia. Hubbard had gained experience and credibility carrying private, last-minute, first-class mail to outbound transpacific steamers, and rushing mail from incoming steamers at Victoria to the trains in Seattle.

The B-1 was powered by a Hall-Scott L-6 water-cooled engine, producing 200 horsepower. It had a top speed of ninety-five miles an hour, could climb 3,500 feet in ten minutes, and land at a comfortably slow fifty miles an hour. With only slightly more than seventy-five miles separating the two cities, Hubbard could pick his holes in the weather. When the sturdy plane was retired from service eight years later, it had flown 350,000 miles and worn out six engines.

In spite of Eddie Hubbard's success in flying the mail with the B-1, Boeing's Washington D. C. representative, Joe Hartson, was getting nowhere in his attempts to gain orders for the plane. However, he finally landed a contract to rebuild and modernize DH-4 de Havilland observation planes. The original wooden fuselage structure was replaced with a new and revolutionary Boeing-designed welded steel tubing structure. Boeing modified 298 of these airplanes for the army, earning a profit on every unit.

The spark of creativity continued to burn brightly in the two-man engineering department, but Claire Egtvedt was concerned that there was no chance to embark on a new venture. He decided to confront Ed Gott with his dilemma. Gott had been appointed to president when Bill Boeing moved to chairman in May 1922. Going to Gott's office, Egtvedt found Boeing there also.

"We are building airplanes, not cement sidewalks," Egtvedt began. "If you want to build cement sidewalks, then you can do away with engineering. Just mix the materials, pour them into a form and collect your money. But if you want to build and sell airplanes, you first have to create them. That takes research and development and testing and engineering. The airplane isn't half what it ought to be. Can't we hire a few engineers and try to build a future?"

Ed Gott seemed about to reply when Boeing spoke, nodding. "I think Claire is right."[1]

Although Egtvedt gained confidence after Boeing's unequivocal support, there was no way to get original designs into production.

At McCook field in Dayton, Ohio, where the purchase decisions were made for army airplanes, others had their own ideas of what was needed. I.M. Laddon, design engineer at McCook, had dreamed up a mammoth armored attack plane known as the GAX. A triplane with two Liberty engines, it bristled with guns. The engine nacelles and bodies were completely covered with heavy armor plate. For the safety of the gunners, armored windows were incorporated, consisting of slotted steel plates which rotated to allow gunners to see a flickering view of the outside—similar to motion-picture shows.

Boeing built ten of these giants during 1920 and 1921—a plane four times the weight and seven times the horsepower of the B&Ws.

The army had not called for any new pursuit plane competition. Anxious to get something moving, Egtvedt launched an intense review of the limitations of the current designs. He watched young pilots go through mock combat games, quizzing them for the important features of an ideal fighter. To a man, they called for a machine stripped for action. Light—maneuverable—fast—the attributes still demanded in modern fighters. Egtvedt pored over details. The possibilities excited him, and he became convinced they could build a machine good enough to sell itself.

When Egtvedt and Marsh were satisfied with their preliminary design concept, they went to Bill Boeing for approval. "What I'd like to do is to go out on our own to build the best pursuit we can," Egtvedt said, "our own pursuit, using our own money."

Boeing was on his feet, looking over Elliott Bay toward the Olympic Mountains. Egtvedt kept up the momentum. "We should go to all the sources available," he continued, "here and abroad, to get information and data. We wouldn't have to put in all the contrivances and devices that the Air Service thinks up. It would be designed for one purpose only—combat work."

Boeing didn't even ask how much the project would cost. He spun around. "That's exactly what we should do," he said emphatically. "Do it on our own. Keep it secret. Develop the best pursuit that can be built. Then we'll take it back to Dayton and show them what we can do."[2]

While the new pursuit design was incubating, the company continued to seek business to keep the factory busy. When the army called for bids on a sizeable order of MB-3A pursuit planes, Boeing was ready. The plane was a design of the Thomas-Morse Airplane Company of Ithaca, New York, with an airframe similar to that of the famous French Spad fighter. Although this model emerged too late for combat, it was the outstanding American fighter design of the war period.

Thomas-Morse had already completed and delivered 50 machines at the time of the new bid request—and was well along on the learning curve. The order was a potential plum—200 planes—the largest ever placed.

Boeing officials did some plain and fancy figuring, submitted their bid, and held their breaths. The bid was considerably below the next lowest.

While the losers smugly watched to see Boeing go on the financial rocks, the company dug in. The total order was delivered in a six-month span between July 29 and December 27, 1922—at a profit. As Bill Boeing had predicted in 1919, the company never looked back.

In the back room of a barber shop on Pico Boulevard in Los Angeles, on June 21, 1920, Donald W. Douglas formed the Davis-Douglas Company. David R. Davis, a wealthy sportsman, had provided the financial backing to build a one-only, Liberty-engined plane for an attempt to be the first to fly across the continent nonstop. A rented second floor of an old planing mill served as the factory.

At the time, Douglas was the sole employee of the new company. Soliciting help from associates with whom he had worked at the Glenn Martin Company in Cleveland, he soon expanded the work force to six.

The year of 1920 was late when measured against many of the other pioneers in the fast-moving airplane industry. Nevertheless, this nucleus of six men grew to become one of the largest and most famous aviation companies in the world.

Donald Douglas was well prepared for the task. An engineering genius, he abandoned his love for ships at an early point in his career, and embarked on aviation. Born in Brooklyn, Douglas initially followed in the footsteps of his elder brother, entering the Naval Academy at Annapolis in 1909. With his interest shifting from ships to airplanes, he resigned in 1912, prior to graduation, to begin his career in aeronautical engineering, a science, most of which had yet to be developed.

Enrolling as a student at MIT, the young Douglas was told he would require the full four years to graduate, despite his work at the Naval Academy. Douglas replied stoutly, "I'll do it in two years." And he did.[3]

When Douglas was graduated from MIT, Louis Bleriot in France, had already built more than 800 planes of 40 different types.

Impressed with Douglas' ability, the faculty at MIT, offered him his first job. Carrying a grand title, "Assistant in Aeronautical Engineering," the position paid an annual stipend of $500.

Remaining at MIT for only one year, Douglas aided Commander Jerome Hunsacker in the design of the first truly efficient American wind tunnel, and in 1915 he accepted an engineering position with the Connecticut Aircraft Company, working on the first dirigible to be built for the United States Navy.

Meanwhile, out in Los Angeles, Glenn Martin had started a new company to build the army's first training and bombing planes. Martin needed a chief engineer, and having heard excellent reports on a young man named Donald Douglas, invited him to join the Martin Company.

However, Douglas had itchy feet, and a year later moved back to the East Coast, joining the U.S. Signal Corps as its chief civilian aeronautical engineer, to supervise the task of adapting heavy engines to light planes. The solution was apparent—the planes required redesigning—a venture exactly suited to Douglas' liking.

Martin also moved to the East, forming the Glenn L. Martin Company in Cleveland, in March 1918. One of his first recruits was Donald Douglas, who became chief engineer on the MB-2 bomber program.

Douglas' yearning to go on his own intensified, and believing that financing would be easier in Los Angeles, he resigned and headed West. The result was the Davis-Douglas Company.

The single airplane, the *Cloudster*, with a mission to be first on a nonstop flight across the United States, never came close, landing in Texas with a stripped timing gear. By the time the plane was transported back to Los Angeles and refitted for a second attempt, history overtook the program. Just as the *Cloudster* was ready to take to the air, Army Lieutenants Oakley Kelly and John Macready landed in San Diego in a Fokker T-2, the first to span the U.S. nonstop. The date was May 3, 1923, a day to remember—the idea of flying regular flights from coast to coast began to occupy the minds of many in the new industry.

Douglas was able to win an order for three torpedo planes for the United States Navy, the DT-1. However, he was fresh out of money to begin the project, and the government would not make a payment until the first plane was partially completed. Even with a $120,000 order in his pocket, he was helpless to proceed. Finally convincing Harry Chandler of the *Los Angeles Times* of the worth of the project, Douglas was able to borrow $150,000 from the bank—with the signatures of Chandler and nine other prominent Los Angeles businessmen as collateral.

The Davis-Douglas Company was disbanded. In its place was formed the Douglas Company, and in 1922, the forty-two-man organization moved to a large, vacant building on Wilshire Boulevard in Santa Monica, an abandoned movie studio of the Herrman Film Corporation.

Orders for torpedo planes increased. At the time, General Billy Mitchell—in command of the United States air forces at the close of the war—had thrown down the gauntlet to the navy, claiming that battleships were obsolete—sinkable by air-carried torpedoes.

By 1923, Egtvedt's visionary fighter had been transformed to reality. The XPW-9 pursuit, embodying a welded steel tubing fuselage and a number of other innovations, became the prototype for a long series of army and navy fighters. The Boeing-designed oleo landing-gear struts represented a first for production military aircraft. The radiator was mounted in a tunnel beneath the engine, another first that was widely copied. With a Curtiss 425 horsepower engine, it had a top speed of 160 miles an hour, as compared to the MB-3A's maximum of 140. Its absolute ceiling of 22,850 feet compared to the MB-3A's ceiling of 21,200.

With the introduction of its PW-9 pursuit, Boeing began to carve out a reputation of leadership in military aircraft production. Modifications—through a D Model—continued to improve performance. A navy version, designated as the FB, incorporated a hoisting hook, arresting gear, and improved landing gear for carrier operations, followed. A still later spin-off design, the FB-4, was an experimental model with a Wright P-1 air-cooled 450-horsepower engine. It was not long before the navy turned entirely away from water-cooled engines.

The Boeing philosophy, transmitted to Egtvedt and his engineering staff, and now firmly entrenched throughout the company, was to keep reaching for a piece of untravelled sky. Thus, in 1923, with the PW program barely started, Louis Marsh and E.N. Gott journeyed to Washington, D.C. to discuss the navy's requirements for a completely new trainer. A few months later, the NB-1 emerged—built entirely on speculation.

The plane was dramatically different from anything that Boeing had ever built. It was a two-place biplane with a two-bay wing structure, possessing an extreme degree of interchangeable parts to enhance maintainability. Both wings and ailerons were interchangeable, from upper to lower, and from right to left. It could be readily converted from a primary to a gunnery trainer, and provisions were made for interchanging land and sea gear.

The original NB-1 was the first Boeing plane to be powered by a radial engine—the Lawrence J-1 nine-cylinder 200-horsepower unit—which preceded the Wright Whirlwind, later incorporated on the navy FB-4. The plane, noted for its ease of flying, was designed as a non-spinnable airplane, and no one ever succeeded in spinning it as originally rigged. This novel feature caused the original design to be rejected by the navy—requiring a spinnable machine for training purposes. The difficulty was overcome by incorporating several changes, including a longer fuselage.

The engineering staff continued to build, the University of Washington contributing the major share, including Jack Kylstra, later to become a project engineer, and Leslie R. Tower, making his mark as a test pilot.

Boeing's new successes seemed to assure the survival and growth of the company, however competition, always brisk, would become increasingly formidable.

1. Harold Mansfield, *Vision*, (New York: Popular Library, 1966), 24.
2. Ibid., 26.
3. Frank Cunningham, *Sky Master*, (Philadelphia: Dorrance & Company, 1943), 53.

Philip G. Johnson 1894–1944
President 1926–1933 and 1939–1944.

6

Airmail Comes of Age

In the summer of 1923, a smartly dressed young army officer walked into the former Herrman film studio on Wilshire Boulevard in Santa Monica. He introduced himself as Lieutenant Erik Nelson, and asked to see "Mr. Donald Douglas." His mission was to discuss designing and building four airplanes capable of flying around the world. Douglas was away in the east, but a rush wire brought him back in a hurry.

After enthusiastically listening to the army's proposal, Donald Douglas sat down at his drafting board and designed the *Douglas World Cruiser*, an airplane based partly on his successful DT series torpedo planes, but incorporating many new features. The DWC's were designed to operate either as land or sea planes.

Under the direction of Major General Mason M. Patrick, the flight had been planned for specific purposes:

To demonstrate the feasibility of aerial communication and transportation between the various continents; to make the people of the world conscious that aerial transportation was able to meet any and all conditions under which it might be forced to operate; to arouse interest in aircraft as a vital force in the marts of commerce; to prove that planes could operate off the beaten path of regular established air routes and where no other means of modern transportation could operate effectively and efficiently; to show that aircraft could be kept going despite varied climatic conditions and that its days of "pampered flying" were in the past.[1]

The Army Air Service had been planning the flight for many months. It was to leave from Santa Monica, cover some twenty-two countries and approximately 25,000 miles, and return to Santa Monica in six months. Each plane had been named after a prominent city: the *Boston*, the *Chicago*, the *Seattle*, and the *New Orleans*. On March 17, 1924, the planes were ready, and after a two hour fog-bound delay, they headed north for Seattle. Difficulties on the first leg caused postponement, and the official start became the Sand Point Flying Field on Lake Washington. The date was April 5. Pontoons, installed at Seattle, remained on the planes until they reached Calcutta, where they again became land planes. Leaving Hull, England, the pontoons went back on for the hazardous, multi-hop trip over the Atlantic. After again becoming land planes at Boston, they flew to Santa Monica, landing amid an acre of roses on September 3. On September 28, the around-the-world flight was officially completed, when the planes returned to Seattle.

Actual air time was fifteen days, eleven hours and seven minutes. Two of the original four planes made the entire circuit. The *Seattle* hit a mountain peak near Dutch Harbor, and the *Boston* capsized and sank during towing after an oil pump failure had forced it down near the Faeroes on the leg to Iceland.

With the postwar slump fast fading into history, the country was in a vibrant mood. Calvin Coolidge, who completed the late Warren G. Harding's term, and was reelected in 1924, proclaimed that "the business of America is business."

Mail, carried by air, can properly be said to date from May 15, 1918, when army planes flew between Washington, D.C. and New York City on an experimental arrangement with the Post Office Department. Later in the year, on August 12, the Post Office Department assumed complete control of the airmail program, building up a system of fourteen domestic routes.

In 1925, after passage of the Kelly Bill on February 2, airmail was contracted to private operators. On November 7, Postmaster General Harry S. New announced the first route awards: Boston–New York; Chicago–St. Louis; Chicago–Dallas–Fort Worth; Salt Lake City–Los Angeles; and Elko, Nevada–Pasco, Washington. All five were operational by mid-1926.

Graduating from Yale at age twenty-three, Juan Trippe was a serious individual, who most considered would become a banker. On the contrary, he was determined to make a business out of aviation. He decided to buy some planes and start an airline. In 1922, Trippe organized Long Island Airways, capitalizing it at $5,000, putting up half himself, and selling stock for the rest. Flying was still only slightly faster than crack trains or cross-country busses. It was even slower when the handicaps of no flying in bad weather nor at night were considered—and no landing in the centers of cities. None of these drawbacks dampened Trippe's drive.

When hard times caused the collapse of Long Island Airways, Trippe continued to bid on airmail contracts. He charged ahead, forming new companies in rapid-fire order: Alaskan Air Transport, Buffalo Airlines, Eastern Air Transport, Colonial Air Transport, and more—each time bringing together groups of men, arranging financing, laying plans. Trippe was on a fast learning curve.

When his Alaskan Air Transport failed to get a contract for mail, he formed Eastern Air Transport on September 25, 1925. Two days later they submitted a bid for the New York–Boston airmail contract. Unsuccessful, he merged with his competitor, Colonial Airlines, changing the name to Colonial Air Transport. The moment the merger was announced they secured the contract. Upon signing, Colonial had no planes, no employees, no route system, and no landing fields. Trippe hired men, negotiated for aircraft, rented fields, and planned for the future.

He ordered four trimotors; two Fokkers and two Fords, announcing the order as the largest for commercial aircraft ever placed in the United States.

There was much to learn. Day after day, Trippe watched at the dirt airfield in New Brunswick, New Jersey as the airmail planes came in from the other side of the continent, and when they landed, he quizzed the pilots about their problems. One of the pilots he talked to was Charles Lindbergh.

Colonial Air Transport, still without its trimotors, commenced airmail service between New York and Boston on July 1, 1926, using single engine machines.

The Boeing fighter series, created in the tradition of building the best product, had put the company on a sound financial basis. With an expanded engineering department, Egtvedt found it possible to do a substantial effort in preliminary design, creating the Model 40.

The single place "40" was completed in the summer of 1925. Powered by a 400 horsepower water-cooled, V-type Liberty engine, it had a cruising speed of 125 miles per hour, a range of 550 miles, and a service ceiling of 15,700 feet.

The plane embodied novel features of structure and arrangement that were intended to make it highly desirable for commercial purposes. Its fuselage consisted of three sections: an engine section of welded steel tubing, readily detachable; a wood monocoque midsection of two-ply veneer, with spruce plywood bulkheads, ash ribs, and mahogany outer planking, which provided two mail compartments clear of any structural members or cross wiring; and a steel tail section of welded tubing.

During the rush of activity on fighter planes, few had paid much attention to the part of Bill Boeing's original charter which called for "acting as a common carrier of passengers and freight by aerial navigation." Eddie Hubbard had gone to California where flying was accelerating. Phil Johnson wanted to get him back. He visualized a mail and passenger airline around Puget Sound, including Victoria and Vancouver, B.C. Boeing was enthusiastic, directing Johnson—who had been appointed president in February, after the departure of Ed Gott—to invite Hubbard to rejoin Boeing. There was no immediate response.

Model 40 Series—1925–1931
First steel welded tubing fuselage structure.

Opportunities were again perceived by Alan Lockheed and John Northrup. They revived their operation in 1926, renaming it the Lockheed Aircraft Company, and moving their headquarters to Hollywood.

The result of their new efforts was an eye-catching, high winged monoplane called the Vega, which vaulted into international prominence, pushed by promotional pizzazz that was to become the Lockheed hallmark.

Promotion, in pure Hollywood style, was seized upon by Alan Lockheed as the way to proceed. He persuaded George Hearst of newspaper fame, to buy his first Vega, who entered it in the 1927 Dole race from California to the Hawaiian Islands. In spite of the catastrophic loss of the first Vega toward the end of the race, the sleek new plane had attracted worldwide attention.

A few months after Hubbard received Johnson's letter, he appeared in Seattle, bursting with an idea of his own. The United States Post Office, in November 1926, had announced plans to put its Chicago-to-San Francisco airmail route up for bids for private operation.

Johnson was away from the office, and Hubbard went to Claire Egtvedt. "This is the opportunity of a century, Claire. I've got all the figures on mileage and pounds of mail carried. If you can produce the planes, I know we can operate them successfully."

Egtvedt, taken by surprise, reminded his old friend that he was talking about a huge undertaking. "It's a lot of country. The distances are great, as you know. You'd have winter blizzards to contend with, and all that."

"We could do it."

"You'd have to fly at night. Are the beacons in, all the way?"

"Every twenty-five miles."

Thinking of the airplanes that would be needed, Egtvedt found himself tumbling fast. "We could modify the '40,' I expect. Probably we could make room for a couple of passengers and still have space for the mail."

Egtvedt's mind raced, thinking how he could redesign the plane with a new Wasp air-cooled engine to replace the heavy water-cooled unit. He estimated he could save 200 pounds. After reviewing the performance details, they decided to go to Bill Boeing for approval.

Harold Mansfield describes that encounter:

After laying it all out for him, Boeing was silent. "This is something foreign to our experience," he finally ventured.

"I've logged 150,000 miles on the Victoria route without trouble," Hubbard said, "and made money at it."

"I think you're talking now about something far different. This is over the whole western half of the country. You've got mountain ranges and winter storms to contend with. It would be a mighty large venture. Mighty risky."

They went over it all once more. When there was nothing more to say, Egtvedt and Hubbard departed. "It was a good try," Egtvedt said.[2]

But there was a disposition in Bill Boeing that did not show behind his stern look. It had strong roots, going back to the phrase he had inserted in their original articles of incorporation, and to the fact that he liked to finish what he had started. He knew he had the resources. By now his men had built a good reputation. If anyone could, they could do it. He found it difficult to avoid acknowledging this, as he tossed through the night. By morning the idea had taken control.

Boeing arrived at the plant early, eager to go over the figures one last time. The Post Office would allow up to $3.00 per pound for the first 1,000 miles and thirty cents for each 100 miles beyond that. The figure Egtvedt and Hubbard had come up with was $1.50 per pound for the first 1,000 miles and fifteen cents for each additional 100.

"Those figures look all right to me," said Boeing finally, deci-
sively. "Let's send them in."[3]

In January 1927, word came back that Boeing was the low bidder—extremely low. The nearest bid was $2.24. The postmaster
general doubted that the Boeing bid was realistic. Other companies had assured him, he said, that the mail could not be carried for
such a low figure, and he did not want a bankrupt carrier on his
hands. Thus, he demanded the full $500,000 bond to insure per-
formance.[4] Bill Boeing personally underwrote the bond, and on
January 15, the contract was awarded. On February 17, 1927, the
Boeing Air Transport Company was incorporated, the second step
in fulfilling the original charter of July 15, 1916.

The plan called for building a fleet of twenty-five planes, to be
ready on the line in five months—by July 1, 1927. The men bent
to the task, the chance of realizing their dream within reach.

The redesigned plane, designated the 40A, had a fuselage constructed entirely of welded steel tubing, covered with fabric, replacing the combination steel and wood construction of its
predecessor. The landing gear had been redesigned, adapting the
new Boeing oleo shock absorbers to commercial use. The wings
were redesigned with a new airfoil section for improved performance. The plane was equipped for night flying. Accommodations
for two passengers were provided in the fuselage behind the engine firewall, and the cargo capacity was increased to 1,200
pounds.

Everything was coming up roses in 1927. The 15 millionth "tin
lizzie" Model T Ford rolled off the Detroit assembly lines; the
"iron man," Lou Gehrig, hit three homers in one day and Babe
Ruth hit sixty for the season; Al Jolson starred in the first "talkie"
moving picture; Gene Tunney retained his heavyweight boxing
title against Jack Dempsey in the famous "long count" match; and
two army fliers, Lieutenants Lester Maitland and Albert
Hegenberger flew from California to Hawaii, the longest ocean

flight on record. However, history would record May 21 as the day in 1927 which overshadowed all other events.

On that day, a lanky, softspoken aviator landed his single place Ryan monoplane at Le Bourget Airport in Paris. Flying alone, Charles Lindbergh had completed the first nonstop flight from New York—and the future of air travel had suddenly become a subject of common conversation.

At Boeing, the race to build the mail planes finished with a hair-thin margin. On June 30, exactly on schedule, all twenty-five planes were gassed and waiting on the line, ready for the official start, the midnight transfer of the mail at Omaha to the new airline—the Boeing Air Transport Company. The next day, the line inaugurated passenger service.

Harold Mansfield captures the aspirations and anxieties of that period in aviation history:

The first passenger to fly in the Model 40A was a courageous Chicago newspaper woman, Jane Eads, of the *Herald and Examiner*. She was the center of attraction at the Chicago airfield—in high heels, knee-length business suit, feather boa and felt cloche—headed for the clouds. At 9:30 P.M., on July 1, in the harsh white of arc lights, Pilot Ira Biffle helped Miss Eads up on the step pad of the lower wing and through the low door to the tiny cabin between the two wings. Biffle jazzed the motor twice and pushed out into the black.

Jane's heart palpitated as she began her role of trail blazer in a new form of transcontinental travel. The pilot, out of sight and out of hearing in the open cockpit behind, seemed far away. Alone in the night, behind the constant drone of the motor, Jane found companionship for a time with a thin crescent moon beyond the left wing. Now and then a sparkle of light drifted by in the black below. She wasn't sleepy. She turned the switch on the glazed dome light in the ceiling. It was cozy, the sea green of the little walls broken only by the sliding window on either side. She let in the cool air. This was fun, she thought.

Later the crescent disappeared and Jane began to feel rocky. The plane tilted and tipped, then dropped as in a hole. She wasn't sure if it was supposed to act this way. Then with a hard jolt she realized they were landing. At Iowa City she admitted, "I was scared."

They passed over Des Moines without coming down. A city without buildings, just strings of jewels. The flight over western Iowa was under a canopy of stars. It seemed strange that the sky should be lighter and more real than the earth below. The plane flew straight and steady into the western night. The changeless roar of the engine was strong, sweet music now to Jane Ead's ears. How odd, how wonderful, she thought, to be settling for the night up here. She found the leather-cushioned seats just large enough to curl up on, kitten fashion, and it was peace.

The landing jolts of Omaha awakened her. Reporters were there to interview her. "I could fly forever," Jane glowed. "I love it." She transferred to a new plane, piloted by Jack Knight. Shoving off at 1:45 A.M., Knight wished her a "merry trip," and she called back gallantly, "Same to you—and a safe one."

Before morning the air grew choppy. Great flashes of lightning lit up the sky. The cracking streaks seemed to be breaking all about them. The plane was lifted and thrown about. Jane put her head on her knees and tried not to think about falling. Then it ended as suddenly as it had begun. There was a yellow fringe on the horizon behind, which grew and flooded the earth with a golden glow. She remembered how a pilot had told her he never knew why the birds sang so sweetly until he saw his first dawn from the sky. They came down at North Platte, then lifted again for Cheyenne, with the sun setting fire to the edge of the clouds on the horizon ahead.

Out of Cheyenne, past the bald, rippling foothills, she could see in the distance the snow-crested magnificence of the Medicine Bow range. Hugh Barker, the new pilot, pushed the mail plane higher and higher. Jane grew drowsy and her legs were heavy with the altitude and the bumping. The road seemed as rocky here as it was below. They skimmed past Elk Mountain and into Rock Springs.

A veteran now of ups and downs and the vast, changing topography of the States, Jane flew on past the white flats of the Great Salt Lake country, the forbidding waterless gulches of Nevada, the ultramarine blue of Lake Tahoe, the yellow hills beyond. Suddenly the hills opened into San Francisco Bay. Twenty-three flying hours after leaving Chicago, Jane Eads put her feet on California soil, like an explorer who had discovered a new world—air transportation.[5]

The new airline made money. With public interest focused on air travel in the wake of the Lindbergh flight, the sky trail to California had come to stay. Finding that air travel was not a certain way to the grave, more and more passengers purchased tickets.

Winter proved to be tougher for the pilots, with snow piled deep in the Rockies and unpredicted blizzards sweeping in without warning. They were tracking the weather by telegram, but many times the weather closed in and they had to come down—following railroad tracks or known valleys and passes. There was a burning need for two-way radio communication.

Major differences developed between Trippe and the president of Colonial, and after a vote by the stockholders, Trippe was bought out and left the airline.

He set out to form a new company, raising $300,000 and incorporating as Aviation Corporation of America on June 2, 1927. Trippe was managing director, with authority to bid on any airmail route he selected, and was authorized to invest into a newly formed New York corporation called Pan American Airways. Pan American did not own any planes nor did it have much money, but it had the inside track on the Key West–Havana, Cuba mail contract—soon to be awarded.

Trippe hammered out a deal with Pan American, in which his Aviation Corporation of America held 45 percent of the stock—a major fraction—with Atlantic, Gulf and Caribbean also holding a portion.

The Fokker trimotor, ready at the last minute, made the first official flight ten days later, on October 28, 1927, carrying a load of mail weighing 772 pounds.

The tiny airline with the prestigious name operated out of a three-room office suite at 100 West 42nd Street in New York City.

Although Havana was only ninety miles away, in hazy or rainy weather, pilots often had difficulty finding it. They had no navigation except the compass, and they measured wind direction and velocity by judging the amount of foam on the peaks of the waves 1,500 feet or more below.

By perseverance, involving pioneering efforts by Thorp Hiscock of Boeing Air Transport, and Hugo Leuteritz of RCA, who later joined Pan American, the two-way radio problem was solved—but the pilots had to accept the worst heresy of all—taking navigational orders from the ground.

With the support of Charles Lindbergh, everybody's hero, Trippe won the mail contract throughout the Caribbean. His daring feat, braving the North Atlantic alone, more than any other single event, sparked a new boom in infant airlines throughout the United States.

1. Frank Cunningham, *Sky Master*, (Philadelphia: Dorrance & Company, 1943), 152.
2. Harold Mansfield, *Vision*, (New York: Popular Library, 1966), 27.
3. Ibid., 30.
4. Contracts were awarded primarily based on financial strength, and bid bonds of *up* to $500,000 were demanded in all cases.
5. Mansfield, *Vision*, 31.

7

Charter Consummated

On the national scene in 1928, Herbert Clark Hoover, accepting the Republican nomination for President, promised "a chicken in every pot, a car in every garage." He was elected by a landslide in November.

The Boeing Airplane Company was beginning to enjoy an international reputation as a meticulous builder of both military and commercial airplanes.

A trip through the crowded factory buildings on the Duwamish in the early part of the year would reveal more types of airplanes than one could count on the fingers of both hands. There were F2B-1 and F3B-1 single-seater navy fighters; PW-9D single-seater army pursuits; an XP-7 experimental pursuit; B-1D and B-1E flying boats; the big new Model 80, a series of 40-C mail-passenger planes; the Model 83 and Model 89 prototypes of the army P-12 and the navy F4B series of single-seat pursuits and fighters; and on the engineering drafting boards, the famed Model 95—first commercial transport to have a bolted, combination steel and dural framework—designed exclusively for carrying the mail.[1]

On October 31, 1928, the Boeing Airplane Company, jointly with Boeing Air Transport, Inc. and other individuals, purchased control of Pacific Air Transport, Inc., which had established a Seattle–Los Angeles mail and passenger route.

Pacific, which began service in September 1926, flew two Fokker Universal cabin planes, five Travel Air biplanes, two Ryan monoplanes, and one Romair biplane—all equipped with Wright Whirlwind engines. A parent company was formed known as the Boeing Airplane and Transport Corporation—of which the Seattle factory was a subsidiary.

The parent company then reorganized on February 1, 1929, forming the United Aircraft and Transport Corporation, the largest organization of its kind in the United States. The new corporation included the Boeing Airplane Company; the Hamilton Standard Propeller Corporation; Northrop Aircraft Corporation, Ltd.; the Pratt & Whitney Aircraft Company; Sikorsky Aviation Corporation; the Stearman Aircraft Company; and the Chance Vought Corporation. In addition to those manufacturing companies, the new giant included Boeing Air Transport, Inc.; Pacific Air Transport; and Stout Air Services; as well as United Aircraft Exports, Inc.; United Airports Company of California, Ltd.; the United Airports of Connecticut, Inc.; and the Boeing School of Aeronautics.[2]

As constituted, the new corporation included everything from manufacturing airplanes, engines, and propellers to operating airlines and airports; a school—and even exports.

W.E. Boeing became chairman of the new corporation, and F.B. Rentschler of Pratt & Whitney became president.

Thus, slightly more than a decade after he founded the company, Boeing witnessed the fulfillment of his visionary charter.

Bigness was the criterion that seemed to attract widespread attention as airplanes quickly captured the imagination of an increasing segment of the public. Boeing was being looked to as the epitome of the biggest—and the best.

When the PB-1 was launched not long after the Model 40 mail plane prototype, it was the largest navy plane yet constructed in the world. Six times the weight of the B-1, this new giant carried a crew of five, and was equipped with two Packard 2A-2500 water-cooled engines, each rated at 800 horsepower. It boasted four-bladed propellers—one a pusher and the other a tractor, with the two engines mounted back-to-back. The cruising range of more than 2,000 miles represented a spectacular advance, ideal for the navy, which was beginning to focus on the vast two-ocean shoreline, inadequately patrolled by surface vessels. New design innovations also appeared on the PB-1. The wings were of metal construction—fabric covered—with beams of welded steel tubing and ribs of aluminum alloy—the first use of aluminum in Boeing airplanes.

The bread and butter machines after the "40" series were fighter and pursuit planes for the army and navy, however, the really exciting competition during this period was to increase passenger capacity in commercial models. The goal, set by Juan Trippe, was to at least double on each succeeding new design.

The last of a series, the 40B-4 carried four passengers. Then in 1928, Boeing claimed a huge chunk of the future sky with the Model 80. Designed to carry twelve passengers with a new degree of comfort, the plane quickly became known as the "Pioneer Pullman of the Air."

The "80" had reclining seats, adjustable to four positions; a lavatory with hot and cold running water; forced ventilation and heating; an insulated and soundproofed cabin; a small buffet; large windows of non-shatterable glass; dome lights; and wall lamps.

Powered by three 425-horsepower Wasp engines, the "80" was not the first of the trimotors. It was preceded by the Ford and eight-passenger Fokker F-7, which made its first flight for Pan

Model 80 series—1928–1930

Boeing's *Pioneer Pullman of the Air* carried 18 passengers and a crew of two, establishing the 27 hour, coast-to-coast Boeing Air Transport service over the mid-continent route.

American on the Key West–Havana route the previous October. However, it was the most advanced passenger transport in the air at that time.

Juan Trippe was beginning to move mountains. In January, he hired the "Lone Eagle," Charles Lindbergh, as a technical adviser. Lindbergh became a welcome ambassador from the U.S. in Central and South America. The previous December, he flew to Mexico at the invitation of the president of that nation. Greeted by joyous crowds, he was entertained over the Christmas holidays by U.S. Ambassador Dwight Morrow and his daughters and then continued on a goodwill tour of South America. While greeting dignitaries, he also charted air routes and scouted for accessible landing sites. When he returned to the United States, he was awarded the Congressional Medal of Honor by President Calvin Coolidge.

Trippe had planned well. Having gained the aura of "flag carrier" for the U.S. in Latin America, he forged ahead. West Indian

Airways, the principal Caribbean carrier, sold out to Pan Am. In Mexico, he purchased Mexicana; in Peru, Huff-Daland Duster, renaming it Peruvian Airways; in Chile he organized Chilean Airways; in Colombia, be bought out SCADTA, the Colombo-German Air Transport Company; and finally, to finesse the Grace Steamship Company, who dominated a substantial portion of South American trade, he worked out a merger—creating Pan American Grace Airways—which came to be known as Panagra.

At a time when no domestic airline had yet managed to span the United States—first accomplished on October 23, 1929—Trippe was ready to push his planes out along ten thousand miles of routes. Soon he would be seeking bigger airplanes—and new engineering innovations—the Boeing hallmark.

It was not long until Boeing produced an improved version of the Model 80, announcing the 80-A, capable of carrying eighteen passengers and 898 pounds of cargo. The twenty-seven-hour coast-to-coast Boeing Air Transport service over the mid-continent route was established, and on-board stewardesses were employed for the first time. In all, sixteen airplanes of the Model 80 series were built, the last being the special deluxe Model 226 which was delivered to the Standard Oil Company of California.

Aviation marched with seven-league boots in 1928. In April, French pilots Costes and Le Brix landed at le Bourget, completing a 45,000 mile around-the-world flight. Also in April, aviators Koehl, Hunefeld, and Fitzmau piloted a Junkers from Ireland to New York, in the first East–West flight over the Atlantic—flying into the teeth of the prevailing winds. In June, Amelia Earhart, first woman to dare the Atlantic, made a successful crossing in a multi-engined Fokker, accompanied by two male pilots. In October, the first ship-to-shore delivery of transatlantic mail was accomplished when a seaplane was launched from the westbound French Line steamer, *Ile de France*, carrying sacks of registered mail and photographs to Boston. In

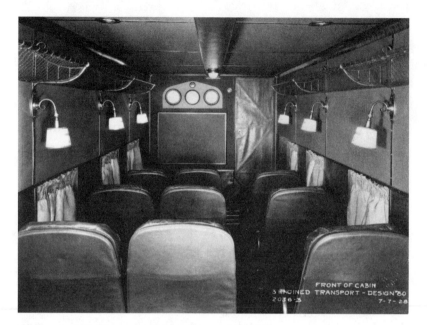

Model 80A Interior

October, Harry Tucker made a new coast-to-coast record of twenty-four hours, fifty-one minutes in his Yankee Doodle monoplane, and in November a British flier hit 319.57 miles per hour in a seaplane.

In 1928, orders came in for the Vega from all sides. Lockheed was already living up to its modern motto: "There is a tide in the affairs of men, which when taken at the flood, leads on to fortune...."

The rush of orders forced Lockheed to seek a new location and they moved to a larger site in Burbank.

The Vega was followed by a parade of new airplanes: the underslung-wing Sirius, which Lindbergh used to fly from Washington, D.C., all the way to China in a series of carefully planned and publicized hops in 1931; the Altair, a two-seated airplane; and the Orion, with an enlarged, seven-seat cabin.

In every case, the introduction of an innovation was accompanied by heavy fanfare. Lockheed's location near the movie capital of the world was a magnificent bonus in its promotional efforts. They sought additional publicity from the achievements of the many trailblazing aviators of the era; including George Wilkins, Amelia Earhart, Roscoe Turner, and Wiley Post, all of whom set and broke speed and distance records in Lockheed planes. The boast of the company in its advertisements, "It takes a Lockheed to beat a Lockheed," was beginning to cement a vision of invincibility in the Lockheed name.[3]

Caught in their own private enthusiasm, awash with favorable publicity, Lockheed concentrated too heavily on the headline-grabbing, but potentially low-profit, low-volume markets. In addition, left unattended was the reawakening military market of the United States government.

After a series of catastrophic events, both on a private and a national scale, which included the stock market crash of 1929, Lockheed, by then a struggling subsidiary of the Detroit Aircraft Holding Company, an early conglomerate that had bought its way into a number of aircraft companies, found itself bankrupt.

"'I have an idea, Claire,' said Eddie Hubbard, now operations vice-president of the Boeing airline, when the two men were sharing a hotel room after the 1928 Los Angeles Air Races. 'Why shouldn't we go entirely to metal when we build our next transport?' We have to line the mail compartment with metal anyway, so the mailbag locks won't tear the fabric. We have to put metal plates up front for accessibility to the engine controls. Why not go metal the whole way, nose to tail?'

"Hubbard's quick hope and confidence were born of gallant hours in the open cockpit, alone in the sky where there was room for uncluttered thought. It was this stimulus that Claire Egtvedt needed. Egtvedt laid a piece of stationery on the dresser, drew the front view of a wing, long and slender, his imagination at work.

"'If the body's going to be metal, the easiest way to make it is perfectly round,' he said, sketching. 'Set it here on the wing. Here's an airplane with minimum drag.'

"He had drawn a circle for the body, on top of the single wing. That was all there was to it, a low-wing monoplane.

"'It gets rid of all the wires and bracing on the wings.'

"To Hubbard it looked too simple. 'Where's your landing gear?' he asked.

"'You could pull the gear up into the wing after you get off the ground. Dragging that thing through the air costs more than all the mail you carry.'

"'Do you think we could build that?'

"'It's only a question of whether we could afford the cost of working it out.'"[4]

Egtvedt felt that the corrugated-metal, "flying washboard" surfaces used for the body construction on the Ford and the German Junkers trimotors had to be eliminated. He wanted the skin to be perfectly smooth on the outside. But, without the corrugations, more stiffening would be required on the inside and the skin would have to be heavier. No one had much experience with this kind of structure.

When Bill Boeing saw the sketch, he was impressed with the cleanness of the design, and highly interested in pursuing it further. He wondered if they could get to work on it as a secret project, as they had done with the pursuit plane, and bring it out as a surprise.

Egtvedt listened, fairly jumping inside. He said he'd have the engineering department investigate.

1. *Boeing News*, June 1937, 4.
2. First Annual Report to the Stockholders, United Aircraft & Transport Corporation, for the year ending December 31, 1929. Boeing Archives.
3. David Boulton, *The Grease Machine*, (New York: Harper & Row, 1978), 25.
4. Harold Mansfield, *Vision*, (New York: Popular Library, 1966), 39.

8

The All-metal First

T he idea of an all-metal airplane was mind-boggling in 1928. Stress analysis for wings was still a relatively unsophisticated science, and no one knew how to reliably assign structural loads to the skin.

At Boeing, the chief engineer was Charles N. "Monty" Montieth, a graduate of MIT in aeronautical engineering; also a pilot, serving as instructor at Kelly Field, Texas; and chief of section in the Air Service Engineering Division at McCook Field, Ohio—all of this prior to coming to Boeing.

Egtvedt's proposal had Montieth shaking his head. Highly regarded professionally, he had written the textbook on aerodynamics being used at West Point as well as at many universities. He had also watched his friend, Lieutenant F.W. Weidermeyer fall to his death as the center section support gave way on an experimental airplane with such a structure.

Reluctantly, he advised Egtvedt that it would be unwise to go ahead with the project.

Montieth was sharp, competitive, and eager to continue leadership in innovation, however he was painfully aware that engineers' mistakes bury them. In his textbook, he had written, "It must be as simple and as cheap as is possible to build."[1]

In the airplane business, always at the cutting edge of technology, the conflict of boldness and caution haunted the waking hours of those who sought to create new designs. The next innovation, a retractable landing gear—on the surface a straightforward engineering progression—harbored hidden hazards. A simple malfunction, resulting in one or both gears failing to extend, meant almost certain catastrophe.

As the days went by, the comfortable alternative to a low-wing monoplane—a high wing, externally braced arrangement—became increasingly less satisfying to Montieth. Keenly aware that leadership—indeed survival—depended on innovation, he initiated a substantial preliminary design effort, gaining encouragement from Bill Boeing's unflagging confidence.

The low-wing, all-metal design, with its smooth, clean lines, quickly captured the imagination of the engineers, and the alternatives were abandoned.

Bill Boeing was elated—there was something almost magic about an idea that appeared at the right place and the right time. His words on that occasion have served to guide and inspire Boeing engineers from that day forward—almost a catechism for developing a winner every time.

"We must not dismiss any novel idea with the cocksure statement that it can't be done," he said in an interview. "We are pioneers in a new science and a new industry. Our job is to keep everlastingly at research and experiment, and let no new improvement pass us by. We have already proved that science and hard work can lick what appear to be insurmountable difficulties."[2]

Montieth had become a disciple. He decided to go all out and

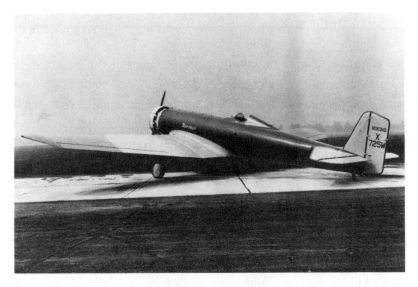

Monomail—1929–1930
First modern air transport.

make the best of it. According to Boeing's wishes, the project was kept secret until it was time to join the wings to the fuselage, accomplished at the airfield a mile south of the plant and in view of the public. Enthusiastic fans crowded close to the fenced-off area. Not at all like any airplane seen before, it had a slender, round, smooth body resting on a silver wing. Constructed almost entirely of durals, the first high strength aluminum alloy family, the *Monomail* had come alive. It was powered by a single, air-cooled 575-horsepower, Pratt & Whitney, Hornet engine.

In spite of all the innovations and sleek lines of the Monomail, the plane still retained an open cockpit, a concession to the pilots, obsessed with the idea that they must be on the outside.

The first Monomail, the Model 200, was not equipped to carry passengers, but had three cargo compartments with a total capacity of 220 cubic feet, providing for a normal payload of 2,300 pounds. In the second airplane, the Model 221, the center cargo compartment was converted into a passenger cabin with accommodations for six. Both models were later modified to carry eight passengers. The open cockpit remained.

With the Monomail taking its flying paces at the direction of Eddie Allen, famous test pilot and aeronautical engineer, it was quickly apparent that the next limitation to speed and performance was the propeller. The pitch of the blades could only be changed on the ground. They needed a steep pitch in the air to get the high speeds that the plane was capable of, but to take off, the pitch should be flat. After extensive experimentation, Allen chose a compromise setting, and the Monomail, one of the most revolutionary airplanes in history, made its maiden flight on May 6, 1930.

The year of 1930 was also notable for the maiden flight of another kind—the launching of the *Boeing News*. The January issue announced the aims and purposes of the new publication:

"Not many years ago the Boeing Airplane Company, housed in a small building with thirty employees, represented all of the Boeing aeronautical activities. The few men and women employed in this one building were, of course, in intimate touch with all phases of the business.

"Today we have a far-flung organization, whose business includes the manufacture of airplanes, operation of the two longest mail lines in the United States, a subsidiary manufacturing plant in Canada, a flying school at Oakland, to mention only our major operations.

"It is my belief that the Boeing family has grown so rapidly, our activities are so varied, our personnel so separated, that the time has come when all of us should be kept informed about what the other groups are doing. That explains *Boeing News*.

"We trust that *Boeing News* will be informative and entertaining and serve a useful purpose in knitting our family of 1,500 employees into one group actuated by the desire to be of service to each other and to the public."[3]

The announcement was signed, "P.G. Johnson, President."

Thus, its creation developed from the simple need for communication. The editor, Harold Crary, was the Boeing advertising and publicity manager. As Crary, who later became United Air Lines vice president for sales, recalls:

"I was a newspaper man...and my observation at the Boeing plant was that too many people in the plant just didn't know what was going on. When I first proposed an employee newspaper, P. G. Johnson, then president, and Mr. Boeing took kindly to the outline I submitted. Both had seen the need for better plant intelligence. A new era was at hand and the Boeing Airplane Company and the Boeing Transport System learned they had to practice the art of communication."[4]

Boeing News became much more than a mere chronology of events. Indeed, it gave the employees a heightened feeling of participation, importance, and belonging.

In spite of the stock market crash on "Black Thursday," October 24, 1929, Boeing sailed along, riding a crest of production orders into the early thirties. They were good years. On the basis of navy tests with the XF4B-1, a Boeing prototype, beginning as the Model 83, which featured bolted aluminum tubing in place of welded steel tubing, the Army ordered nine as the P-12. This was the first order of a 586 plane production run of F4B/P-12 machines. The Model 218, which served as the prototype for the F4B-3, was the first Boeing airplane to see action against the Japanese. One 218 was purchased by the Chinese government, and in 1932 it was attacked by three Japanese airplanes. Two of the enemy craft were shot down before the pilot of the 218 was killed. Export versions were also purchased by the governments of Brazil and Siam, and the tiny fighters became well known throughout the world. Several commercial models were sold to private operators, and one was acquired by the U.S. Department of Commerce.

The bolted aluminum-alloy construction was also incorporated in the Model 95, an airplane designed specifically to carry cargo and mail. Twenty-five of these planes were produced for three airlines: Boeing Air Transport, National Air Transport, and Western Air Express.

Progress in aviation continued around the world. In January 1929, Commander Richard E. Byrd explored 1,200 miles of the Antarctic by plane, and the U.S. Army craft, *Question Mark*, stayed aloft for 150 hours and 40 minutes—refueled in the air. During the flight, the Fokker trimotor took on fuel several times from a sister ship and would have stayed aloft longer if an engine had not failed. Two decades later, it was Boeing who developed the first sophisticated aerial refueling system. Known as the "flying boom," the technology provided the U.S. Air Force Strategic Air Command essentially unlimited range for its heavy bombers.

On April 26, 1929, British fliers completed a record, nonstop, 4,130-mile trip from London to India.

At home on February 17, 1929, Universal Air Lines reported showing a film during a scheduled flight, and on July 7, Transcontinental Air Transport inaugurated cross-country service, with passengers traveling by plane during the day and sleeping on trains during the night. The airline took customers from New York's Penn Station to Glendale Airport, outside Los Angeles. The first coast-to-coast, all-air service, began on October 23—from New York to Los Angeles in thirty-six hours—with an overnight stop.

The year was notable for other events. The Lone Eagle married Anne Morrow, Babe Ruth hit his 500th home run, Charlie Chaplin was runner-up to Janet Gaynor in the first Academy Awards ceremony in Hollywood, and in China, Canadian archeologist David Black discovered the 400,000-year-old bones of Peking Man.

The Monomail cruised at 140 miles per hour, and with increasing significance of aerodynamic drag on performance, the issue of the open cockpit eventually had to be faced.

The first 80A trimotors had provided for the pilots to sit inside the enclosed cabin, a situation which they strongly disliked. They wanted to be able to look out, lean over for a glance at the ground—to follow a fence line or a railroad track. The pilots complained so strongly that one of the trimotors was modified to install an open cockpit atop the square nose. The airplane, one of a kind, designated the 80B, did not last long. After a few trials at the higher speeds, the comforts of being inside the cabin began to outweigh the thrill of the open cockpit, and the airplane was converted back to an 80A.

The Monomail was not a celebrated airplane in terms of production, but was the spawning ground for still further advancements. It evolved to the twin engined B-9 bomber, carrying two 30-caliber machine guns and four 600 pound bombs. A commercial version, the Model 247, followed.

With the stock market crash, the United States plunged into the Great Depression. Unemployment soon hit eleven million, eventually reaching 25 percent of the work force. The Hoover Administration took an upbeat view, proclaiming that "prosperity was just around the corner." With a landslide victory in November 1932, President Franklin D. Roosevelt promised a "new deal" for the American people, announcing that "the only thing we have to fear is fear itself." At Boeing, the plant was busy turning out fighters—and looking to future products.

At noon on February 8, 1933, the silver-bright 247—a twin engined monoplane, fifty-four feet, four inches long and weighing 13,000 pounds—lifted from Boeing Field and winged out over Puget Sound on its first test flight. Its retractable landing gear, first in the commercial industry, had been well proven on the Monomail. Soon it was to incorporate the controllable pitch propeller, developed by Frank Caldwell of Hamilton Standard.

Model 247 Interior

For the first time, the interiors took on a modern look, many features still retained in today's airplanes.

The ten-passenger plane won instant acclaim. "They'll never build 'em any bigger," said a triumphant Monteith.[5]

The capability of the 247 was increased with a further series of improvements, finally evolving to the 247D. This model was the first twin-engined transport monoplane able to climb with one engine out, while fully loaded.

United Airlines—incorporated on March 28, 1931—a part of the giant United Aircraft and Transport Corporation, purchased a fleet of 247D airplanes, operating coast-to-coast and border-to-border. Spanning the U.S. became a matter of twenty hours—with only seven stops.

A total of seventy-five airplanes of the 247 series were manufactured, two purchased by the German airline, Deutsche Lufthansa in Hamburg.

The 247 design won Bill Boeing the 1934 Guggenheim Medal

Model 247 Series—1932–1935

First standard design for contemporary transport airplanes. Carried ten passengers, two pilots, and 400 pounds of mail.

for successful pioneering and advancement in aircraft manufacturing and transport.

In this instance, first and best was not sufficient in the rapidly changing marketplace. The aircraft industry was sharpening its teeth. Technology, sometimes inching along, and at other times breaking its bonds with a sudden leap, was a constant companion—and a constant adversary. One could never be certain what competitors were hatching in their design rooms and wind tunnels.

Donald Douglas continued to expand his organization, and in 1929, they moved to a new building near Clover Field in Santa Monica. The Douglas Company became the Douglas Aircraft Company, an identity which it maintained for nearly forty years.

United Airlines, flying the Boeing 247D, with its modern features, quickly gained dominance of the air travel industry.

United's competition wanted a larger cabin to accommodate the expanding demand. It was time for another leap forward. Trans

World Airways approached Douglas to design an airplane that would out-perform the 247D.

The product—ready for its test flight on July 1, 1933—was the twelve passenger DC-1. The six-ton, all-aluminum plane represented the hope for Douglas to wrest commercial supremacy from Boeing. The ensuing dogfight was still going strong in the nineties.

The DC-1, a one-and-only, was improved and redesignated the DC-2 before it entered airline service. The plane immediately began an assault on aeronautical records. In March 1935, a DC-2 established a new transcontinental record of twelve hours and forty-two minutes from west to east, and in 1936, an east–west record, against prevailing winds, of fifteen hours and thirty-nine minutes, traveling at a speed of nearly 200 miles per hour.

Douglas gambled on the DC series, setting the price far lower than the initial cost of production—counting on a learning curve which would reduce costs dramatically with a large production run. Further, the initial development cost of the DC-1 ($307,000), had to be recovered. With the planes selling for about $65,000 each, the first twenty-five netted a loss of $266,000.

The gamble paid off. The seventy-sixth plane raised the program out of the red, and by June 1938, some 132 DC-2 planes had been delivered. In the meantime, the DC-3, with a nominal configuration of twenty-one seats, was introduced.

With the DC series, Douglas achieved undisputed world leadership in the production of commercial airplanes. A total of 10,629 DC-3s were manufactured, including over 10,000 military versions, that were churned out of Douglas factories during World War II as C-47s, R4Ds, and Dakotas.[6]

A legendary flying machine, the DC-3 represented the greatest single airplane model that the world had produced. On December 17, 1985, the airplane celebrated the fiftieth anniversary of its first flight. At the time, aviation historians estimated that between 1,500 and 2,000 DC-3s were flying with scheduled airlines, or serving the air forces of many developing countries. Others were engaged in agricultural pest control and private chartered flights.

In 1935, Donald Douglas received the Collier Trophy for development of the DC-2, and in January 1940, joined William E. Boeing in the select group of aviation pioneers to receive the Guggenheim Medal.

From the introduction of the DC-3 in 1936, until the start of World War II in 1939, U.S. air travel increased by 500 percent. DC-3s and DC-2s carried nearly 90 percent of all U.S. air traffic, and were operated by thirty foreign airlines.

A favorite story told about the DC-3s' war days took place in the Far East:

"Major General Jimmie Doolittle rode out of China after his famed 1942 Tokyo raid in one of China National Airline's amazing DC-3s. The aircraft, piloted by Captain Moon Chin, stopped in Burma on its way from Chungking to India to pick up refugees. After sixty passengers had been crowded aboard, the pilot reluctantly shut the door, feeling the plane's overload was great enough. When the aircraft landed in India, twelve additional passengers climbed out of the aft baggage compartment. That adds up to seventy-two passengers in a twenty-one seat airplane—a 340 percent load factor!"[7]

In Burbank in 1932, with orders completely stopped, and the employment down to four, a federal receiver put Lockheed up for sale, valuing its assets at $129,961.

Allan Lockheed, excited by the opportunity to buy back the company he and his brother had founded, desperately sought to raise $100,000 for a bid, when to his dismay, he found that receivers had already accepted an offer for the astoundingly low figure of $40,000.

The new buyer, Robert Ellsworth Gross, an investment banker with no knowledge whatsoever of flying or the production of airplanes, had purchased a bargain. Robert Gross invited his younger brother, Courtland, to join the company as deputy chairman.

Gross had a lot of catching up to do. For his $40,000 he had acquired floor space, a few boxes of spare parts, some blueprints, the total labor force of four people—and the Lockheed name. The goodwill in terms of world renown was probably worth tenfold what Robert Gross had paid for the company.

It was a good match. Gross had the knack for playing the market, knew how to keep his finger on the pulse of national trends, and immediately sensed a long-range future for commercial airplanes—which had come of age for mass travel.

Gross was in the right business to raise the capital that was so necessary to get on the track. He returned the Orion to production and began a blitz of the overseas commercial markets—so far neglected by almost everyone.

Swissair became Lockheed's first overseas customer, followed by many of Europe's emerging airlines.

In a short eighteen months, Lockheed produced a challenge to its competitors, rolling out the all-metal, twin-engined ten-seater known as the Electra Model 10. As a result of spending over three times the $40,000 he had invested in the company—in research and development—Gross had accomplished his objective in one grand stroke. The new plane incorporated all the modern refinements: retractable landing gear, trailing edge flaps, and variable pitch propellers.

By the end of 1935, forty machines had been sold, half of them to the overseas market.

Robert Gross had the gut feeling to exploit new developments in the tried and true Lockheed tradition. The corporate complexion—and the corporate conscience—was being indelibly molded to fit the personality of its boss.

The final leg of the "Big Three" in commercial airplane manufacturing had emerged.

In Seattle, with United Airline's competitors turning to the DC-3 and the Electra Model 10, there were no orders in sight for the 247D, beyond the initial seventy-five. Boeing was quickly reduced to third in commercial airplane sales.

1. Charles Monteith, *Simple Aerodynamics and the Airplane*, (Washington, D.C.: Army Air Corps, 1925), 5.
2. Harold Mansfield, *Vision*, (New York: Popular Library, 1966), 42.
3. *Boeing News*, January, 1930, 1.
4. K.L. Calkins, *An Analysis of Labor Relations News Coverage...*, (Seattle: University of Washington, 1968), 3.
5. Mansfield, *Vision*, 46
6. DC-3 DAKOTA NEWSLETTER, Douglas Aircraft Company, 17 December, 1985.
7. DC-3 FEATS—FACT OR FANCY, McDonnell Douglas NEWS, 17 December, 1985.

Claire L. Egtvedt 1892–1975
President 1934–1939, Chairman 1939–1965.

9

Clipped Wings

The Boeing Airplane Company never flinched in the face of the trials of the marketplace. Bill Boeing had passed the torch of pride in the product to every level in the organization. It was left to the political and legislative processes to bring the company to its knees—indeed coming within a hair-thin margin of forcing it out of business.

In 1934—just when Boeing sorely needed its strength to beat the new competition—the huge United Aircraft and Transport Corporation was ordered to break up. Three major entities remained: the Boeing Airplane Company, the United Aircraft Manufacturing Corporation, and United Airlines, separating airframe manufacturing, engines, and airline operations into individual companies.

Bill Boeing, disillusioned and bitter, sold his stock and retired from the company. He was never to return to the aircraft business except for a short time during World War II as a consultant.

Inevitably, Boeing left a legacy of integrity and rockhard ethics with those who followed him. His never-say-die attitude during his eighteen years as the leader of the company, was epitomized in a motto which was formalized from some of his earlier remarks:

> *I've tried to make the men around me feel as I do, that we are embarked as pioneers upon a new science and industry in which our problems are so new and unusual that it behooves no one to dismiss any novel idea with the statement that "It can't be done." Our job is to keep everlastingly at research and experiment, to adapt our laboratory results and those of other laboratories to production as soon as practicable, to let no improvement in flying and flying equipment pass us by.[1]*

The Boeing Airplane Company, after the breakup, consisted of the parent company, incorporated in Delaware, and two subsidiaries: the Boeing Aircraft Company in the state of Washington, and the Stearman Aircraft Company in Kansas.

Boeing Aircraft Company of Canada, Ltd., remained as a subsidiary of the Boeing Aircraft Company of Washington.

Claire Egtvedt, named president of the Boeing Airplane Company with the departure of P.G. Johnson, inherited the smallest—and the most fragile—of the three new corporations. The first annual report of the restructured company covering the four months from September 1, 1934 to year end, recorded a net loss of $225,977 on gross sales of $1,116,627.[2]

A new and experimental navy fighter and army pursuit didn't sell well. A twin-engined bomber competition was won by the Glenn Martin Company, and there was no chance of getting back into the bomber business without a new model.

Egtvedt wanted to build an experimental twin-engined bomber and a matching twin-engined transport. There was no money. In fact, when the legal separation was completed and the books rationalized, cash available for operations was down to $582,000, most of it needed to meet payroll and other obligations for the remainder of the year.

After reaching an all-time high of 2,275 employees in May 1933, the payroll dropped to 600 by late summer in 1934.

Valuable, experienced employees had been laid off, perhaps never to be retrieved. However, those were dedicated people clinging to a dream—certain that given the opportunity—they could produce another winner. Some employees came in to offer a plan of spreading out the work—one group on for two weeks and then off for two—thus preserving the core of expertise. When the plan was adopted, many of them came to the plant to work on their own time—with no thought of being paid. They represented the hard core of the organization. Where was there to go but up?

This was an example of the sometimes inexplicable loyalty which Boeing employees felt for their company. Bill Boeing had left an organization behind that refused—as he had—the notion that it could not be done. That concept was embodied in the simple idea that, if they built the best product, the customer would respond and buy it.

With the dissolution of the United Aircraft and Transport Corporation, Boeing and its subsidiaries were left without any foreign representation. Early attention was directed to this potentially fruitful market area.

Egtvedt had invited Wellwood Beall, an exuberant young engineer who had been an instructor at the Boeing School of Aeronautics in Oakland, to join the sales department, and almost immediately, he received instructions to go to China to endeavor to sell some pursuit planes. Beall, with degrees in both mechanical and aeronautical engineering from New York University, had

P-26 Series—*Peashooter*—1932–1936

The P-26A was the first all-metal pursuit to go into production for the Army, rated as one of the fastest air-cooled fighters in the world. Top speed 234 mph, range 635 miles, service ceiling 27,400 feet.

made an auspicious entry into industry, starting as assistant chief engineer with the Walter M. Murphy Company in Pasadena, California, prior to his position at the Boeing school.

The P-26 *Peashooter* had been a great success with the U.S. Armed Forces. Boeing decided to try to market the little plane on an international basis as the Model 281. In the late summer of 1934, as Far Eastern Sales Representative, Beall headed for Canton to visit the Chinese Air Force. In July 1935, the Chinese purchased eleven airplanes. After coming off the production line in Seattle, the planes had to be disassembled, crated, and shipped to China. It would be necessary to have a Boeing man on site who could not only set up the airplanes, but also train the Chinese pilots to fly the machines and the Chinese mechanics to service them.

Beall found the man he needed in Shanghai, Herbert D. Poncetti, better known as Nemo. Poncetti accepted Beall's invitation to join the company to take part in the field assignment, promptly setting sail for Seattle to learn what the Model 218 was all about.

When Poncetti returned to China late in 1935, he was Boeing's first unofficial field service representative. At the time there was no such organization.

The impact and importance of the *Boeing News* began to be felt as the company grew. Indeed, it became the most powerful single force in welding together the Boeing spirit.

Beginning monthly, the *News* was to be used not simply for informing but for influencing—as Johnson had stated—"for knitting the family into one group." While *Boeing News* worked hard at the job, it could not disguise the inequalities within the company at times. The paper even pointed out the harsh realities of managing a labor force in the feast-or-famine environment of the airplane industry.

K.L. Calkins, in a study of labor relations at Boeing, observed:

The cruel impersonality of work planning charts was just one cause for grumbles by hourly paid employees in 1933. These grumbles stemmed from a very basic fear—job security. In 1933 there were many reasons for an hourly worker to look to a union for help. Hourly work lacked the dignity and honor that salaried work enjoyed. Salaried men at Boeing had sick leave privileges, a broader insurance program, vacations, hot water in the washroom, and regular working hours. Hourly men could be called to work whenever their services were needed and sent home when they were not needed. A union might help control the sometimes unequal, and, it seemed to many hourly workers, unfair distribution of wages.[3]

In the 1920s, many U.S. companies had adopted policies of welfare capitalism to develop loyalty to the company among employees and to discourage union organizing. Company management involved itself in planning educational programs for improving an employee's chances of promotion; low cost food service was introduced; free or low cost medical services were offered; stock purchase or profit sharing plans started; recreational programs organized by the company; vacations with pay became common; sick leave was offered. The impact of these offerings was to dampen union activities.

In the airplane manufacturing industry, no such benefits were considered, and at the Boeing Airplane Company, for factory employees, there was only a health contract with a local clinic and an occasional bonus on Christmas. In spite of the paucity of benefits, there was little visible effort to organize the workers. Employment was too tentative, hinging on follow-on production orders, or the introduction of a successful new program.

The National Recovery Act of 1933 gave Boeing production workers the impetus they needed to unionize. Under its terms, the National Labor Relations Board (NLRB) was formed, with regional boards in each part of the country. In 1934, fewer than one in twenty American workers belonged to a union.

Some factory employees, impatient for a labor union, wrote to the Seattle Regional Board in early March requesting a plant election. The Board called for such an election for March 15, 1934. The aeronautical workers A.F.L. union won every one of the four shop employee positions on the five-man committee.

Notwithstanding this impressive beginning, labor organization at Boeing was still three years away from gaining significant bargaining power.

Looking back from 1934, the late twenties and early thirties were halcyon years. For that brief period, the company was national in scope, multi-product deep, and growing with undiminished confidence.

Now, even *Boeing News* became a victim of the severe downturn. In November, it suspended publication.

1. Boeing Archives.
2. *REPORT TO THE STOCKHOLDERS*, The Boeing Airplane Company, 1934, 6.
3. K.L. Calkins, *An Analysis of Labor Relations News Coverage...*, (Seattle: University of Washington, 1968), 6.

10

The
Dreadnoughts

Integrity, innovation, and product excellence were destined to be rewarded. Boeing, and the company he created, had built a blue ribbon reputation in the minds of the planners at Wright Field. Thus, it was inevitable that any new request for procurement would include Boeing on the bidders list.

In the spring of 1934, the lowest point in the company's history since the days of bedroom furniture, Claire Egtvedt received a call from Brigadier General Conger Pratt, chief of the Air Corps Materiel Division at Wright Field in Dayton, Ohio. The general requested Egtvedt to attend an important meeting on May 14. The subject was secret.

General Billy Mitchell had startled the military world in July 1921, when he and his fellow aviators sank the former German battleship Ostfriesland with six 2,000-pound bombs in just twenty-five minutes. On the occasion, an observer remarked, "A bomb was fired that will be heard around the world."[1]

Billy Mitchell had touched a nerve in the military hierarchy, getting their attention, but finding little response. Arguing futilely for a separate air arm, he accused his superiors of "incompetency, criminal negligence, and almost treasonable administration of national defense."[2]

In 1925, General Mitchell was court-martialed for insubordination, violation of good order and military discipline, and suspended from rank for five years without pay or allowances. He resigned before the sentence was carried out. Even President Coolidge declared his opposition to a large air force, calling it a menace to peace. Coolidge upheld the suspension, but restored the allowances and granted him one half his monthly pay.

In 1945, General Billy Mitchell was posthumously restored to service with the rank of major general, and awarded the Congressional Medal of Honor in recognition of service and foresight in aviation.

Planners at Wright Field were stimulated by the promise that air power seemed to offer, and a few young visionaries pushed for more emphasis on bombers. Perhaps the most enthusiastic of these pioneers was a young lieutenant by the name of Leonard "Jake" Harman. He had become a Billy Mitchell disciple, and his goal was to see that the Air Corps developed better, long-range bombers. The key in Jake's book was range.

The battleships that were sunk by Billy Mitchell were close to the coast. In a real fight, they would be far out at sea, safely out of the range of airplanes—according to the admirals. To get greater range, one needed an increase in size, translating into a bigger wing and bigger power plants.

The all-metal structure offered new promise, but there remained the question of factor of safety. How close to the line could they dare push the design?

Normally, you took what range you could get, after determining how heavy a structure was required, and how large a power plant was available.

Harman thought perhaps the design process was being done backwards, suggesting that the baseline should be established according to mission requirements, instead of what was currently possible. His concept gained support with his superiors, and a list of desired future bomber categories was conceived.

Category One was a seventy-five foot wingspan airplane with a gross weight of 15,000 pounds. Such a plane was already in the inventory. The Army Air Corps had taken delivery of seven Boeing B-9 airplanes which represented the state of the art. Those advanced twin-engined bombers, utilizing technology developed on the Monomail, had shown exceptional performance—outrunning the pursuit airplanes of their day.

Category Two called for a 100-foot wingspan and 40,000 pounds gross weight; Category Three, a 150-foot span and 150,000 pounds; Category Four, 200 feet and 250,000 pounds.

In the fall of 1933, the Air Corps budgeted a project for a 5,000-mile range bomber in Category Three, skipping Category Two entirely—reaching into the future as far as they dared.

General Pratt sent the proposal to Washington, recommending that Wright Field be authorized to put all its experimental budget into this single project.

In Washington, Air Corps chief Benny Foulois took General Pratt's double-sealed secret envelope to a meeting of the general staff, strongly endorsing the proposal. "A plane with a range of 5,000 miles could protect Hawaii and Alaska," he said. "I think it is highly important that we undertake this as an experimental project."[3] The general staff agreed.

"The purpose of this meeting," General Pratt began on May 14, 1934 in the curtained, carpeted, brass-filled briefing room at Wright Field, "is to discuss a procedure under which the Air Corps will consider proposals for the construction of a long-range airplane suitable for military purposes—an airplane weighing about thirty tons, to carry 2,000 pounds of bombs a distance of 3,000 miles." Egtvedt caught his breath, glancing over to C.A. Van Dusen of the Martin Company, who appeared equally startled.

The general continued, "Before I go further, may I ask if you gentlemen are interested in discussing such a project?"[4] Everyone nodded.

Pratt outlined the preliminary data, requesting cost estimates to be submitted by June 15 in order to award a design contract.

Back in Seattle, a special area was partitioned off in the engineering building. It was classified secret. Preliminary design studies were initiated immediately for a 150-foot wingspan, four-engine, giant monoplane. Project A was born. The plane was so revolutionary that new engineering would be required throughout. Montieth was shaking his head over the project. A year earlier he would have branded it as pure fantasy.

Decisions were made quickly in 1934. On June 28, a design contract was awarded and the project organized. Jack Kylstra was named project engineer. A wooden mock-up of the forward section, including the control cabin and other elements, was constructed. If the design data and the mock-up looked good enough to the Air Corps, a contract would be awarded for building an experimental plane.

Wright Field personnel became a common sight at the Boeing plant as they consulted and mulled over the design details.

Some of the proposed features taxed the imagination. The wing would have a passageway large enough to permit crawling out to the engines in flight; there were six machine gun turrets; a flight deck in place of a cockpit, with positions for a flight engineer, a radio operator, a navigator, and two pilots; sleeping quarters for the crew; a landing gear weighing 3,800 pounds. Wright Field even wanted a kitchenette with a hot plate and percolator.

Project A was an experiment—nothing more. Its purpose was to learn how to build a maximum size airplane, and it could be years before such a plane would be ordered in large quantities—if ever. The award called only for a design study. What the Boeing factory desperately needed was a hardware contract.

United Airlines, seriously studying a Boeing design for an improved twin-engined machine, was concerned that the proposed airplane's performance was not sufficiently better than the DC-2s being flown by the competition. "Why not go to four engines?" they inquired.

The question reinforced a growing conviction in Egtvedt's mind that four engines were inevitable. Twenty-one years had elapsed since Igor Sikorsky, famous Russian aviator and aircraft designer, had developed and flown the first four-engined airplane. The date of that historic flight was May 13, 1913.[5] The *Grand*, Sikorsky's first four-engined airplane, flew less than ten minutes on its initial flight, however from that day, four-engined flight was indisputable, and technology had moved forward in the ensuing decades.

Progress demanded bold action. Competition was becoming keener, but there was plenty of blue sky still to be conquered...*let no new improvement pass us by....*

Events quickened. On August 8, 1934, a circular was issued from Wright Field with the specifications for the next "production" bomber. "Bomb load 2,000 pounds; desired top speed, 250 miles an hour; range, 2,200 miles; a crew of four to six." Interested companies were requested to submit bids for construction of up to 220 airplanes.

The word production danced in Egtvedt's brain. He began to envision a fleet of flying dreadnoughts, capable of defending themselves in the sky as they carried heavy bomb loads to distant targets.

Meanwhile, on May 19th, in Russia, the biggest airplane in the world, amidst much fanfare, made its first flight. The giant *Maxim Gorky*, with eight engines, had a wing span of 260 feet—64 feet greater than a 747—and a crew of twenty. When the pilot of an accompanying fighter plane decided to liven things up with a barrel roll, he came crashing down on top of the *Maxim Gorky's* wing, causing the huge plane to disintegrate in the air.[6] The world wrote the airplane off as a stunt.

Preliminary design of the four-engined transport for United was proceeding well, and a Model 299 bomber was in the concept stage. The circular said "multi-engine," possibly limited to two-engined machines in the minds of the Air Corps. Trimotors might also be a possibility. Egtvedt flew to Wright Field to inquire.

"Would a four-engined airplane qualify?" he asked. Major Jan Howard, the engineering chief, looked up quickly, squinted, then smiled. "Say now." He looked at the circular. "The word is 'multi-engine,' isn't it?"[7]

Back at the plant, work was kicked off on the four-engined bomber. The company's position was more tenuous than ever. They were operating in the red.

But there was a prospect of building 220 bombers. The risk was loss of the company. All the resources of manpower and equipment—and borrowed money—would have to be sunk into a single, costly experiment.

Egtvedt sought guidance from his friend and counselor, William M. "Bill" Allen.

Allen hailed from the almost unknown town of Lolo, Montana, in the Bitterroot Mountains thirty miles south of Missoula. The son of a mining engineer, he graduated from the University of Montana in 1922 with a B.A. degree. After receiving his law degree from Harvard University, he came to Seattle in 1925 to start law practice with the firm of Donworth, Todd & Higgins. His first major assignment was legal advisor in the formation of Boeing Air Transport in 1926, and he quickly became the "company lawyer."

Egtvedt, in the spirit of past Boeing innovations, wanted to build the airplane on speculation, fly it to Wright Field, and demonstrate the performance that he was confident they could build into it. He explained to Bill Allen that there would be many unknowns, problems currently unsolved. The preliminary design study on Project A was already proving that.

Allen was neither an engineer nor a pilot, but he had a way of focusing the central issue. "Do you think you can build a successful, four-engined airplane in a year?"

"Yes, I know we can," Egtvedt responded firmly, after only a moment's hesitation.[8]

On September 26, 1934, borrowing to the limit, the board of directors voted $275,000 to design and construct the Model 299, to be delivered to Wright Field for trials the following August. The entire Boeing work force was reorganized on a one-job, maximum-effort basis.

Wind tunnel testing of models produced encouraging predictions—the top speed should hit 235 miles per hour and the range would be 3,000 miles. That good news stimulated the seventy-three engineers assigned to the project—sustaining them in their wearying seven-day week schedule.

The road was strewn with controversies and compromises—and innovations. Young Edward C. Wells, fresh out of Stanford University's engineering school, where he graduated with great distinction, was the assistant project engineer.

At the age of 23, Wells had been in charge of preliminary design for the Model 299, after a key assignment on the P-26 Peashooter. Many years later, when an interviewer noted this remarkable career milestone, Wells laughed and said, "We were all young then."[9]

By December, the major share of drawings were in the shops, and assembly was begun. Then they ran out of money. The board raised another $150,000 to finish the airplane. In mid-1935, the body and wings were ready to be moved to Boeing Field for final assembly. Everything was under canvas. Boeing's expensive secret must be well kept until the opportune moment. Rumors were rampant about the new mystery ship.

During that same period, again in a double envelope marked secret, Wright Field sent a contract to construct the giant Project A airplane.

The month of July at the hangar at Boeing Field, was as tough a month as Boeing work crews had ever seen. Even Fred Laudan, the factory superintendent, checked in on first shift and out again at the end of the second shift around midnight. In the final week, shifts were not observed—the crews simply worked as long as they could stand up—to meet the July 28 flight date.

The curious, awed public had their first look at the sparkling battle giant, arrayed with its five machine gun blisters, reporters immediately dubbing it an aerial battle cruiser.

Before sunrise, on Sunday, July 28, test pilot Les Tower checked out the airplane, and prepared for takeoff. Mansfield describes the event:

A cluster of men stood at the edge of Boeing Field, shivering a little in the morning mist, their hearts and the soles of their feet catching the rumble of four idling engines at the far end of the field. The rumble grew to a burning, firing roar and the big form was moving toward them down the runway, racing past them. Les Tower lifted her slowly, surely, over the end of the field. As though timed by a stage crew, the sun popped over the ridge of the Cascades, its brightness glistening on the polished wings that streaked to meet it, and the 299 was a receding speck in the sky.

Claire Egtvedt closed his eyes and smiled. Design engineer Bob Minshall turned to Ed Wells, who had been promoted to project engineer for the 299. "That's it Ed. Great work."[10]

With the test flights successfully completed, on August 20, 1935, at 3:45 A.M., the 299 was off for a nonstop flight to Dayton, Ohio. On board were Les Tower, engine man Henry Igo, and mechanic Bud Benton. Exactly nine hours after leaving Seattle, they were coming down at Wright Field. The plane had made the 2,000-mile flight in record time, averaging 252 miles per hour.

Claire Egtvedt and Ed Wells were waiting. They informed the crew that they were three hours earlier than expected.

The 299 was not alone—a Martin B-12 and a Douglas B-18, both twin-engined aircraft, were there also—but attention was focused on the radical new four-engined design.

Preliminary flight tests were excellent. The staff at Wright Field was eagerly following the progress of the tests—speed, endurance, time of climb, service ceiling, structure, design, power plant, armament, equipment and maintenance.

One morning in October, with a takeoff that should have now been routine, the plane seemed to be climbing too steeply. Abruptly, it pitched straight up, falling off on the wing, dropping and straightening out—but not enough. Billowing flame and smoke enveloped the plane as it hit the ground, with the fire trucks already speeding toward it.

Jake Harman, now bombardment project engineer, heard the sirens, and someone shouting "299." He raced out, hailed a field car, and rushed to the site. Fire trucks were pouring foam on the burning plane. Harman jumped onto a flatbed truck, yelled at the driver, Lieutenant Giovanelli, to back it into the burning mass. Pulling their coats over their heads, with arms shielding their faces, the two men dashed into the inferno and dragged out Major Pete

Hill, the pilot, and Les Tower. Lieutenant Don Putt, the project test pilot, face gashed and burned, had jumped out the front end. Two other crew members scrambled out the back. Major Hill died that afternoon. Les Tower, who had been on board as an observer, was badly burned, but expected to survive. The rest had lesser injuries.

Examination of the wreckage revealed that the plane had taken off with the control surfaces locked. The tail surfaces were so large that locks were put in place on the ground to guard against whipping in the wind. Having forgotten to remove the locks before takeoff, the crew had doomed the plane.

Under the rules, the 299 was ineligible for the final judging—it had not completed all the tests.

Egtvedt was devastated. Boeing treasurer, Harold Bowman, back at the plant, gazed mournfully at the overdrawn bank statement. Les Tower rallied, but took the accident personally, blaming himself for not removing the control locks. The overbearing remorse took the fight out of him, and suddenly he was gone.

Rumors came from Washington that the 299 was too big for a human being to handle—that the Douglas B-18, a bomber version of the DC-3, would win the competition. Egtvedt clung to Dayton and Washington in an all out attempt to salvage the program.

The 600 employees were already thinking about a bleak Christmas, when the news came that the B-18 had won the production contract. Now they were certain.

However, the 299 had gained many converts in the Air Corps and in Washington. A service test order was placed for thirteen airplanes, plus a fourteenth for structural test. The new plane—the B-17—became the *Flying Fortress*.

Fabrication of the giant XB-15, the designation for the Project A design, continued—and was completed in 1937. *Old Grandpappy*, the one and only, was 26 feet longer than the Model 299, and had a 36-foot greater wingspan, at the time representing the largest bomber ever built. On July 30, 1939, the XB-15 broke the world record for weight lifting held by the *Maxim Gorky*.

1. *Chronicle of the 20th century*, (New York: Chronicle Publications, 1987), 282.
2. *Flight: A Pictorial History of Aviation*, 1953, 99.
3. Harold Mansfield, *Vision*, (New York: Popular Library, 1966), 50.
4. Ibid., 50.
5. Igor Sikorsky, *The Story of the Winged-S*, (New York: Dodd, Mead & Company, 1938), 86.
6. James Gilbert, *The World's Worst Aircraft*, (New York: St. Martin's Press, 1975), 99.
7. Mansfield, *Vision*, 53.
8. Ibid., 54.
9. E.C. Wells, interview by Donald S. Schmechel, June, 1986.
10. Mansfield, *Vision*, 55.

11

The Ocean Queens

The world was just about the right size for Juan Trippe, and he needed a bigger airplane to conquer its skies.

Early in 1929 he reached an agreement with Sikorsky to build two giant four-engined airships, designated the S-40—each costing $125,000. A third was optioned.

In April 1931, the first S-40 rolled out and began flight testing. With a range of 1,500 miles, the 58,000-pound amphibian could cruise at 115 miles per hour, flying at 13,500 feet. Trippe named the new planes *Clippers*. Speed was reckoned in knots, and time according to bells. The fifty passengers sat in Queen Anne chairs upholstered in blue and orange, in a walnut cabin with blue carpets.

On Columbus Day, October 10, 1931, Mrs. Herbert Hoover christened the *American Clipper* with a bottle of water from the Caribbean Sea. A new era in ocean flying had begun.

On November 19, 1931, the S-40 flying boat took off from Miami on its maiden flight to Panama with paying passengers on board. Charles Lindbergh was at the controls.

A hot meal was served aloft, the first prepared in an American overwater aircraft galley. Passengers dined at real tables draped with linen tablecloths, using heavy silverware. Service was performed by a uniformed steward.

Lindbergh was pleased with the airplane—but not satisfied. The S-40 was based on the twin-engined S-38, upgraded to four engines. He wanted a completely new airplane. Contemplation as to the next step in design occupied most of his thoughts. Thus, high above the Caribbean, while Sikorsky ate his lunch, Lindbergh turned the controls over to copilot Basil Rowe and drew sketches on the menu. He wanted a range that would take them at least from San Francisco to Hawaii, a distance of about 2,500 miles.[1]

Trippe had set his mind on crossing oceans. He searched the world for undiscovered islands suitable for landing spots; considered artificial floating islands; aerial refueling; and even catapults operating from ships in the open sea. He studied the idea of additional engines, but increasing the number beyond four seemed to be going in the wrong direction.

The Germans had already developed the DO-X, a huge flying boat with twelve engines. Built in 1929, it had accommodations for sixty-nine on a luxurious shipboard scale. In May 1932, the DO-X made a successful crossing of the South Atlantic to Brazil, then flew island-by-island to New York, where it circled triumphantly over Manhattan. After refueling, it returned to Germany via Newfoundland. In spite of the apparent success, the plane simply had too many fuel-gobbling engines to warrant continued development.

Still, Trippe was arrogant enough to rate nothing as insoluble, and five months before Lindbergh and Sikorsky made the sketches

for the S-42, he had sent letters to all six prominent U.S. manufacturers, asking them to design a high-speed multi-engined flying
boat having a cruising range of 2,500 miles against 30-mile headwinds and providing for a crew of four together with at least 300
pounds of mail. Four of the six manufacturers told him he was
dreaming. But Sikorsky agreed to study the proposal, and the
Glenn Martin Company of Baltimore, did likewise.

The S-40 was test flown by Lindbergh on August 1, 1934.
With a full load, the new flying boat averaged 157.5 miles per hour
over a 1,242-mile course. The absolute range was 2,540 miles—
with no passengers.

By year end, Trippe had three Sikorsky S-42s and three Martin
M-130s about to be delivered, and he kept staring at the globe. It
appeared he would have to challenge the Pacific at its widest
point—via Hawaii. He stretched a piece of string between two
points on his globe, measuring it to translate the inches into hours
in the air.

The following spring, the S-42 took off for Hawaii on a proving flight. On return, heavy headwinds nearly spelled disaster. The
calculated maximum time the plane could remain in the air was
twenty-one and one half hours. When it landed in San Francisco,
it had been in the air for twenty-three hours and forty-one minutes. Testing with a gauge stick, the flight engineer found no
measurable fuel, reporting, "Just about damp at the bottom. I don't
think we could have made it once around the bay."[2]

The S-42 went into service in Latin America and Trippe asked
the factory to stretch its range.

In Baltimore on October 9, 1935, the first of the new Martin
M-130 flying boats was turned over to Pan American, and on Oc-
tober 21, the airmail contract for flying the Pacific was awarded.
Pan American was the sole bidder.

Trippe announced, "This flying boat will be named the *China
Clipper*, after her famous predecessor which carried the American
flag across the Pacific a hundred years ago."[3]

On November 22, 1935, the *China Clipper* inaugurated regular service across the Pacific, flying the Honolulu–Midway–Wake–Guam–Manila–Hong Kong route. The *Phillipine* and *Hawaii* Clippers, second and third of the Martin flying boats, were delivered shortly thereafter, and by December, the planes had established weekly service.

Around the world history was moving in giant strides. In Europe, the seeds of war began to sprout as Chancellor Adolf Hitler renounced the Treaty of Versailles. Heinrich Himmler, chief of the SS, took command of Germany's concentration camps. Mussolini's armies invaded Ethiopia, and in China, Mao Tsetung embarked on his 6,000 mile Long March from Kiangsi Province to Yunnan.

At home, the United States officially recognized the Communist government of the Soviet Union, and the Roosevelt Administration initiated a number of programs to bring the nation out of the Great Depression. A watershed year for new legislation, 1935 brought forth social security—perhaps the single most far reaching socio-economic statute of the twentieth century. The National Labor Relations Act also became law—prohibiting employers from interfering with a worker's right to join a union, requiring management to recognize unions, and directing management to bargain collectively with them.

Egtvedt had been considering the possibility of doing something with a commercial adaptation of the XB-15, but he was acutely aware of the plant limitations for building big flying boats, which the market seemed to be demanding. Financing also presented a major problem. With stockholders expecting a profit, 1935 ended in a loss of $334,000—even worse than the previous year. Nevertheless, construction of the fourteen flying fortresses simply demanded additional facilities—and he was driven by a certain confidence in the future.

Planning was initiated for acquiring a new plant site. There had been a persistent rumor that a California company had offered Boeing the lease of enough land for a new factory for ten years, free of charge. A pioneer truck farmer, by the name of Guisseppe Desimone—an ardent Boeing fan—took the rumors seriously and didn't want the company to leave Seattle. He had settled on the rich bottom land along the Duwamish, the prime location for a new facility.

No land was for sale in the area. Farming had been good for the Desimones, and Guisseppe had enough land to part with "40 acres for Boeing and the future of the Pacific Northwest."[4] He sold the land to Boeing for $1.

In April 1936, the company announced its intent to construct a modern assembly building on the site. This 61,750-square-foot addition represented nearly a 20 percent increase in floor space. With the Duwamish river immediately to the rear, and a railroad spur in the front—adjacent to Boeing Field—the new fabrication facility would be accessible by land, sea, and air. Named Plant II, it was occupied in November. The old Heath facility became known as Plant I.

Not long after Wellwood Beall went to China to sell pursuit planes, Captain Eddie Musick flew the S-42 flying boat to Hawaii and there was a rumor that China and the U.S. would be linked by regular air service before the end of the year.

Beall, poised and confident with his invariably flashy bow tie and trim mustache, had been quickly accepted by his peers as a man of exceptional insight. He insisted that air service over the Pacific was at least ten years away, dismissing the rumor as a lot of poppycock.

It was not long before Beall began to have second thoughts. When Pan American put the first of their three Martin flying boats into service in the Pacific, he realized his off-the-cuff prediction was far from the mark. Taking a tour of the factory where the XB-15 wing was being assembled, even Beall was awed by its massive beams and trusses—more like a bridge than an airplane.

For one fleeting instant a vision of a giant flying boat flashed through his brain—much bigger than the Martins, and capable of carrying at least fifty, perhaps seventy passengers to China.

In the days that followed, Beall tracked the XB-15 progress and studied the details. Unable to contain his personal enthusiasm any longer, he went to chief engineer Bob Minshall, proposing that the company get back into the flying boat business. He wanted to submit a Clipper design to Pan American—utilizing the XB-15 wing.

"We've already discussed that," Minshall told him. "Claire and I talked with Pan American about it." He showed Beall a letter dated February 28, 1936, from Frank Gledhill, the Pan American vice-president and purchasing agent, asking if Boeing would be interested in submitting plans for a long-range four-engined marine aircraft built around engines of 1,000 to 1,250 horsepower.

"Great. That's right in the XB-15 class," Beall said.

"I know. But we can't do it."

"Why not?"

Minshall spelled out the problems—money, facilities, manpower. "Look at the date they want the drawings. We're up to our necks now." Minshall looked tired. Responsibility was putting furrows in his round, full face.

"I'd like to work on it if that would help," Beall said.

"We've already written Gledhill that we won't be able to enter."[5]

Beall went away disappointed. The huge wing seemed so right for a flying boat. He was only the service engineer, it was none of his business—but the idea continued to haunt him. He could not put it out of his mind. He began making drawings at home on the dining room table.

The concept slowly came into focus. Night after night, Beall labored over his drawings, starting with the wings and tail, then the hull—the flight deck and the passenger cabin. Beall took the sketches to Minshall. He was impressed, promising to talk with Egtvedt. Reaching Egtvedt in Dayton by phone, he got the green light, and they requested an extension of the deadline for submitting bids to Pan American. Gledhill agreed, and Beall was assigned to the new program.

After some intense working sessions, the specifications for the airplane were established. The giant seaplane would be 106 feet long with a wingspan of 152 feet, and standing over 27 feet in height. The cavernous hull would accommodate seventy-four passengers with a crew of six. Grossing 82,500 pounds, the big ship would have a range of 3,500 miles.

Gledhill had sent his letter to the six top aircraft manufacturers in the country. In Baltimore, the letter angered Glenn Martin. After furnishing the *China Clipper* and its two sister ships, he thought he deserved a better deal. The first three had been manufactured at a loss, and he expected to make a profit from re-orders. He wanted to improve the design or be granted a contract on favorable terms. From Bridgeport, Connecticut, a similar reply was received from Sikorsky. Trippe only shrugged, and Boeing was the sole bidder.

In Pan American's headquarters in the Chrysler Building in New York, and the Barclay Hotel, Egtvedt, Beall, and aerody-namicist Ralph Cram hammered out the cost and performance guarantees. On June 21, 1936, a $3 million contract for six Model 314 Clippers was signed, with an option for six more.

With the news of the Boeing contract, Martin was furious, claiming that Gledhill and Trippe had ruined him. Trippe replied in pat phrases: "We're businessmen. We can't have friends. We can't be in the position of according favors. We have to look at each deal on a cold-blooded business basis."[6]

Back at the plant, there was work to be done. Hiring began to pick up. The company found many of its new recruits in the waves of dispossessed farmers from the dust bowl who migrated to the coast. They were green—knew nothing about building airplanes—but they were eager and ambitious, willing to work hard for a few dollars. Boeing expanded its training program—always one of its strong commitments—to meet the need.

On September 23, 1935 the International Association of Machinists issued a charter to a union local at the Boeing plant in Seattle. With the new National Labor Relations Act, now law, the number of union members grew. The union president, 68-year-old Milton W. Potter, with a committee of others, approached Boeing management that month to seek a wage agreement. After much discussion, a contract was negotiated. The company asked the NLRB to certify that the union had a majority membership among the eligible employees. The union was certified and the company signed a union shop contract covering production workers.[7]

Another milestone was passed in April 1936, when *Boeing News* began publication again, with Harold Mansfield hired as editor and publicity manager. Mansfield, destined to play a unique role in Boeing's history, had served as a reporter for the *Post-Intelligencer*—Seattle's morning newspaper—for a brief period, after graduating cum laude from the University of Washington in 1934.

By 1939, the union founded its own newspaper, the *Aero Mechanic*, official house organ for the Aeronautical Industrial District 751.

The first of the Pan American Clippers was approaching the zero hour for launching in late May 1938. Most of its 500,000 parts were now in it. Factory manager Fred Laudan, quick stepping, quick talking, was all over the plant and in and out of project engineer Ed Duff's office to see about final changes.[8]

Edmund E. "Ed" Duff was not easily ruffled, even though he was fairly new compared to Laudan, having joined Boeing after graduating in mechanical engineering from the University of Washington in 1928.

Carpenters had to cut away the whole back side of the assembly building so the hull could be dollied out to the newly built dock where high derricks could attach its wings. Out there it looked for the first time like an airplane.

A national radio network had its microphone set up on the dock on May 31, the day for launching. Harold Mansfield reported from the scene:

Tide tables set an insistent deadline of 5:00 P.M. for the ship to hit the water, so there would be ample depth to get out through the shallows and link up to a barge for the trip down the waterway and into the bay. Lowering it into the water would be a delicate operation. When the hour struck, the ship began to move and the radiomen were on the air.

"This mighty triumph of American enterprise, this great Flying Clipper ship that will span the Atlantic and the Pacific carrying the flag of the United States to world supremacy in the air, is being lowered majestically into the water here in Seattle." The announcer spotted Laudan coming by.

"The vice-president and factory manager of this plant, Mr. Fred P. Laudan, is directing the operation. We are going to ask him to say a few words to our nationwide audience." An assistant grabbed Laudan's arm and coaxed him to the microphone. "Mr. Laudan, what does this occasion mean to you?" The harried Laudan spared one glance from his ship. "To me? It means just one big headache." Hurriedly, an aide summoned him away.

Newspapermen from the East arrived for the flight. Jim Piersol, the *New York Times* reporter, and something of an aeronautical engineer, wore a skeptic's scowl. "The tail is too small for all that airplane," he said.

"Quit worrying," said Beall. "It's been tested. It's based on the XB-15 and that's doing all right."[9]

On Wednesday, June 1, Eddie Allen revved up the four 1,200 horsepower Wright Cyclone engines and began taxi tests. After some harrowing experiences in getting fuel and ballast adjusted in the huge plane, the taxi tests were deemed satisfactory by Allen. The following Tuesday, the Clipper was loaded to a gross of 77,500 pounds, just 5,000 pounds under its maximum, and ready for takeoff.

"At 6:17 P.M., the great roar of the Cyclones sounded across the water and Eddie Allen was moving toward the picket boats. The watchers raced ahead to stay parallel. Salt spray in the face and high excitement aboard, they bounced through the waves as the big-hulled flying boat roared past them, sailing high on the step. Everything was rushing—water, wind, airplane. Ahead, the great hull skimmed the surface, lifted up, steady into the air, up and up into the northern sky. Yells of applause broke into the freshness of the wind. They watched the flying Clipper sail out of sight.

"After a thirty-eight minute flight, Eddie Allen landed on Lake Washington, where further testing was to be based. Beall caught up with him later in the evening. 'We had power to spare,' Eddie said, 'but when I got off the water I couldn't turn. There's just not enough rudder for that big body. When we got to 2,000 feet, I used power on one side for a wide ten-mile turn.'"[10]

The 314 went back to the wind tunnel. The tail was changed to a double, and finally to a triple configuration. The sponsons, sometimes called sea wings, which replaced the pontoons, also required redesign to improve lateral stability during takeoff. They were expensive changes.

The cost of research and engineering for big airplanes was escalating. The original Model 299 had taken 153,000 man-hours of engineering. The Clippers took 380,000, representing the largest engineering program ever undertaken by Boeing up to that time.

The first Clipper was delivered in January 1939—late—a result of the extensive testing required to reconfigure the tail and sponsons.

Model 314 *Clippers*——1937–1941

The *Ocean Queens* were designed for Pan American for both transAtlantic and transPacific routes. The largest airplane then flying, it carried 77 passengers, with 40 berths.

On March 3, 1939, having flown nonstop to Washington, D.C., the first Model 314 was christened the *Yankee Clipper* by Mrs. Franklin D. Roosevelt at Anacostia Naval Air station. There was no champagne at the christening. She used a gold trimmed bottle of water gathered from the Seven Seas by Pan American.

Regular passenger service, New York to Marseille, was announced for June 28. A timetable was printed, and fares were established: $375 one way, $675 round trip, and the first ticket was sold to W.J. Eck, who was from Washington, D.C., and had applied for ticket No. 1 ten years before. On takeoff day, he waved the ticket, bragging that he had been offered $5,000 for it.[11]

The *Yankee Clipper* was the largest airplane then flying. Its propellers cut an arc fourteen feet, ten inches in diameter. It had a maximum range of around 4,275 miles at 150 miles per hour, and it could seat up to seventy-four passengers, or sleep forty in berths. It had two decks, both carpeted, the upper deck being used exclusively for the crew. The lower deck contained five passenger compartments, plus a dining room seating fifteen people, plus a kind of honeymoon suite self-contained in the rear. There were separate dressing rooms for men and women, each with its own toilet, and the gentlemen's toilet contained—for the first and last time in commercial aviation—twin service units. Commercial aviation would never know such luxury again.

The Clippers were also employed on the Hong Kong route and made the first connection with Africa. Pan American exercised its options for the second contingent of six airplanes, designated 314As, with greater fuel capacity, increased power and a passenger load increased by three—to seventy-seven.

During World War II, the total fleet operated as C-98s for the army and as B-314s for the navy. They carried priority passengers and priority cargo only. Admirals and generals flew—kings and queens of beleaguered nations flew—such as Wilhelmina of the Netherlands and George of Greece. Roosevelt himself flew, becoming the first incumbent president ever taken aloft.[12]

1. Robert Daley, *An American Saga*, (New York: Random House, 1980), 103.
2. Ibid., 156.
3. Ibid., 166.
4. *Boeing News*, 19 December 1986, 3.
5. Harold Mansfield, *Vision*, (New York: Popular Library, 1966), 63.
6. Daley, *An American Saga*, 224.
7. K.L. Calkins, *An Analysis of Labor Relations News Coverage...*, (Seattle: University of Washington, 1968), 12.
8. Mansfield, *Vision*, 71.
9. Ibid., 72.
10. Ibid., 75.
11. Daley, *An American Saga*, 243.
12. Ibid., 335.

The Four-engine Era

The beginning of Boeing's third decade in July 1936, marked a major transition in the airplane manufacturing business. The four-engine era had been opened with the Model 299 and the giant XB-15.

The flying boats, result of determined pioneering by Juan Trippe and innovative response by industry, epitomized by the Clipper Queens, were soon to conquer the last bastion of angry ocean, the North Atlantic—and nowhere in the world would be out of reach by airplane.

In September, although only a nucleus of the worldwide organization which was destined to develop, a service unit was formed, with Wellwood Beall in charge. Nemo Poncetti, having returned from his assignment in China, was hired into the Field Service Section of the Service Unit. From the beginning, this organization dedicated itself to providing customers with the best service in the world.

Thus, early in its corporate life, service became one of the principal pinions upon which The Boeing Company stood. The others: integrity, quality of product, technical excellence, and attention to people as the key resource.

In 1936, powerful forces signaled dramatic change around the world. On March 7, German infantry goose-stepped into Cologne, and the Rhineland—established as a demilitarized zone after World War I—was reoccupied. Three weeks later, a plebiscite gave Adolf Hitler a 99 percent vote of confidence. In November, Japan's Kursu and Italy's Ciano met with Hitler in Berlin, where they signed an anticommunist pact pledging cooperation against the spread of Soviet influence.

In Spain, civil war erupted in July, when General Francisco Franco, leader of the Fascist troops, vowed to press on until he had installed himself in Madrid.

In Africa, Ethiopia's defense against Italy crumbled, and the capital of Addis Ababa, jammed with refugees, was about to fall. Benito Mussolini boasted, "Italy at last has her empire."

In Asia, Canton demanded war on Japan, seeking to rally all of China.

As the year drew to a close, Foreign Secretary Anthony Eden of Great Britain warned Hitler that his country would fight to protect Belgium.

In the U.S., Franklin D. Roosevelt won reelection by a landslide, defeating Alfred M. Landon in the greatest outpouring of voters in the nation's history.

The U.S. Army general staff met in Washington, D.C. to discuss bombardment airplane procurement policy.

The Air Corps had a quantity of twin-engined Douglas B-18s on order, and thirteen four-engined Boeing B-17s, with a fourteenth to be used for structural testing. In Category Four of the development list made up in 1933, the mammoth, 164,000 pound XB-19, more than two and one-half times the gross weight of the XB-15, was being designed by Douglas.

At the meeting, the merits of very large airplanes received intense discussion. No country had or was likely in the near future to have an aircraft capable of attacking the United States. The twin-engined B-18 was equal to any mission assigned to the Air Corps and was much less expensive than the proposed four-engined airplanes. Many felt that the planes were getting too big for the materials of construction. In the final report to the chief of staff, it was concluded that concentration on big bombers was inconsistent with national policy and threatened duplication of the function of the navy, which was assigned to protect the country beyond 200 miles from its shores. At this juncture, the future of the B-17 looked bleak.

In Dayton, Jake Harman was still lobbying hard to get more bombers.

"Colonel Oliver Echols, the Air Corps engineering chief, called him in. 'Look, Jake,' the colonel said, 'I have an idea. We aren't going to get any more than thirteen B-17s for awhile. We could make it fourteen, if we made a flying airplane out of the one that is supposed to be used for structural tests. I doubt that we need those tests. Why don't we use that airplane to put in turbo-superchargers for high altitude?'

"Harman thought it was an excellent idea. The engine turbo-supercharger, developed by Dr. Sanford Moss of General Electric with the aid of Wright Field engineers, utilized a turbine wheel driven by exhaust gases. The turbine was used to pump high pressure air into the engines for increased power at thin-air altitudes.

"'What would turbos do for the speed of the '17'?" Echols asked.

"Harman got out his slide rule and worked the numbers back and forth. 'At 25,000 feet, maybe 290 miles an hour.'

"'Get hold of Claire Egtvedt and find out if Boeing will do it. I'll see if I can dig up the money.'"[1]

Bold innovation proved once again to be king of the industry. In one corner of the engineering department at Seattle, a few drafting tables were separated from the rest by a glass partition. On the door was a sign—*Restricted Area—Preliminary Design*. Ed Wells was in charge.

"Every so often Claire Egtvedt would go down and lean over Ed Well's table. This time he had a new question. Did they have enough information on turbo-superchargers to put them on the B-17?

"Ed said he wasn't sure, but that he could get it.

"'Oliver Echols wants to equip the static test ship for high altitudes.'

"'How high?'

"'Twenty-five or thirty thousand feet.'

"'Not cabin supercharging?'

"'No, just engines.' But Egtvedt added, when they discussed it further, that he didn't think they could always be partial to the engines. The people in the airplane needed air as well. Something would have to be done sooner or later about supercharging the passenger cabin."[2]

The issue of whether to use the fourteenth Y1B-17 for structural test or for high altitude flying with the new turbo-superchargers was settled partially by chance. On a routine test flight, one of the production airplanes stalled. During the recovery maneuver, the loads on the wings were so great that the wings were bent. There was no need for further testing.

The modified airplane was called the Y1B-17A, and operating altitudes were increased to above 30,000 feet. The "A" performed so well, validating the high altitude bombing capability, that thirty-nine of the new supercharger-equipped planes were ordered—designated as the B-17B.

The year of 1936 witnessed another milestone. A suggestion contest was initiated in September, whereby cash awards were given for ideas to improve some aspect of company operations. The suggestion system became a permanent Boeing feature, another of the mechanisms which provided individuals at all levels the opportunity to develop their identity with company products and to further its competitiveness.

Preliminary design, a small, select group, was the gestation center for new projects—always shrouded in a certain aura of secrecy. All the manufacturers had them. At Douglas, experimental machines came out of an area called "The Holy of Holies," and at Lockheed, "The Skunk Works."

The latest new Boeing project was announced on George Washington's birthday in February 1937, when it was revealed that Transcontinental and Western Air, Inc., had ordered six airplanes of a Model 307. It was named the *Stratoliner*.

Everywhere the coming four-engined transports became a subject for lively dialogue. A center spread Boeing ad in the March 15 issue of *Time* proclaimed: "The 4-Engine Era is here!"

With the boast, "Boeing has always built tomorrow's airplanes today!" the ad noted that the Boeing production line currently contained FOUR-ENGINED BOMBERS, FOUR ENGINED TRANSPORTS, AND FOUR-ENGINED 'CLIPPERS.'[3]

Shortly following, Pan American announced they would purchase two Model 307s completely equipped for flying in the substratosphere, and descriptive stories of the vast possibilities opened up by the new type of plane, flowed from the pens of pundits.

With a gross weight of 42,000 pounds, the Model 307 accommodated thirty-three daytime passengers, in addition to a crew of four, and twenty-six passengers on overnight flights, with upper

Model 307 *Stratoliner*—1939–1940
The ill-fated pioneer of high altitude pressurized cabin flight.

and lower berths for eighteen, and reclining chairs for the remaining eight. The cargo capacity was 3,750 pounds, greater than the entire payload of the two-engined airplanes in service at the time. Powered by four Wright G-100 series Cyclone engines, capable of developing a total of 4,400 horsepower, the plane would cruise easily at over 200 miles per hour, attaining a speed of 250 at high altitudes.

The pressurized cabin, a spectacular first, augured well for Boeing to wrest the commercial leadership from Douglas.

The extra speed attainable at high altitudes—with sea-level comfort for the passengers—and berths for night flying, made the airplane unique in the commercial field.

On December 31, 1938, Eddie Allen and a crew of four took the first Stratoliner into the air. Tests went well.

An electric atmosphere pervaded the engineering department—they had scored once again with a first in the industry.

There are times, however, when brains and guts are not enough. Technology plays no favorites, and the elusive edge of innovation can evaporate like the morning mist. Luck—a double-edged sword—can deliver fame and fortune, or can as easily, turn what appear to be golden opportunities into black despair.

The Stratoliner, ahead of its time and full of promise, was pushed too far in its test program. In March 1939, two representatives of the Dutch airline, KLM, were in Seattle to fly the airplane. They posed a very improbable flight situation, inquiring what would happen if two engines were out on the same side and the rudder was full-over for maximum yaw. When Boeing aerodynamicist Ralph Cram replied that there was no reason for that maneuver with such a big ship, Dutch engineer Albert von Baumhauer was not satisfied. They decided to try various angles of yaw, and measure the forces on the control column.

Later that bright Saturday afternoon, the sheriff's office called to report that a giant plane had crashed in the foothills of Mt. Rainier. During the test, the plane had approached stalling speed and gone into a spinning dive. An eyewitness reported that the plane had fallen out of the sky in pieces.

Sheriff's deputies had taken test pilot Julius Barr's body out of the pilot's seat; von Baumhauer's from the copilot's seat; chief engineer Jack Kylstra, Ralph Cram, Earl Ferguson, and five others from the remaining wreckage.

Robert "Bob" Minshall, chief engineer—newly elected to the board of directors—who was in charge, held his head and wept.

An old timer, Bob Minshall had joined the engineering department in 1918. He attended the University of Washington on a part-time basis, receiving a degree in civil engineering in 1923. Chief test pilot Eddie Allen, who was hired a few months after the maiden flight of the Stratoliner, came into Minshall's office shortly after the crash investigation was completed.

"'We have the opportunity here that exists nowhere else, Bob. We've come to the point where we need extensive research. Not

just on the ground but in the air—flight and aerodynamic research.'

"Minshall was interested.

"'Now,' Eddie's finger shot up enthusiastically, 'you can't do
that sort of thing in small airplanes. You have to carry all kinds of
instruments and equipment. Here you are with a stable full of big
airplanes. You're the ones to do it.'

"'Just what do you have in mind, Eddie?'

"'The day when you build an airplane and call in a pilot like me
to test it is over. There should be a full-time, fully staffed department constantly carrying on this flight research, and the same department should carry on a constant program of wind tunnel
research. The two go hand in hand. They should both be a part of
designing the plane, not just testing it.'"[4]

Minshall discussed Allen's proposal with Egtvedt, and soon a
department for aerodynamics and flight research was created, with
Eddie Allen as the director.

Gathering a staff for his new department, in 1939 Allen hired
George S. Schairer, a brilliant young aerodynamicist from
Swarthmore College, who earned his masters degree at MIT. He
was destined to leave his mark on Boeing airplane projects for the
next thirty-eight years.

The thrust of the 307 program was blunted by the crash investigation. Only ten Stratoliners were built, five of them taken into
the Army Air Corps as C-75s during World War II, where they
pioneered the Air Transport Command's transatlantic routes.

Before the C-75s were returned to their private owners, they
completed some 3,000 ocean crossings and logged more than
45,000 hours in flying to every corner of the world.

Donald Douglas reached his quarter century mark in the aviation industry on July 6, 1939. A year earlier, he had developed a
prototype for the DC-4, a four-engined commercial transport
known as the DC-4E, which embodied many new advances in the

state of the art. The DC-4 represented another giant step in commercial aviation. Roughly three times the size of the DC-3, the plane could carry forty-two passengers in a pressurized, soundproofed cabin. For the first time, the tail wheel was replaced with a nose wheel, providing a level platform for the plane on the ground.

Shortly after the announcement, forty airplanes had been ordered by domestic airlines—but none were delivered. After Pearl Harbor, with an urgent need for military transport, the Army Air Corps took over the orders, and the airplane went to war as the C-54 *Skymaster*. The thousands of hours of wartime flying proved the big plane, and assured Douglas of a continuing claim to the postwar commercial sky.

The impact of the DC series on market share was boldly highlighted in the figures released from the Civil Aeronautics Authority in July 1939. Scheduled commercial aircraft in service and in reserve for the top three manufacturers were: Douglas, 183; Boeing, 45; and Lockheed, 42.

1. Harold Mansfield, *Vision*, (New York, Popular Library, 1966), 68.
2. Ibid. 68.
3. *Time*, 15 March, 1937, Centerfold.
4. Mansfield, *Vision*, 82.

13

The Flying
Fortress

Boeing was in over its head. The first
nine months of 1939 showed a loss of $2,600,000. Money would
be needed—and quickly.

With the Clippers posting a loss, the Stratoliner dead, and
General Echols reporting that the War Department in Washington had turned down his request for funds for four-engined
bombers for fiscal 1940–41, it was difficult for officials at Boeing to
find any silver lining in the dark clouds.

At Douglas, the DC-3 was being manufactured for both foreign
and domestic operators, with deliveries averaging six aircraft per
month. The B-18A was in production, with orders on hand for 217

airplanes. France had placed an order for 100 DB-7s, an improved version of the 7B twin-engine attack bomber built for the U.S. Army. A further refinement of the DB-7 design, the A-20A, was well advanced, and 123 airplanes were to be built for the Army. Finally, the U.S. Navy had ordered 144 SBD scout bombers.[1]

Lockheed, with the eleven-passenger, Model 14 Super Electra, turned a profit in 1936—the first since 1929. With a continuing sure sense for image building, the company promoted the round-the-world flight of Howard Hughes in 1938. With a crew of four, Hughes established a new record of three days and nineteen hours. The world shrank, and sales boomed. The fourteen-seat Model 18 Lodestar followed. That airplane put Lockheed in the big time to stay, appearing in the war as the *Ventura* bomber.

By 1937, Gross was steering his company toward the war, which he believed was certain to involve the United States, in spite of the firm declaration of neutrality by President Roosevelt.

Following his instincts, Gross sent his brother, Courtland, to England in 1937 to attempt to interest the British in a modified Super Electra to serve as a medium-range bomber. At the time, the British were sold on diplomacy as the solution to the demands of Nazi Germany, and Lockheed came up empty-handed.

Not one to be squeamish about customers, Gross took his offers to the Germans, again returning with no orders. The Germans said "no thanks, our aircraft industry is quite adequate." He even tried Japan, where he had better luck, concluding a contract on the eve of war in 1939.[2]

Undaunted by his limited success abroad, Gross turned back to the needs of the United States. His engineering department had grown both in numbers and in expertise, including a talented visionary, Clarence "Kelly" Johnson.

Johnson's first creation was one that captured the imagination of friend and foe alike in World War II, becoming one of the growing symbols of American air power, the P-38. It was dramatically different from any airplane that had ever flown. With a raised tail, twin booms extending from the two engines, all the way back to the tail, and only a central bubble for a fuselage, it was not only wildly beautiful, it performed. Quickly gaining the moniker of *Lockheed Lightning*, the plane went into mass production.

The British market did not evade Lockheed for long. In 1938, the British sent a delegation to the United States, visiting the major aircraft builders to determine how they could supplement their own industry.

According to a Lockheed legend, the five-day advance notice of the arrival of the British team gave them sufficient time, working around the clock, to build a plywood model of a bomber version of the Model 14 airplane.

Without fanfare, a production order for 175 machines was placed, for a contract value of $25 million. The airplane was named the *Hudson*. Orders added—and multiplied.

Lockheed formed two subsidiaries to help deal with the production demand; the Vega Company, also in Burbank, and a British assembly plant at Speke, near Liverpool. Later in the war, more assembly bases were set up in Northern Ireland, Scotland, and Australia. Lockheed had already drawn the lines, in rough crayon, for multinational operations to come.

Work was also continuing on the Excalibur Project, a planned thirty-passenger answer to the latest version of the DC-3 and the Stratoliner. Designated the L-44, the airplane became the nucleus for preliminary design studies by Kelly Johnson for a still larger airplane. The audacious target was for transcontinental range and a speed of 300 miles per hour.

Multimillionaire Howard Hughes, who had then gained control of Trans World Airlines, encouraged Lockheed to go forward, ordering nine while the airplane was not much beyond the doodling stage.

The product was the *Constellation*. When Pan American placed a rival order—for forty planes—Hughes increased the TWA order to forty. Thus, both Lockheed and Douglas had guaranteed themselves firm positions in the postwar commercial airplane market—even before the United States entered the war.

Angry currents flowed in Europe and Asia, with events marching to a quickened cadence. On September 5, 1937, the streets of Nuremburg were lined with storm troopers, as hundreds of trains converged on the city, bringing 600,000 German soldiers to hear their Fuhrer. On February 4, 1938, Adolf Hitler named himself as supreme commander of the German armed forces, and in March, followed his columns of tanks into Austria. By September, a four-power conference in Munich reached an agreement to divide Czechoslovakia, and German troops goose-stepped unhindered into the Sudetenland. Neville Chamberlain, prime minister of England, announced that the agreement "would bring peace in our time."

In March 1939, Madrid fell to General Francisco Franco, and the Spanish Civil War was history. In May, Hitler and Mussolini signed a "pact of steel", pledging mutual support.

After stunning the world with a nonaggression pact with Stalin on August 23, Hitler sent a mighty German force of 1.25 million men across the Polish border on September 1. Russian troops invaded from the east two weeks later. On September 3, 1939, Britain and France declared war.

In Nanking, Chiang Kai-shek and Mao Tsetung agreed to fight together against their common enemy, Japan.

At Boeing, it seemed inconceivable that the B-17 would not be ordered in large numbers. What was needed was an all-out effort to organize for mass production.

Lawyer Bill Allen went to talk things over with Claire Egtvedt. "'Why don't you try to get Phil Johnson back in the company?'" Allen suggested. Phil had been gone since the time of the breakup of the United Aircraft and Transport Corporation in 1934. "'The need now is production. That's Phil's long suit.'"[3]

In August 1939, Johnson came back as president, and Egtvedt became chairman of the board. Recognizing the increasing importance of public relations, Johnson appointed Harold Mansfield to the new post of public relations manager.

While the initial B-17B was yet to be delivered, scheduled for July 29, 1939, Boeing was requested to work out a license agreement with Consolidated in San Diego to start up a second production line. Consolidated responded by promising a new airplane—larger and faster than the four-year-old Boeing design. Herein lay the latent hazard that plagued all manufacturers of airplanes. As soon as a new technology was committed to production and significant funds invested in hard tooling, competitors could offer riskless, incremental growth with zero investment. Those offers became known in the industry as "paper airplanes."

When the first $50 million of Roosevelt's rearmament program was authorized by Congress, the Consolidated program was given the green light, launching a direct competitor for the B-17—the B-24 *Liberator*.

Timing for the U.S. armed forces had also become crucial. With Congress routinely turning down appropriations for long range bombers as "aggressive"—with a potential of embroiling the U.S. in "Europe's war"—September 1, 1939 forced a complete rewrite of the rules of engagement.

A study ordered by Chief of Staff Malin Craig, to be delivered to his desk before his term expired—coincidentally on September first—made some sobering recommendations. The report hit the desk of General George C. Marshall, new chief of staff, the same day that Hitler's legions had begun the crushing defeat of Poland.

The report sounded a clear warning that naval forces and coastal guns were no longer sufficient to protect the United States. The bottom line spelled out the need for a flexible, long range air fleet. Marshall appointed General Frank Andrews—a strong advocate of the Flying Fortresses—as chief of operations on his staff.

The impact hit Wright Field like a tornado. Not only was the fire lit under B-17 procurement, but urgent discussion began on a "big bomber" which had previously been limited to the dreams of bomber enthusiasts.

The official notice reached Boeing on February 5, 1940. The circular requested that all interested companies submit proposals within one month of receipt, for a 5,333-mile-range high-altitude, high-speed bombardment airplane, designated as the R-40B.

Although some were already viewing the B-17 as a stopgap airplane, the need had become urgent. In the fall of 1939, thirty-eight of a still newer version, the "C," were ordered, for delivery in 1940. Flat-panelled gun positions replaced the blisters to reduce drag. Horsepower was boosted. More armor plate was added. The B-17C was the first of the series to see action. A British RAF squadron used them in its attack on the German battleships *Scharnhorst* and *Gneisnau* in the harbor of Brest.

Close on the heels of the "C" came the "D," with leak-proof bladders in the fuel bays and still more powerful engines—now up to 1,200 horsepower. Speed hit 300 miles an hour.

When Paris fell on June 14, 1940, General Echols called in Boeing eastern representative Jim Murray and Don Euler, chief of preliminary design, to discuss the new superbomber.

Then, turning to the Flying Fortress, he announced. "All previous estimates are obsolete. We'll contract for 512 B-17Es. But there'll be lots more later."[4]

The "E" came out in 1941. The 30-caliber machine guns were replaced with 50s, and installed in the tail for the first time. In addition, a Sperry ball turret replaced the belly gun position, and a powered turret was installed on top of the fuselage. George Schairer's enlarged dorsal fin design, developed for the Stratoliner, was incorporated to improve stability on the bombing runs.

When Pearl Harbor was attacked on December 7, 1941, Jake Harman called. "Start building airplanes," he said.

"How many," asked Phil Johnson.

"My instructions are you just start building. Never mind the

B-17 Series——*Flying Fortress*——1936–1945

The workhorse of the American bombing of Germany in World War II. A total of 12,731 were built; Boeing produced 6,981, Lockheed 2,750, and Douglas 3,000.

schedules. Tell us how much money and what things you need and when."[5]

Boeing acted quickly, developing a multi-line production plan. The fuselage was built in four sections, and the wing in five. These sections were complete—finished as to electrical wiring, control cables, and hydraulic tubing. Even the linings and equipment were installed prior to joining.

Assembly lines were established at both Douglas and Lockheed. In 1942 the "F" model came out, and finally the "G." A new chin turret, pioneered on the "F," became standard equipment. More than 400 additional design improvements had been incorporated.

Although not destined to break into the big three in

B-17 Engine and Wing Line

Final Assembly, Boeing Plant II, Seattle, at peak production, World War II.

B-17 Fuselage Line

commercial airplane production, Consolidated was a giant in building military airplanes. Put together in 1923 from remnants of one of the largest manufacturers of World War I airplanes, Dayton-Wright Company—and one of the smallest—Gallaudet Aircraft Corporation, Consolidated was largely the efforts of one man—Reuben "Reub" Fleet.

Eventually, Consolidated became the world leader in the production of training planes, and built a seaplane dynasty with the U.S. Navy—manufacturing hundreds of PBY *Catalinas*, as flying boats, and hundreds more as amphibians.

For Major Fleet, Consolidated Aircraft was his third career. Graduating from Culver Military Academy in 1906, he was active in the National Guard in his home town of Montesano, Washington, while operating a successful real estate and timber business. In 1917, at the age of thirty, he enlisted in the Signal Corps of the U.S. Army. Already a captain in Company G of the Washington National Guard, Fleet was soon promoted.

On May 15, 1918, Major Rueben Fleet was put in charge of the U.S. airmail service. After the war, he served nearly four years as contracting officer and business manager of the Air Service Engineering Division, at McCook Field, Dayton, Ohio. Fleet brought a number of the key people at Wright Field with him to Consolidated.

The B-24 went forward at a feverish pace. The March 30 contract called for first flight in nine months, before the end of 1939. The B-24 had innovations of its own, including a tricycle landing gear, first for a large bomber. Although the Liberators were used extensively in Europe, primarily on the longer strikes, its predominant deployment was in the Pacific.

In 1943, Consolidated merged with Vultee, forming Convair, one of the largest integrated aircraft manufacturers of the war period.

Headlines extolling the exploits of the Flying Fortresses in raids over Germany, left the Liberators in their shadow—nevertheless, the airplane enjoyed the largest production run by far of any

American aircraft. A total of 18,481 Liberators were built, more than half at the two Convair plants at San Diego and Fort Worth.

As a footnote to history, Consolidated very nearly missed existing at all. In 1922, when Major Fleet decided to leave Wright Field to begin a new career, he had three job offers: Clement M. Keys, president of Curtiss offered him a job as advisor on aviation matters; Gallaudet Aircraft Corporation offered the position of vice-president and general manager; and Bill Boeing—whom he had known in the lumber business—made the same offer.

In 1942, the Seattle Division, for its B-17 record, and the Wichita Division, for its Kaydet trainer, gave Boeing the honor of being the first airframe manufacturer to be selected by the U.S. government for the joint army-navy "E" award for excellence.

At Seattle, the average number of pounds of airframe produced monthly, per square foot of direct floor area continued to increase, with an average of 3.23 pounds in 1943—compared to the aircraft industry average of 1.3 pounds, and the next best heavy bomber plant of 2.5 pounds. In direct man-hours per pound of airframe produced, the 1943 average was 0.9 man-hours, versus an industry average of 3.6, and the next best heavy bomber plant average of 1.1 man-hours.[6]

Labor turnover was unusually high, primarily due to military induction and enlistments. To replace these men, the company began early to employ and train female factory workers. In March 1942, about 2.6 percent of the factory employees were female. Housewives came to work in droves, and by December 31, 1942, 42 percent of the factory work force in the Seattle plant was women. In 1943 the percentage peaked at over 50 percent.

Rosie the Riveter became the domestic hero of the war years, and a proud badge for women workers. At Boeing, 20 percent of all employees were riveters. Wearing colorful bandanas, they brought a new dimension to the work force, forming closely coordinated teams of two—riveter and bucker.

***Kaydet* Series——1938–1945**

The *Kaydets* were the most widely used primary trainer for the U.S. armed forces in World War II. Boeing Wichita Division manufactured 10,346 of these two-place biplane trainers.

Engineering, a profession generally considered to be an exclusive arena for men, took a major upswing in female employees during the war years. In 1942, Mary Ellen Russell joined Boeing as the first of the new wave. Russell, a graduate in mathematics from the University of Washington, with a masters degree in geology, was still spending part of her time working toward a doctor's degree in mathematics.

Boeing developed a tradition of encouraging their employees on all levels for continuing education. Thus, leaves of absence were almost always granted for this purpose.

The "Forts" saw action in every theater of operations in World

Rosie the Riveter

Rosie and her bucker, riveting B-17 wing front spars.

War II. Volumes have been written about their exploits—and their integrity.

The key to their phenomenal performance was the wing, which came through the entire series with no major structural changes. The B-17G, last of the series, had an empty weight of 36,135 pounds with a gross of 49,000, having grown from its prototype with 22,657 and 32,432 pounds respectively. As the power was increased, the body grew, armor and firepower was added; the loading on the wing simply went up.

Since stress analysis was not sufficiently sophisticated to reliably include the wing skin as a load-carrying member, all the stresses were taken into account in the internal structure. In reality, the wing skin carried major loads.

Seemingly incredible events attested to the quality of design and manufacture that Boeing people had built into the Flying Fortresses.

On January 27, 1942, *Werewolf* limped home from a raid on Brest on one engine—after the other three had been knocked out by enemy flak and fighter guns.

On October 17, 1942, *Flaming Jenny* returned to its base in England from a raid on northern France with flames raging from nose to tail, left outboard wing and number one engine gone—it had flown through a thicket of ack-ack, fought off dozens of Nazi fighters, and sustained more than 2,000 bullet holes.

Perhaps without the Flying Fortresses, the Nazi production capability—and its war machine—would have survived, with frightful consequences.

1. Crosby Maynard, *Flight Plan For Tomorrow*, Douglas Aircraft Company, 1962.
2. David Boulton, *The Grease Machine*, (New York: Harper & Row, 1978), 29.
3. Harold Mansfield, *Vision*, (New York: Popular Library, 1966), 83.
4. Ibid., 91.
5. Ibid., 98.
6. *Annual Report*, The Boeing Airplane Company, 1942, 6,7.

14

The B-29

In May 1941—the last commercial airplane on order, a Model 314 Clipper—was delivered to Pan American. Boeing turned its entire energies to the war.

With the factory going all out on B-17 production, the engineering department keyed to the R-40B superbomber. In order to have a prayer of meeting the 5,333-mile range target, drag would have to be reduced drastically. They started on the nacelles.

Someone suggested putting water-cooled engines inside the wings—eliminating the nacelles entirely—with the propeller shafts sticking out in front. When the engine manufacturers said they could design a flat engine, the idea seemed plausible, but after weeks of design effort, Ed Wells reported that they could only promise 4,500 miles of range.

He didn't like the design—there was no way to retract the landing gear, and the structure was poor around the engines. The wing was already thicker than they liked. Wells arranged a brain-storming session with George Schairer and Wellwood Beall.

Schairer had an idea. "Had you thought of going at it the other way around? The wing itself is the biggest item of drag. Instead of enlarging it to install the engines, why not make the wing as thin as we can, and then go to work cleaning up the nacelles?"[1]

Subsequent studies showed that a thin wing would give them the range—and the speed went up dramatically.

There was only one problem, and it was major. Such a wing required a loading nearly double the thirty-five pounds per square foot that had long been considered the upper limit.

To achieve the required loading, the traditional truss structure was discarded. In its place, the modern wing evolved—spanwise spars at the leading and trailing edges—connected by chordwise ribs. The result was a structural box, which relied heavily on skin loading.

As an aid to lift, a huge flap was incorporated. To reduce drag even further, flush countersunk rivets replaced the old round heads in the nacelles, and the main landing gear was retracted flat into the wing.

With the German fighter force increasing its ferocity with every new battle, the Army Air Corps pushed for more guns, more armor, more bombs. The original design target of 48,000 pounds grew to 85,000. Echols latest wish list would add still another 26,000 pounds.

Wells was not at all comfortable with the way things were going. *Is this the airplane we should be building?* he asked himself. He thought of Claire Egtvedt's counsel: *honesty of purpose.* Could he honestly get behind this airplane?

Minshall suggested they work on an alternative smaller airplane in parallel, and Wells directed his engineers to start a new design. The more Wells looked at the alternative, the less he liked the big airplane. Finally he and Minshall went to see Phil Johnson.

"'We don't feel right about the big airplane,' Wells told the president. 'Maybe we should drop it and submit a smaller one.'

"Phil Johnson recognized Well's quiet sincerity. On the other hand, he knew what the customer wanted.

"'Now Ed' he said, 'if you *had* to make a good airplane out of this, could you do it?'

"Wells looked at Johnson. He thought for a moment, then answered, 'Yes.'

"Johnson smiled. 'Let's submit it and win the competition.'"[2]

On May 11, 1940, Beall took the latest design data to General Oliver Echols at Wright Field. Don Euler stayed, waiting for the result. Suddenly, Major H. Z. Bogert, acting chief of the experimental engineering section summoned him.

"We're giving you a contract to cover engineering and wind tunnel models and a wooden mock-up of your plane. We're designating it the B-29.

"Push it. Cut the red tape. Move. We may want two hundred of them."[3]

Euler reeled from the office to phone the plant. Two hundred! They had never built a B-29.

In September 1940, developmental contracts were awarded to Boeing for the XB-29—and to Consolidated for the XB-32. Wing spans were 141 feet for the XB-29 and 135 feet for the XB-32. The huge Douglas XB-19, delayed in development—with new technology passing it by—was discontinued. The one and only XB-19 flew on June 27, 1941, serving as a flying laboratory for later innovations.

More changes—and more additions—went into the XB-29. The gross weight went up to 120,000 pounds, the wing loading to 69 pounds per square foot.

In a walled-off portion of Plant II at Seattle, the first XB-29 began to take form. Construction was under way in Wichita, Kansas, on a huge plant that would produce the planes.

General Echols requested Wellwood Beall to come to Washington for an urgent meeting.

Model B-29—*Superfortress*—1942–1945
The B-29 was the air power of the Pacific in World War II.

"'The United States government,' said Echols, 'is about to spend more money on one project than any other project of the whole war. This project is the B-29. We haven't even flown the airplane. We're worried about the tremendous risk if it doesn't pan out. Now you're the chief engineer of the Boeing Airplane Company. We want to know, really—the survival of the whole country may depend on this—we want to know what you really believe in your heart, whether that will be a good airplane or not.'

"Beall took a deep breath. Here and now was the test of vision and courage. He thought of the step-by-step progress that had made the B-29 possible; of the men who had made it possible; their faith; their devotion to a goal that they knew was vital. The 1,800 men in the engineering department were as one on this airplane. These men *were* the airplane. Their work on the first B-29 was mostly done now. It only had to be proved.

"Beall looked Echols in the eye. 'Yes,' he said. 'It's really going to be a good airplane. If you'll give us first priority on test facilities and let us do all the testing we want to do, when we want to do it—flight testing, system testing, all kinds of testing—if you'll assign us the airplanes to do this, I'll guarantee that we'll get you successful operating airplanes.'

"Echols went in to see Hap Arnold, commanding general of the Air Corps. 'All right,' said Echols when he came back. 'We'll do what you ask.' Then he laid out a production program that would cost $3 billion."[4]

Three companies would build the superbomber. The B-29 became America's secret white hope—not just an airplane now, but a giant program and a faith.

The Air Corps had hedged its bets to the end. Consolidated had been awarded a contract for three XB-32s and 13 additional airplanes for service test. The XB-32 *Dominator* looked like a scaled up Liberator, with a twin tail. The Air Corps had other ideas. The big dorsal fin on the B-17 was providing exceptional stability during bombing runs, so they contracted with Boeing to develop a single tail for the B-32. Thus, George Schairer's innovation, first used on the Model 307 Stratoliner, became the standard design on a major competitor's airplane.

Consolidated had contracts for over 1,500 production airplanes, but after 114 were built, the contracts were terminated. Some of the planes were used for training, and before the end of the war, 15 saw action in the Pacific.

More aerodynamic research and testing was conducted to develop the B-29 than on any previous Boeing airplane. The new wing gave the B-29 no more drag than the B-17, in spite of its much greater size. The flaps, which constituted almost 20 percent of the total wing area, were the largest ever used on any airplane up to that time. The B-29 was the first altitude conditioned four-engined heavy bomber, and the first airplane to have a complete remote-control gun aiming and firing system.

The B-29 went through eight major design changes on paper before construction was begun. When all the design modifications were completed, the range was increased to nearly 6,000 miles. The top speed was raised from 248 to 363 miles per hour, and the maximum bomb load increased from 5,800 to 20,000 pounds.

At Renton, on the south end of Lake Washington, near Seattle, a completely new plant was rising—not for B-29s, but for a strange new bird for the navy. With submarines and surface raiders preying on shipping on both oceans, aerial reconnaissance was the only way to patrol the vast areas involved. The navy wanted an airplane that could remain aloft for three days and nights without refueling in the air.

For that mission, Boeing designed the XPBB-1, an experimental bomber and patrol airplane, named the *Sea Ranger*. Three-fourths as large as the Model 314 Clippers, the huge flying boat had only two engines, and when fully loaded, was unable to take off under its own power. To achieve the marathon missions, the plane was designed to be catapulted into the air.

Taking the empty plane up on her maiden flight on July 9, 1942, test pilot Eddie Allen reported excellent handling characteristics. However the program was overtaken by fast moving events. Originally conceived as a successor to the Consolidated PBYs— the backbone of the navy air patrol fleet—its 158-mph cruise speed was its Achilles heel. Shortly after December 7, 1941, the Japanese attacked Dutch Harbor in Alaska. The slow moving PBYs were downed like sitting ducks—and the Sea Ranger was dead. The project was canceled, and the plane, renamed the *Lone Ranger*, faded into history.

Production workers continued under the contract originally negotiated with the Aero Mechanics Union in 1937. During the war years, company–union relations were governed by the War

XPBB-1 *Sea Ranger*—1942

The *Sea Ranger*, designed for long-range patrol bombing, was capable of staying aloft for 72 hours. A one-and-only, it became known as the *Lone Ranger*.

Labor Board. However, at one point in February 1943, union members walked off the job in protest of the board's delay in granting a wage increase. It was the first work stoppage in Boeing's twenty-seven-year history. The union's half-day march to city hall in Seattle, achieved the desired results. The War Labor Board granted the increase.

At the University of Chicago, working under the top secret, $2 billion Manhattan Project, a group of physicists led by Enrico Fermi, achieved the first controlled nuclear reaction with fissioning uranium. The die was cast for the marriage of this awesome new weapon to the B-29.

The XB-29—first of the new breed—named the *Superfortress*—rolled out of the Plant II factory in September 1942. After packing it with measuring equipment, Eddie Allen and a crew of seven took the airplane into the air for its maiden flight. The date was September 21.

Eddie came back with an eloquent smile. "She flies," he announced.[5]

Manufacturing for mass production had already begun, and the newly completed plant at Renton, no longer needed for navy airplanes, was assigned to the exclusive production of Superforts.

As flight testing continued, power plant troubles surfaced. In the first twenty-six hours of flight time, engines had to be changed sixteen times, carburetors were changed twenty-two times, and the exhaust system had to be redesigned.

On December 30, flying the second airplane off the line, Allen and his crew were running feathering tests when a fire developed in number four engine. They were lucky. After smothering the fire with their last CO_2 bottle, a half mile from the field, number four engine flared up again just as they rolled to a stop. The ground fire trucks were able to extinguish the flames before they got to the fuel tanks.

Engine problems persisted. Allen felt they should discontinue flight testing until more laboratory and design studies were completed. But there was a war on. The weekly casualty lists were grim reminders. Testing continued.

On February 18, 1943, a day which found the Boeing executive staff gathered in the boardroom for their weekly meeting, an urgent call was piped to the anteroom. Ed Wells slipped out to answer it. He reappeared at the door, face ashen.

"The tower just got a message from Eddie. They're coming in with a wing on fire."[6]

The airplane was over Tacoma, about thirty miles south of Boeing Field when the fire started. They were able to extinguish it with the CO_2 bottle. Allen elected to return to the field. The wind was from the south, and he headed over Seattle to come in from the north. A second fire broke out when he was turning for a final approach. The fire got to the fuel tanks just as the plane neared the runway.

Losing altitude rapidly, and with one wing completely ablaze, the plane crashed into the Frye meat packing plant, a five-story, brick building adjacent to the field.

It was standard procedure on test flights to wear parachutes, and a moment or two before the crash, three men bailed out in a desperate—and futile—attempt to save their lives.

The other members of the eleven-man crew perished in the fire—along with more than a score of people on the ground—primarily employees in the plant. Eddie Allen was still strapped in—at the controls—fighting the doomed machine to the last.

Father of three, at forty-seven, Allen was regarded as "the greatest test pilot aviation has ever had."[7] His first connection with Boeing was in 1927—flying the mail. He worked as a free-lance pilot for many years, testing products of a number of leading airplane manufacturers. In 1939, he joined Boeing, however he was still loaned to others for critical testing. In fact, on January 9, 1943, scarcely two months before the fatal crash of the XB-29, Allen had flown the Lockheed Constellation on its first test flight. "His hand on the controls cut first-flight insurance rates in half."[8]

The next day, at the McDermott building, a rented facility in downtown Seattle, where the B-29 engineering project was housed because of shortage of space at Plant II, the entire force increased its normal 51.5-hour week to 74 hours. Certain features of the wing and nacelles were redesigned to provide internal ventilation, preventing the accumulation of explosive fuel vapors.

A memorial went up at Plant II, where Allen's dream began its first increment. A new wind tunnel, the first to be located at any Boeing plant, was dedicated on April 22, 1944. Appropriately, it was named the Edmund T. Allen Wind Tunnel and Aeronautical Research Laboratories.

The nearly 9,000 hours of wind tunnel testing which went into the B-29 design had been accomplished in other tunnels. Sometimes it was necessary to tuck a model under their coats to shield it from the curious gaze of others as the engineers hopped around the country from tunnel to tunnel.

The wind tunnel at the University of Washington was a resource of value beyond estimation. Originally donated by William E. Boeing in 1919, the tunnel was described in a local newspaper at the time:

"A fully equipped research laboratory in aerodynamics, having as its purpose the advancement of the scientific aspects of aeronautics, is to be presented to the University of Washington by W. E. Boeing, Seattle capitalist, aeroplane enthusiast and sportsman.—

"The laboratory will be one of three of its kind in the United States, and will consist of a steel-lined wind tunnel about six feet square and seventy-five feet long."

In Wichita, Kansas, 200 acres of prairie had been transformed into a vast manufacturing plant, teeming with 29,000 employees: converted farm hands, housewives, and shopkeepers. The first Wichita-built B-29 was in the air in June, 1943.

Early in the delivery program, the *Battle of Kansas*, an effort to work out the manufacturing bugs which developed as a result of getting parts from so many different places, was fought. In March 1944, the first combat ready Superfort was loaded. There seemed to be no end to the materiel going aboard. Earl Schaefer, general manager of the Wichita plant was there.

"How heavy are you loading these?" he asked.

"135,000."

"135,000! Do you know the maximum gross is 120,000?"

"Yeah, we know. Your maximum on the B-17 was 48,000. We flew at 60,000 all the time in England."[9]

The planes were loaded to 135,000, and later to 140,000 pounds.

Early one morning late in March, Colonel Jake Harman took off for India, the first leg toward establishing bases in China, and on June 15, sixty-eight B-29s departed from handmade runways in Chengdu to bomb the steel works in Yawata, Japan.

By early 1945, massive firebombing raids were being made over Japan, with B-29s based in the Mariana Islands. In a single raid on March 9, 1945, 334 B-29s attacked Tokyo, raining fire that appeared to nearly destroy the city.

Finally, at 9:15 A.M. on Monday, August 6, the *Enola Gay*, a Superfort piloted by Colonel Paul W. Tibbets Jr., released *Little Boy* over Hiroshima, wiping out more than four square miles—60 percent of the city of 343,000 inhabitants.

Less than 1,000 miles to the south, the U.S. Tenth Army was still landing soldiers on the Hagushi beaches on Okinawa. The thin Missouri twang of President Harry Truman came on the radio—announcing the cataclysmic event which had taken place at Hiroshima. Although they had no comprehension of the power of an atomic bomb, the soldiers knew intuitively that Operation Olympus—the landing of 1.5 million troops on the Japanese beaches, scheduled for the following November—would not occur. For a few brief moments their main concern was to avoid being killed by the flak falling all around—from the guns of supporting ships—which had erupted in a literal fire-storm.

Three days after Hiroshima, *Fat Man* was dropped, destroying Nagasaki, and on August 15, Japan surrendered.

A total of 3,970 Superforts were built; 2,766 by Boeing, 668 by Bell, and 536 by Martin. That magnificent battle-plane took its place as a major instrument of both war and peace in a century in which mankind stared at oblivion—and oblivion blinked.

1. Harold Mansfield, Vision, (New York: Popular Library, 1966), 83.
2. Ibid., 90.
3. Ibid., 91.
4. Ibid., 106.
5. Private Communication.
6. Ibid.
7. *Time*, 1 March 1943, 56.
8. Ibid., 18 January, 1943, 72.
9. Mansfield, *Vision*, 137.

William M. Allen 1900–1985
President 1945–1968, Chairman 1968–1972.

15

Postwar
Challenges

At Lockheed, the four employees of 1932 had blossomed to over 90,000 by the end of World War II. Production was equally impressive. Lockheed produced 2,900 Hudsons and 2,600 Venturas in addition to 10,000 P-38s.

When the war ended, Lockheed was the largest defense contractor in the Western world. Inevitably, in 1945, the company was one of the first to be dropped out of military production. Initially viewed as a disaster, the event was actually a fortunate one, putting Lockheed at the forefront in the postwar commercial market.

That enviable position was the result of timing, foresight—and plain luck. On April 17, 1944, fifteen months after Eddie Allen—on loan from Boeing—flight tested the Constellation, Howard

Hughes flew the initial production model from Burbank to Washington, D.C., in a record time for a commercial airplane of six hours, forty-three minutes, and thirty seconds.

Pearl Harbor and the entry of the United States into the war had not halted, or even interrupted, the development work on the Constellation, as it had done on its major competitor, the Boeing Stratoliner. TWA and Pan Am waived their rights to early production units, and the Army Air Corps took delivery and converted them into troop carriers. Thus, production of the world's largest, fastest, and most sophisticated airliner was continued during the war.

By the end of 1945, 20 Constellations had been sold to TWA, 6 to BOAC, and 5 to other airlines. Yet to come were orders for 105 more, valued at $75 million—sold to Pan American, Eastern, and American in the United States—and to both Air France and KLM in Europe.

Lockheed's continuing attention to advancements in fighter airplanes also paid off. As early as 1942, Kelly Johnson had proposed that the Army Air Corps get involved in an attempt to produce a jet fighter. Finding no interest, Robert Gross nevertheless kept the research project alive, and by the end of the war was able to marry a British de Havilland turbojet engine to Lockheed's prototype fighter. The F-80 *Shooting Star* was the result. Rapidly on its heels followed the *Starfire*, those planes becoming America's first operational jets.

Douglas was in an excellent position to challenge the Lockheed Constellation for commercial air transport leadership. Incorporating the latest technology developed during the war, and distilling the experience gained from millions of flying hours with the DC series, Douglas quickly brought out the DC-6.

A DC-5 had been designed at about the same time as the DC-4—and somewhat to the confusion of historians—was produced first.[1] Many of the systems and structural developments of the

DC-3 were adapted to the DC-5, but the overbody, high wing configuration resulted in a greater empty weight, penalizing payload and range. Only twelve DC-5s were manufactured.

On November 24, 1946, the first DC-6, a beefed-up, speeded-up, descendant of the "DC" line, was delivered to both United and American Airlines.

The DC-6 boasted a sophisticated cabin control system, providing for a 5,000-foot altitude environment, while flying at 20,000 feet.

By the end of 1944, Douglas had booked orders for 175 of their DC-6 model. Soon to follow were the DC-6A and "B."

With Boeing bombers in the news for six years, at war's end, the company was hardly viewed as a producer of commercial airplanes. President Phil Johnson even hedged his bet that there would be an orderly return to a new market of civil air transportation after the war ended. With his exposure to the bedroom furniture business following World War I in mind, he ordered an engineering unit to look into a non-aircraft postwar line. Included in those studies were a low-priced automobile, as well as kitchen and bedroom equipment.

The company had returned to profitability in 1940—earning $374,655—representing 1.9 percent of sales. Then, in 1941, with sales soaring five-fold, net profits leaped to $6,113,143.

This pleasant state of affairs was not to continue. In spite of unprecedented production, profits were extremely low during the remainder of the war years, with a disappointing downhill trend. In terms of sales, the company realized net profits of 1.35, 0.91, and 0.86 percent, respectively, for the years 1942–1944. The 1941 peak earnings of 6.3 percent, highest in the history of the company, were not achieved again until 1980.[2]

Two new types of military aircraft had been completed during 1944: the XF8B-1, a navy fighter plane designed specifically for long range carrier strikes against Japan, and the C-97 military transport, a double-decked aircraft for transporting troops and cargo.

The XF8B-1, a 20,000-pound gross weight machine with a top speed of 432 miles per hour and a range of 3,500 miles, was a very ambitious project. Known as the "Five in One", because it was to serve as a fighter, interceptor, dive bomber, torpedo bomber, or horizontal bomber, the plane never reached production. When the B-29s became operational, long-range carrier strikes were scratched.

The C-97 was a hybrid. Utilizing the wing, power plant, landing gear, empennage, and the lower half of the fuselage of the B-29, a new, larger diameter, upper lobe was designed, creating an inverted figure-eight cross section. With a retractable ramp in the rear, and a crane hoist running the entire length of the upper deck, the plane was capable of loading outsize cargo. Four ambulances or two 105mm howitzers could be carried. The airplane could transport 130 fully armed men; or when converted into a flying hospital, 79 litter patients with their attendants and medical supplies. One of the three XC-97s set a new coast-to-coast speed record from Seattle to Washington, D.C., of six hours, three minutes and fifty seconds, averaging 383 miles per hour. The Army Air Force placed an order for ten service test models.

When the war ended the Boeing Airplane Company did not even have a president. Phil Johnson died of a stroke in September 1944. Claire Egtvedt, in the office of chairman, resumed active management of the company and started the process of finding a president. They offered the position to Bill Allen. In addition to his close association with the company from the first day he joined its law firm, Allen had been serving on the board of directors for many years. He was the natural candidate.

Allen, in his modest way, declined, professing not to be qualified. Perhaps he felt the need for engineering expertise in a company dominated by engineers.

In March 1945, the board urged Allen to change his mind. He finally gave a qualified consent, although the decision was made with great reluctance.

He made his own long list of things he would have to do if the board voted him in as president:

Must keep temper always—never get mad.

Be considerate of my associates' views.

Don't talk too much—let others talk.

Don't be afraid to admit that you don't know.

Don't get immersed in detail—concentrate on big objectives.

Make contacts with other people in industry—and keep them.

Try to improve feeling around Seattle toward company.

Make a sincere effort to understand labor's viewpoint.

Be definite! Don't vacillate.

Act—get things done—move forward.

Develop a postwar future for Boeing.

Try hard, but don't let obstacles get you down. Take things in stride.

Above all else, be human—keep your sense of humor—learn to relax.

Be just, straightforward, invite criticism and learn to take it.

Be confident. Having once made the move, make the most of it.

Bring to the task great enthusiasm, unlimited energy.

Make Boeing even greater than it is.[3]

With history as the judge, Allen accomplished all of those things. He was an uncommon man—a leader among leaders. The people at Boeing developed an enduring faith in his ability to guide the company.

The issue of president was not resolved until September 5, 1945. Seven men sat around the boardroom table on that day, busy with their first meeting since Japan surrendered. The main item of business was the election of a new president.

The air force was winding down its orders for the B-29. August production stood at 155 planes, and would be reduced to 122 for the month of September, with 20 per month thereafter. The C-97 had only a tenuous possibility for a long production run. Employment was already down to around 30,000 in Seattle, from a wartime peak of 45,000. By November, employment was expected to be cut again—by one half. Experts in the industry viewed that figure as the critical mass below which the company could not survive.

At the board meeting, the selection committee announced that William M. Allen was the unanimous choice for president. While he was being congratulated, Egtvedt's secretary appeared in the doorway, handing him an urgent note. It was from Bob Neale, factory manager. Word had just been received from the air force that the B-29 schedule was being cut again—to 50 for the current month, then to ten a month until February. Neale reported that most of the 50 were already in the line, recommending that an announcement be made over the public-address system before the four o'clock shift change, to close the plant.

"Egtvedt glanced at his watch. It was three-thirty. He looked at Bill Allen, shook his head, and said, 'Tell Bob that's okay.'"[4]

Allen realized he was in a desperate situation. He needed the team to stay alive, but the payroll was running at a half million dollars a day with no orders on the horizon. He knew intuitively that the potential was there in the guts of the company—the experience that his engineers had accumulated during the war. He decided he must hold that force together.

The C-97 was a logical start for a commercial derivative; however, Douglas and Lockheed had already established firm market positions, in fact satisfying all known customer demand. The price would have to be in the neighborhood of $1 million each to be competitive.

Stratocruiser—1945–1950

A commercial version of the C-97 freighter, the twin-decked, 80 passenger Stratocruiser catered to comfort and class.

Boldly seizing the initiative, without a single order on the books, Allen put his engineers to work to convert the cargo carrying C-97 to a commercial airplane that would be competitive with the successful airplanes already in service. Then he ordered the production of fifty airplanes, instructing his sales department to get busy and sell them.

That was the nature of the business that Allen was destined to lead for the next twenty-seven years, a period that became known as the *Allen Era*.

The product that evolved from that decision was the *Stratocruiser*, a luxurious, four-engined, double-decked airplane. In the Boeing tradition, it incorporated innovations that proved to be its best selling points. The unique lower-deck lounge—joined to the main deck by a circular stairway—and berthable seats, piqued the imagination of the traveling public. The plane cost far too much to build—and sold at a loss—but it accomplished its primary mission—holding the core of the technical and manufacturing force together.

It soon became clear that there would be insufficient work to keep the total engineering force busy for long. In the spring of 1947, the Stratocruiser design effort passed its peak. More than 300 engineers—about 16 percent of the force—hit the streets. In a "one-company" city like Seattle, it meant they had to pull up and get out.

The production run of fifty-six Stratocruisers lasted into 1950. Miraculously, they were all sold. However, the program did not earn a profit for ten years, finally nudging into the black on accumulated sales of spare parts.

1. Crosby Maynard, *Flight Plan for Tomorrow*, Douglas Aircraft Company, 1962.
2. *Annual Reports*, The Boeing Company, 1941–1980.
3. Harold Mansfield, *Vision*, (New York: Popular Library, 1966), 153.
4. Ibid., 152.

16

Labor Kicks the Traces

Close on the heels of the ending of the war—across the country—pent up labor demands caused a rush of work stoppages and strikes. In Chicago, 200,000 meat packers shut down 74 percent of the nation's meat supply in January 1946. Later in the same month, 800,000 steel workers hit the bricks. Elsewhere, General Motors, Ford and General Electric workers struck. The General Motors strike, lasting 113 days, was the longest and most costly in the history of the automobile industry.

Labor unrest at Boeing had been practically unknown. Other than the half-day work stoppage in February 1943, organized labor and management had enjoyed a harmonious relationship since the first contract with the Aero Mechanics in 1937.

The labor climate began to change in the fall of 1945 when workers were laid off as fast as the company could process the notices. It was simply good-bye and good luck. In September, the union rescinded the no strike pledge it had made at the beginning of the war.

The company laid off employees in ascending order of seniority. The agreement provided that each could use his seniority to "bump" any other employee with less seniority on any job, at the same or lower pay, which the senior employee was qualified to perform. The system bred resentment among both employees seeking to exercise their seniority to acquire a job at less pay, and those who were bumped out of a job.

The supervisors were uniquely affected, since most had risen through the ranks. The union protested that the company could not demote supervisors into jobs covered by the labor agreement unless no employee already under union jurisdiction was available. Thus, since they could not displace union men, supervisors effectively lost their seniority rights. When the company protested, the union requested arbitration, and King County Judge, Charles P. Moriarty ruled in the union's favor.

Bill Allen, on the job as president for scarcely two months, was already being tested in his resolve to understand labor's viewpoint. On October 25, 1946, he had no choice but to lay off the 672 supervisors who had bumped union employees.

Many shops ground to a halt, with still more layoffs. Allen asked the union to open negotiations for a new working agreement. In a letter to all shop employees, he wrote:

> *Experience since the termination of the B-29 and other government contracts has convinced the company that the present labor relations agreement has become unworkable to such a degree as to seriously impede progress of the company toward peacetime production and maximum acceleration of employment.*[1]

A depression hit Seattle—32,000 workers had been laid off, there were 61,000 jobless in the State of Washington, and 62,700 veterans were expected home from the war.[2]

Conditions worsened. On November 15, the remaining supervisors did not report for work, and production nearly came to a standstill. Allen took direct action, sending a personal letter to each of the striking supervisors. Most of them returned to work five days later.

In January 1946, A. F. Logan, Boeing wage and salary administrator, announced that amendments to the existing contract had been worked out and agreed to by both parties. One of the amendments, sometimes referred to as a new contract, providing for a 15 percent increase in wages, was approved by the Wage Stabilization Board, a wartime agency that maintained jurisdiction in the unsettled, postwar period. This new contract was to "remain in force until March 16, 1947, or thereafter until a new agreement has been reached by the parties, either through negotiation or arbitration."[3]

Later in the year, Boeing engineers in Seattle formed a collective bargaining organization, the Seattle Professional Engineering Employees Association (SPEEA), declining to call it a labor union, and signed an agreement with the company. In a National Labor Relations Board (NLRB) election, SPEEA was certified as the bargaining agent for the engineers.

Although negotiations were continuing, when the labor contract with the Aero Mechanics Union expired in March 1947, no new agreement had been reached. The company held out for a change in the seniority system to allow transfer of qualified workmen to other jobs on short notice.

K.L. Calkins reports: "The entanglement of the seniority system was like a footrace through a blackberry patch; it was hard to get anywhere without drawing blood."[4]

Allen viewed the problem in starkly simple terms—a necessity to maintain the direction of his work force. To the union, such a concession was like the threatening sword of Damocles.

It was no secret that the company had not made a profit since the end of the war. Although the union fully realized the survival of Boeing was at stake in the severely competitive marketplace, they could not bring themselves to accept any compromise on seniority.

With the stalemate continuing month by month, there was time to breed dissension in the ranks, and a new element entered the picture—the Communist Party.

Harold Gibson, union president, a war veteran with four Bronze stars, and a Presidential Unit Citation, was a devout anti-communist, adamantly rejecting attempted Communist inroads. Nevertheless the Communists' efforts to influence leaders seemed to harden their stand with the company.

Early in April, the union filed a strike vote request with the Department of Labor. Allen began an intense personal campaign to bring reason to the table. He appealed to the employees through *Boeing News*, stating: "...the company is not seeking to destroy seniority. Rather, it is seeking the first essential to job security—a successful, operating company."[5]

The company proposed to exempt 10 percent of the bargaining unit from the seniority provisions so that those employees could be transferred between jobs or shifts as their services were needed.

Even though Boeing attempted to explain the importance of the seniority issue in providing operating flexibility to be competitive, the union members essentially mistrusted the company's motives.

After the concessions were formalized, the proposal was put to a vote at a mass meeting on May 24. It was rejected by a 93-percent margin.

Immediately following the vote there were cries of "Strike!," and "Let's have a strike vote!" When Gibson asked for those in favor of a strike to stand up, the entire audience seemed to rise as one man. The vote to strike passed by 94 percent, however, no date was established for it to begin.

Both sides had much to lose by a strike, but union members gradually convinced themselves that a massive walkout would bring the desired concessions. They failed to recognize the determination of Bill Allen.

In California, workers at Lockheed agreed to a new contract for less money than Boeing workers were already receiving,[6]—and the SPEEA engineers signed a new contract.

In June 1947, the Congress passed the Taft-Hartley Act, an amendment to the Labor Relations Act. Under the act, management was also allowed to file unfair labor practices complaints with the NLRB. Further, Taft-Hartley required a cooling off period of sixty days before striking, and granted the government power to enforce an eighty-day injunction against strikes which threatened national health or safety.

President Truman vetoed the act as bad legislation, and labor raised cries of antilabor. The Senate overrode the veto sixty-eight to twenty-five, reflecting the impatience that had swept the country in the wake of the unprecedented series of work stoppages following the war.

After the passage of Taft-Hartley, President Allen wrote still another letter to all employees, assuring them that the company did not intend to use the new powers of the law to seek undue advantage. "The company earnestly desires to build a sound and friendly relationship with its employees," he wrote.[7]

Nevertheless, Allen let it be known that a strike would be viewed as a breach of contract—a violation of Taft-Hartley. Concerned at the turn of events, Harvey Brown, president of the parent union, the International Association of Machinists (IAM), directed the local union officers to continue negotiations and to explore arbitration.

When the union offered arbitration, the company declined. The impasse continued.

Pressure grew. The company was forced to live with the inefficient seniority system, and union members had not had a pay raise since March 1946.

In January 1948, Boeing submitted a new proposal, offering fifteen cents an hour pay raise, continuation of the union shop, and a modified seniority clause. Negotiations were completed in March and the new contract was put to the membership for a vote. Both parties had agreed to submit certain items to arbitration.

Neither side would accept the other's recommendations for an arbitration panel, and negotiations deadlocked.

Abruptly, the union council voted to give the company a deadline to agree on an arbitration panel—4 P.M., April 16.

Without IAM sanction, there could be no strike, so the company ignored the deadline. The current contract continued in force until a new one was "negotiated or arbitrated." To Allen, a contract was a contract.

Union members, heedless of cautions, were ready to strike. The situation was out of control.

Gibson called for help from International. "Don't let them strike. Hold them back," they told him. "I don't know if I can," he said.[8]

"Garry Cotton, former Lodge 751 president who had advanced to a Grand Lodge representative's position, appeared before the 400 shop committeemen. The issues with the company were virtually settled, he said. There was agreement on pay, vacations, on holidays. The one remaining issue was seniority and it could be worked out without a strike.

"'The shop committeemen told him to go to hell,' recalled Gibson. 'So I stood up. I told them we weren't prepared for a strike. We weren't organized for one and we didn't need one. They started throwing union buttons on the floor.'"[9]

Gibson could not hold them. In an emergency meeting, the union's district council called a strike to begin one hour after midnight on April 22.

Allen was stunned. Then he was angry. He contacted IAM

President Harvey Brown. Had the IAM sanctioned the strike? The answer was no. Allen wired Brown that the company no longer considered Lodge 751 to be the bargaining agent for the employees. The union had broken its contract. Brown suggested that he send a committee from the International to Seattle to discuss the matter, and Allen accepted.

The three-man executive council committee sent from the Grand Lodge called Allen when they arrived in Seattle to arrange for a meeting time. When they told him they wanted Harold Gibson to sit in, Allen refused to meet. He was not going to confer with a man who had broken his word.

The company charged breach of contract and violation of Section 8(d) of the Taft-Hartley Act, which dealt with the requirement for a written, sixty-day notice of proposed termination or modification of a labor contract.

On the day of the strike, Boeing sent everybody home except guards, firemen and other key personnel. When the strike was still in effect two days later, the company announced that the plant was open and everybody was to report on the next work day. The company obtained a court order limiting the number of pickets at each gate and outlawing threats against anyone entering—and began an active, intensive campaign to lure striking employees to work. President Allen was determined to break the strike.

In May the union filed unfair labor practices against the company, complaining that the company had canceled the contract without the sixty days' notice prescribed by the Taft-Hartley Act.

While most of the factory workers stayed out on strike, by June about 2,000 of them had returned, enough to make the work force somewhat effective once again.

The first plane to roll out after the strike was a B-50 bomber, an improved version of the B-29. The rollout called for a plant celebration. The strike had been on for seven weeks. Prestrike employment had been nearly 19,000 and now was back to 5,000, including 3,000 supervisors, engineers and other salaried employees. Allen took the opportunity to invite all employees to the factory apron at Plant II for an important message on the state of the company.

True to his starchily ethic philosophy, Allen did not ask for blind support. In an emotional appeal, he solicited employees to help in its contest with the union, saying:

"...I'm trying to accomplish a fair and honorable result. I only ask for your support if you think that this company is doing the right and proper thing. But if you believe that, then I do ask for your support.

"By the same token, I can say this: that I do not feel that the union in this case is doing a fair thing, a proper thing, or a lawful thing. And under those circumstances, that the union is not entitled to support. And I say it's unAmerican to ask for support under those circumstances."[10]

When Federal Judge John C. Bowen ruled that the strike was unlawful, because the union had not given the required sixty-day notice, the hiring pace—and the bitterness—increased. By July, new hires were running about fifty-fifty with former employees returning to work.

Then in July, the NLRB trial examiner, William E. Spencer, ruled that the clause requiring the agreement to remain in force until a new contact was signed must have limited duration, and therefore Boeing was guilty of unfair labor practices.

Boeing took legal exception to the Spencer ruling and requested a hearing with the full board. In the meantime, they announced that strikers would be rehired to fill available jobs only. Newly hired employees would not be dismissed.

With employment rates continually on the upside, the union, fearful that there might not be jobs for the strikers to go back to, moved to call off the strike. Boeing agreed to reinstate all those on strike who were under the jurisdiction of Lodge 751, and from whom it received applications within two weeks of the strike's end.

After spirited discussion of the conditions on the part of both adversaries, a vote was taken. Strikers voted twelve to one in favor of ending it.

By October, the striker reinstatement was complete, and employment was just over 19,000, slightly more than the pre-strike high. Also, in October, Boeing presented its appeal to the full NLRB, who, about a month later, upheld Spencer's recommendations. Boeing immediately filed an appeal to the Federal Court in the District of Columbia.

It was not until May 1949, that the three-judge Court of Appeals handed down a unanimous decision. The NLRB findings were not founded in law, said the court. Not only had Lodge 751 violated the Taft-Hartley Act, it had also violated its contract with Boeing—and lost its rights to bargain collectively for factory employees.

In the meantime, the Teamsters Union, active in bringing new hires to the company, made an all out effort to win bargaining rights.

In June, the air force canceled its contract with Boeing for the B-54—an advanced bomber succeeding the B-29/B-50 series—in favor of the mammoth Consolidated-Vultee, Intercontinental Bomber, the B-36. A six-engined machine with a wing span of 230 feet, the B-36 was first ordered as an experimental airplane in November 1941. It was given a low priority because of the production emphasis on B-17, B-24 and B-29 models, and did not fly until after the war. A later version of the 384 B-36s built, incorporated a pair of jets under each outboard wing, supplementing the six aft mounted piston engines.

Boeing had already decided to manufacture future military aircraft at the government-owned plant in Wichita, with only flight testing to be completed in Seattle. The move signaled more layoffs in the Puget Sound area, and again there was talk, fear, and speculation that Boeing would move out of the city.

A hard-boiled review could not fail to conclude that a major manufacturing facility would have little chance to succeed in the

Puget Sound area. Cohn, analyzing those considerations in his location theory study of industry in the Pacific Northwest, stated that Boeing continued to exist there for no economic reason whatsoever, but simply "because an individual who happened to live in the Northwest evolved an original product which proved successful."[11] He concluded that there is a strong tendency for such firms to emigrate, or at least to establish branch plants closer to the center of the national market.

Indeed, Boeing management recognized that there were several more advantageous areas for the main production facility than Seattle, however the consequences of cost and disruption always loomed as too large a factor to trigger a move.

One can argue that isolation eventually worked to the company's advantage. With its primary product uniquely capable of delivering itself to any place in the world, in the most rapid fashion yet devised, a major disadvantage of isolation from markets was negated.

In the case of labor, isolation militated toward an extraordinary loyalty—a loyalty which permeated the company for most of its history. The 1948 strike was an exception, exacerbated by a series of unusual local and national conditions.

In July 1949, the NLRB held hearings to determine which union should be recognized as the bargaining agent. Hourly employees voted, casting more than 12,000 votes. The Aero Mechanics Lodge 751 received two-thirds of the total, and the union turned a more friendly face to Boeing.

In January 1950, Lodge 751 was certified as bargaining agent, and on May 22, signed an agreement with Boeing. It contained the raise in pay offered during the strike, more paid vacation, and a weighting of seniority as a deciding factor in promotions "when competence and ability are equal" among two or more eligible employees. Boeing promised to study the seniority issue still further in the future. [12]

The contract was a clear victory for President Allen. Standing firmly on principle, he had fought with every legal weapon at his command. Nevertheless, the bottom line was epitomized in one word—*fairness*. Allen had demonstrated that both sides—labor and management—were equal partners, and added significantly to his public personality as well as the esteem of his associates.

For the factory employees, loss of the union shop was a major blow. Although the union pressed for its reinstatement, they were never again able to retrieve that status.

Bill Allen had given his word to the employees who crossed the picket lines, and a union shop would unravel that pledge. Instead, the contract contained a security clause regarding union membership. New employees could join the union or not, as they chose, but once having joined, they must remain members during the term of the contract.

On May 22, 1950—more than two years after the workers had gone out on strike—a one year contract was signed with Lodge 751, ending the longest and most bitter confrontation in Boeing's history. Seven months later, in Wichita, Kansas, a similar contract was signed with Lodge 70. The strife was behind them, but the scars remained.

1. K.L. Calkins, An Analysis of Labor Relations News Coverage..., (Seattle: University of Washington, 1968), 24.
2. Ibid., 24.
3. *Boeing News*, 21 March, 1946, 1.
4. Calkins, 33.
5. *Boeing News*, 24 April, 1947, 1.
6. Calkins, 38.
7. *Boeing News*, 17 July, 1947, 1.
8. Calkins, 54.
9. Ibid., 55.
10. *Boeing News*, 10 June, 1948, 2.
11. E.J. Cohn Jr., *Industry in the Pacific Northwest and the Location Theory*, (New York: King's Crown Press, 1954), 44.
12. *Boeing News*, 25 May, 1950, 1.

17

The Jet Bombers

What to do about a postwar bomber was a top priority. Ed Wells concluded that speed was the answer. Having watched the tests of Bell's experimental jet pursuit plane at Muroc Dry Lake, California, in September 1943, he directed Bob Jewett, chief of preliminary design, to work up a jet bomber, shaving the wings down to next to nothing to get maximum speed. Robert Jewett, an intense aeronautical engineer from the University of Minnesota, destined to lead the company into missiles and space, put his senior designers to work on the project. In March 1944, they took the design to Wright Field.

"'Would you take speed as a substitute for guns?' Wells asked Oliver Echols.

"'Maybe so,' said Echols. 'If it's fast enough you might get by with just a stinger turret in the tail, and flak protection under the engines.'"[1]

In wind tunnel tests, as they increased the speed, air moving over the leading edge of the wings approached the speed of sound, creating the mysterious compressibility burble which became known as the sound barrier.

George Schairer and his aerodynamics staff had been giving the subject considerable study. "We'll just to have to beat it out in the wind tunnel," he concluded.[2]

The Army Air Force, concerned over the late start the United States had made in jet airplane technology, began pressing for proposals for quick construction of new experimental machines. Ed Wells took the position that Boeing should not propose a design until they learned how to make a successful one—rejecting the conventional approach of simply installing jet engines on a plane like the B-29. He concluded that something entirely new was needed.

While Boeing delayed, Wright Field went ahead with contracts to North American, Consolidated, and Martin for medium-range jet bombers utilizing conventional design.

In May of 1945, aerodynamics chief, George Schairer, as a member of the Scientific Advisory Board of the Army Air Force, had been at the Pentagon preparing to go on a special mission into Germany. The theory of high-speed flight was the hottest new subject, and sweepback seemed to some theorists as the way to achieve it.

The same day that General Gustav Jodl and Admiral Hans Friedeburg unconditionally surrendered the German armed forces to the Americans inside a little red school house at Reims, and Soviet soldiers hung the hammer and sickle atop the gutted Reichstag in Berlin, Schairer's group arrived at Reichmarshall Goering's Aeronautical Research Institute at Brunswick. They found drawings of a model with sweptback wings. There were also charts, columns of figures and wind tunnel testing results. The tests had led to the design of the Messerschmitt ME-262 with a forty-five-degree sweepback—already under construction when the war came to an end.

Wells created an entire new group, selecting George Martin to lead it. Graduating from the University of Washington in 1931 with Phi Beta Kappa and Tau Beta Pi honors, Martin began as a stress engineer. A visionary, and a relentless driver, he proved to be the right man for the job.

On September 13, 1945, the new team had a formal proposal ready for presentation to Wright Field. The proposed plane was radical in design, with a thin sweptback wing and six jets; four blasting from the top of the body, and two more from the tail.

The engineers at Dayton were more than skeptical—they were incredulous.

"Why should the Air Force finance some wild idea George Schairer has?" asked one colonel. "Let's cut out this foolishness."[3]

The armament laboratory brought in some results of firing 50-caliber bullets into the burner section of a roaring F-80 jet engine in a wind tunnel test. The outcome was an uncontrollable blow-torch blasting from the side of the engine. That settled the body-mounted engine design.

Unable to salvage anything from the proposal, the Boeing team went back to the drawing boards. Wells remembered some data that Schairer brought back from Germany—experiments with engines mounted on struts under the wing.

In the face of cries of heresy from the aerodynamics staff, several ideas were tried in the wind tunnel. They tested every position they could think of: below and behind the wing, straight below, above and behind, straight above, above and in front, and below and in front. The last position seemed to work. Subsequent tests and calculations proved it to be almost ideal, with drag no greater than for body-mounted engines. The strut-mounted engines became another Boeing first.

There were still sticky engineering problems to solve. The thin

B-47 With Jato Assisted Takeoff

The B-47 taking off from Boeing Field. The planes were equipped with rocket units for operations from short fields.

wing did not provide sufficient fuel capacity, and there was no good place to retract the landing gear. The retraction problem was solved by designing a tandem, bicycle gear that pulled up into the body, with small outrigger wheels retracting into the inboard engine pods. Adding internal body fuel tanks still did not give the air force the desired range, but the design was sufficiently interesting that they ordered two experimental models—the XB-47.

The year of 1947 witnessed many first flights at Boeing. On June 25, it was the B-50; on July 8, the *Stratocruiser*; and on December 17, most spectacular of all—the XB-47 *Stratojet* literally shot off Boeing Field when test pilot Bob Robbins cut in a bank of the eighteen rocket assist (ATO) units, each of which instantaneously added 1,000 pounds of thrust to the 24,000 pounds that its six engines were producing. (The B-47E, entering service in 1953, produced 43,000 pounds of thrust and carried thirty-three ATO units).

On February 8, 1949, an XB-47 crossed the United States in less than four hours, setting a new speed record of 607.2 miles per hour.

The air force's reluctance was abruptly transformed into unbridled enthusiasm. They had an airplane that flew like a fighter, with a top speed of over 600 miles an hour—fastest known bomber in the world—and a range of over 3,000 miles. With the addition of externally mounted wing fuel tanks, the range was increased to over 4,000 miles.

Boeing manufactured 1,371 B-47s at its Wichita plant, and both Douglas and Lockheed tooled up to raise the total to 2,040. The program was successful beyond Boeing's wildest imagination; however, it did not solve the most pressing requirement of the air force—a truly global jet bomber.

Even before the B-47 flew, Boeing had won the design competition for such an airplane. It was visualized to be twice the weight of the B-47, with wings swept back twenty degrees, and using turboprop engines. However, as the weight went up and up to gain range, the speed went dismally down. The air force wanted the speed of the B-47 with global range, and began studies on aerial refueling. The existing hose-and-drogue-method would not be adequate to transfer the large quantities of fuel being contemplated.

At Wichita, engineer Cliff Leisy had an idea that they could link two planes with a telescoping pipeline, a "flying boom," that would lower from the tanker tail to the nose of the receiver. Experiments continued.

Immediately following the end of the war in Europe, the Soviet Union annexed the eastern half of Poland and northeast Prussia. In the Balkans and its occupied German territory, the Soviets set up Communist regimes, supplanting previous governments. On March 5, 1946, Winston Churchill, speaking at Fulton, Missouri, characterized the state of Europe in somber tones. "From Stettin in the Baltic to Trieste in the Adriatic, an iron curtain has descended across the continent," he declared.[4] The "Cold War" had begun.

The Soviets hinted in November 1947 that they had discovered the secret of the atomic bomb, and real peace in the world seemed more illusory than ever. When the Russians imposed a blockade on Berlin in 1948, the Truman-ordered Berlin airlift—which landed an airplane a minute at its peak—focused once again the need for modern, powerful air fleets. The U.S. Congress appropriated funds for a seventy-group air force, and the need to speed up the development of an intercontinental bomber became urgent.

Wright Field, with the prospect for in-flight refueling becoming a reality, decided to fix the design at 300,000 pounds and settle on turboprop engines.

Ed wells was not convinced. The turboprops were already two years behind their development schedule, and an additional four seemed entirely realistic. He feared they could easily find them-

The Chief Flies With Boeing Jet Bomber—1950

President William Allen prepares to board an early flight of the B-47, Boeing's sleek, six jet bomber. It was a first of a kind for a Boeing president, and Allen's most cherished photo.

selves with an airframe and no engines. However, urgency in the air force was at fever level, and they were intent on awarding a contract for two experimental models. The possibility for Boeing to build a pure jet on its own funds was beyond contemplation.

When the Westinghouse Company revealed plans for a big new jet engine, the potential of jets appeared to be substantially better, and the turboprops comparatively worse. Wells went to Bill Allen. "We've come to the conclusion that the airplane should be jet powered," he declared.

Allen was startled. It would throw the program back, might bring a cancellation. "Isn't this pretty late to be proposing a change like that?"

"I know, Bill, but it just isn't the airplane we should be building."[5]

Ed Wells and George Schairer went to Wright Field to talk with bombardment project officer Colonel Pete Warden about changing to jet engines. He was sold on jet speed from experience with the B-47, but knew the push toward turboprops was strong. "Go ahead and work up a new design with jets," he said. "But we'll have to keep on with the turboprop airplane until we see what can be done."[6]

In July, 1948, the contract came through to build two experimental airplanes with turboprop engines.

Engineers at Seattle worked at maximum effort to put a proposal together for jets without jeopardizing the contract in hand for the turboprops. They found they could get almost as much range, plus better speed without changing the wing or the twenty-degree sweepback. Utilizing a new jet promised by Pratt & Whitney, with a thrust of 10,000 pounds, they brought the speed up to 500 miles an hour. The plane would still be within the 300,000 pound gross weight target. Putting the proposal together, they headed back to Wright Field in October to sell it.

Colonel Warden looked over the data. "I think you need a faster wing," he said, "more sweepback, like the B-47. We've already compromised on range, with refueling. Let's not compromise any more on speed."[7]

Warden was greeted by a surprised silence. Then, Wells responded firmly. "Let us see what we can do to get you some more," he said. Glancing at his watch, he noted it was nearly noon—and Friday. Without hesitation, he promised, "We'll be back Monday morning."[8]

Boeing had sent its top team of engineers to the Field, armed with all the data on both turboprops and jets, complete with wind tunnel results. Wells and Schairer returned to their hotel rooms, where the rest of the team was waiting.

Wells unrolled the drawings. The twenty-degree sweepback suddenly looked conservative. "I think we'd better put this away and start again," he said. They looked at the drawings of a proposed medium range bomber—thirty-five degrees of sweepback.

"Double this in size and you just about have it,"[9] said Schairer resourcefully. Wells spread out drawing paper on the top of the bureau and began making a three-view sketch of the scale-up. Art Carlsen, project, and Maynard Pennell, preliminary design, worked up a weight breakdown. Bob Withington and Vaughn Blumenthal, from the aerodynamics staff, calculated the estimated performance. Schairer laid out the lines of the new sweptback wing. By late that night they realized they had created an airplane. It had the range. The weight was up only a little, to 330,000 pounds. With a wing swept back thirty-five degrees, and a span of 185 feet, supporting eight engines, the speed went up to more than 600 miles an hour. They had achieved Stratojet performance in an intercontinental bomber.

On Saturday morning, Schairer rounded up some balsa wood, glue, and carving tools, and set to work on a model. Wells organized the engineering data and hired a public stenographer to put it into document form. By Sunday night, it was a clean, thirty-three-page, bound report—with scale model attached.

Pete Warden was beaming on Monday morning. "Now we have an airplane," he said. "This is the B-52."[10]

Two experimental planes were built, and the first test flight was made on April 15, 1952. The first production airplane rolled out of the factory on March 18, 1954. In all Boeing manufactured 744 of these giants.

B-52 *Stratofortress*—1952

The eight jet B-52 became the backbone of the United States Strategic Air Force Command, still in active service in the nineties.

No one needs to tell the story of the exploits of the B-52. It wrote its own, providing the backbone of the Strategic Air Command of the United States Air Force for almost four decades.

1. Harold Mansfield, Vision, (New York: Popular Library, 1966), 147.
2. Ibid., 148.
3. Ibid., 157.
4. *Chronicle of the 20th Century*, (New York: Chronicle Publications, 1987), 609.
5. Mansfield, Vision, 174.
6. Ibid., 175.
7. Ibid., 180.
8. Ibid., 180.
9. Ibid., 181.
10. Ibid., 182.

18

The Transition Years

In an uncertain, postwar world, new technology seemed destined to be directed preponderantly towards conflict, however no field of endeavor failed to feel a new surge.

Portents of dramatic change in business and industry were everywhere. One breakthrough was hardly digested, when another—promising to supplant it—stood poised on the threshold.

The war had spawned ENIAC—for Electronic Numerical Integrator and Computer—an extremely sophisticated calculator—invented by IBM. First utilized by the U.S. War Department in 1946, ENIAC worked 1,000 times as fast as any calculator ever devised—operated by a flow of electrons in some 18,000 vacuum tubes—and for the first time, all moving parts were eliminated, with electronic pulses replacing mechanical switches.

Scarcely two years later, Bell Telephone Laboratories announced the transistor, a lilliputian solid-state electronic device about 1/200 the size, and requiring 1/100 of the power of a single vacuum tube—destined to relegate ENIAC and its vacuum tube cousins to the trash heap of industry.

In a time warp of history, two quite disparate events in 1947 dramatically focused the pace of technology in the aircraft industry. Foreshadowing a new era, on October 14, Chuck Yeager became the first human to travel faster than the speed of sound, when he breached that formidable barrier, flying a Bell X-1 rocket plane. Less than a month later, on November 2, Howard Hughes rang down the curtain on the glue and wood technology that had survived a half century, when he took the *Spruce Goose* to the air for its first—and last—flight. A 200-ton, eight-engined giant; with wings, fuselage, and empennage constructed entirely of wood—the world's largest airplane—the *Goose* had one of the shortest flights in history, rising seventy feet off the water before Hughes brought the big bird down to stay.

Turmoil and uncertainty threatened almost every aspect of the aircraft industry in the transition years of the late forties and early fifties. Strikes, material shortages, financial limitations, and locked-in government regulations were not the only concerns.

In July 1947, when President Truman signed legislation uniting all branches of the armed services into a single agency—creating the Department of Defense—a new face was put on the military procurement process. With the Cold War supplanting the heat of battle, United States defense agencies were in an unsettled state, as each postured to gain its perceived rightful share of the defense budget.

The world power balance shifted mightily when, on September 23, 1949, Truman announced that the Soviets had exploded their first atomic bomb. Following close on the heels of that sobering news, on October 1, 1949, Chairman Mao Tsetung proclaimed the birth of the People's Republic of China, a new Communist monolith.

In January 1950, Truman ordered the Atomic Energy Commission to proceed with production of the hydrogen bomb, and proclaimed the beginning of NATO; as eight Western European nations signed the pact, escalating the Cold War yet another notch. Sixteen months later, a raging ball of fire destroyed the island of Eniwetok, when the world's first hydrogen bomb was exploded.

In May, French forces, feeling the sting of the attack of four well armed Viet Minh battalions, appealed to the Americans for aid. Trained by the Chinese, the Viet Minh had gained their support when Mao recognized the new regime as the Democratic Republic of Viet Nam.

In June, the U.N. and the U.S. agreed to send troops to Korea, and General Douglas MacArthur was named to lead the force.

To provide additional brainpower for the new postwar age, the U.S. churned out millions of college graduates. More than half of the 2.5 million students who received degrees in 1947 were war veterans who had studied under the G.I. Bill. An unprecedented number majored in engineering.

Postwar manpower witnessed remarkable changes. Boeing was among the leaders in efforts toward equal opportunities for minorities, helping to secure women's place on the factory floor. Further, during the war, a team of recruiters combed the farms and cotton fields in the South, signing up black citizens to go to work in Seattle. As witness to the success of that program, in 1956, Bertram C. Williams and Gordon McHenry became the first two black supervisors at Boeing, and in 1961 Boeing was one of the first of eight United States corporations that voluntarily joined John F. Kennedy's Plans for Progress program.

At Boeing, Cliff Leisy's flying boom project for in-flight refueling was just entering production—with a high priority—to satisfy the air force requirement for global range for its jet bombers. The concept was fully proven, when, on March 2, 1949, a Boeing B-50 bomber completed the first nonstop flight around the world. Ninety-four hours and one minute after takeoff, the *Lucky Lady* landed at Carswell Air Force Base near Fort Worth, Texas. The plane refueled four times in midair during its 23,452 mile flight, taking on fuel over the Azores, Saudi Arabia, Manila, and Hawaii.

The booms were quickly adapted to the Boeing C-97, which became the KC-97 series. The air force ordered the airplane as its standard tanker, assigning twenty planes to each B-47 wing.

The engineering study group that Phil Johnson initiated for postwar ventures quickly rejected the idea of building automobiles and refrigerators. Nevertheless, diversification remained clearly focused because of the vagaries of military procurement and the uncertain magnitude of the commercial airplane market. Engineering was going forward on a pilotless aircraft project, a ramjet engine, two bomb-lift projects, and a small gas turbine, all under government contracts.

The gas turbine engine seemed promising for both commercial and military applications, and the first contract was received from the navy for turbines to drive generators for electric power aboard minesweepers. Later, the turbine was adapted to a Kaman helicopter and a heavy-duty truck. In 1955, Boeing created an Industrial Products Division, which centered its activities on the Model 502 gas turbine, and by year end 500 units had been sold.

In spite of its success in numerous specialized applications, a mass market never developed for gas turbines and the project continued on a tentative, year-by-year basis.

On July 27, 1949, the world's first jet airliner, the de Havilland *Comet*, made its debut in the skies over Hatfield, England. The sweptwing Comet, powered by four jet engines tucked into the wing-body interface, was Britain's bid to gain world leadership in commercial aviation. With a comfortable, five-year lead, they very nearly succeeded. Capable of carrying thirty-six passengers in a pressurized cabin at 40,000 feet, at speeds in excess of 500 miles per hour, it was almost twice as fast as any airliner in service.

In August 1951, an experimental Douglas *Skyrocket* plane broke all altitude records, climbing to over 72,000 feet above the earth by use of rockets—after being carried aloft by a B-29 bomber. The same month, the *Viking*—a pure rocket—reached an altitude of 135 miles above the desert of New Mexico. Aerospace was close to reality.

Rocket technology was opening up an entirely new field of missiles. Ground-to-air, air-to-ground, ground-to-ground, and air-to-air types were on the drawing boards in America's busy aerospace companies.

When the Germans began launching V-1 buzz bombs against British targets in 1944, General Hap Arnold set up a crash program for 1,000 jet-propelled bombs a month, similar to the V-1s, to be built by Northrup.

Boeing developed a ground-to air-pilotless aircraft (GAPA) under contract with the air force, and in 1946, were firing the needle-nosed missile by the dozens on the Utah salt flats. By 1949, with success achieved, and production imminent, the project was abruptly canceled. A Washington, D.C. decision had put all missiles of 100 miles range or less under army jurisdiction, and the army already had a missile of its own—the *Nike*.

Not to be discouraged easily, Bob Jewett and his preliminary design engineers presented their new electronic guidance system to the air force. The result was a joint proposal by Boeing and the University of Michigan for an advanced ground-to-air missile, which came to be known as BOMARC.

For BOMARC, far more than the guidance system had to be invented. Difficult new problems reared up as the requirements of performance stretched the limits of existing materials and manufacturing processes.

BOMARC
Test Firing at Cape Canaveral January 22, 1958.

Utilizing a fuel and an oxidizer—stored in separate tanks—which ignited spontaneously upon contact, the new missile demanded a containment material with properties not yet achieved by industry. The Armco Steel Company had done laboratory testing of a new stainless steel called 17-7PH, which had demonstrated the corrosion resistance necessary to contain the red-fuming nitric acid oxidizer—while maintaining the high strength necessary for storage under pressure for long periods.

John "Fred" Baisch, a metallurgical engineering graduate from the University of Washington, addressed the problem with the patience and intensity of a surgeon. The result was a tailoring of the new material by heat lot to each tank, essentially introducing laboratory controls into the manufacturing process.

BOMARC went into production, becoming the defensive shield around the northern perimeter of the United States—on instant alert during the early Cold War period. Boeing was in the missile business to stay.

Working as a consultant for Pratt & Whitney during the war years, Charles Lindbergh was also in Germany immediately following the war, seeking information on jet airplane design. Back in the United States, he went to see Juan Trippe, and rejoined Pan American as a technical consultant. A survey was undertaken to determine if the time for commercial jet airplanes was at hand. Although the speed was there, none of the projected jets had sufficient range.

In November 1949, Wellwood Beall sent Trippe a letter in which he called attention to the jet progress in Britain. He pointed out Boeing's extensive experience in large military jet airplanes, suggesting the company was well prepared with the know-how to design and manufacture an "outstanding type" of jet airliner. "All we need for an immediate go ahead is a customer."[1]

Trippe was not the customer Beall was looking for, and neither was any other airline. Commercial jets were being viewed by most experts as having no future because of their short range. Nevertheless, in October 1952, Trippe ordered three Comets. He was one of the few who viewed jets as a way to reduce the cost per seat-mile, as a result of doubling the speed. Nearly everyone else saw the jets as a rich man's airplane—those willing to pay a premium for a super-fast, first class ride. Since the planes would cost over $3 million each, they would have to carry more passengers than any previous aircraft, and should be capable of crossing the ocean non-stop.

To Trippe, the Comet was an economic failure before it entered service. He ordered the three planes to cover himself, actually doubting that Pan American would ever take delivery.

The sleek new Comet did not make an auspicious start. Three units were damaged in runway accidents early in the program. Then, two literally exploded in the air during proving flights.

The day of reckoning came on May 2, 1953, when the third Comet, first to carry passengers, crashed; and the airplane was grounded.

Parts of one of the earlier crashed airplanes were fished out of the Mediterranean Sea, and it was deduced that a small crack had formed in a window frame from the stress of the pressurized cabin. In turbulent air, the flexing of the structure resulted in the crack instantly growing to several feet, rupturing the fuselage.

The reverberations of that crack investigation rolled through the engineering departments and the boardrooms of the aircraft industry around the world. Perhaps there was something fundamentally wrong with sustained, high-altitude, pressurized jet operations.

However, tragic accidents also continued to plague piston engine driven commercial airplanes. At this stage of design and manufacturing know-how, there was still much to learn about producing long-lived airframes. At Boeing, the spotlight abruptly focused on the structures and materials departments to understand the problem of metal failure, and to devise a solution.

The commercial jet age was just around the corner, and it came at a landmark moment in history. Millions of Americans had returned from the war to take up the tools of peace.

Perhaps more than at any time in this century, there was a freshness of beginning—an anticipation of unfolding opportunity. It was a time for testing—a time to be brave with a new kind of courage—a courage of faith in the creation of enterprise.

The Great Depression that had swallowed the dreams of our fathers was cloaked by a curtain of years. Its importance had faded and its sting had healed. Hope was in style. Self esteem was never higher, fear for the future scarcely considered.

The airplane industry stood at the cutting edge of a new era. Two decades lay ahead during which such amazing accomplishments would be achieved, that discussion of them in 1950 would have been branded as pure fantasy.

1. Robert Daley, *An American Saga*, (New York: Random House, 1980), 398.

19

Commercial Jets

The last Stratocruiser was delivered to British Overseas Airways Corporation in May 1950. Wellwood Beall went on the delivery flight for a look at the British Comet. The airplane was in flight status, and BOAC had placed orders for ten. The other airlines of Europe appeared ready to tumble.

Boeing engineering studies for a commercial jet transport had been limited to designing a new fuselage, utilizing a B-47 wing. Dissatisfied with the results, George Schairer suggested taking a fresh approach.

After a more detailed study, a prototype concept evolved—a low winged machine with a nose gear up front and the main gear mounted in the wings, folding into the body. Four single engines would be installed in pods under the wings.

When Bill Allen attended the Farnborough Air Show the following spring, he was startled at the sleek, futuristic appearance of the Comet.

That night, at dinner with Maynard Pennell, chief of preliminary design, and Ken Luplow, sales engineer, Allen confronted them with some hard questions.

"How did you like the Comet?" Allen asked.
"It's a very good airplane," said Pennell.
"Do you think we could build one as good?"
"Oh, better. Much better."[1]

Back in Seattle, the romance of a jet transport seemed to be buried in the hard negatives of no U.S. airline demand for such an airplane, and no interest by the air force. To go ahead could well be a terrible waste of stockholder's money. The production order for the B-52 had not yet been achieved, and there was the reality of where the money would come from, short of more debt.

Allen directed the engineering department to take a look at putting jet engines on a KC-97 to refuel the B-52. The air force was not interested—it would be cheaper to convert B-47s into tankers.

When salesmen Fred Collins and Ralph Bell pressed Bill Allen to order the construction of a jet transport prototype on speculation, he cut them down.

"Whose money are you spending?" he demanded.[2] As an alternate, he continued to push the air force to buy a jet-powered KC-97, feeling it was too good an airplane to pass by.

With the air force showing a deaf ear, Allen went through many weeks of soul-searching, thinking back to that September day in 1945 when he was made president. *Act, get things done, move forward.*

The time had come for a decision. Dictating a list of questions to his secretary, he called a meeting of his department heads. He told them to take plenty of time to reply to his questions. "We don't want to make a mistake," he said.[3]

Six days after the first flight of the B-52, on April 21, 1952, the second meeting—to answer Bill Allen's questions—convened. Jim Barton of cost accounting put the price of a jet prototype at $15 million—equal to four times the total profit since the end of the war. Pennell reported the plane would meet the range requirements of a military tanker and would have three times the work capacity of the C-97. As a commercial airplane, the seat-mile operating cost would be competitive. Schairer said the same prototype could be used to demonstrate both a military and a commercial transport and could provide the performance data needed for production airplanes. Beall said Pratt & Whitney would have the engines. There was sufficient engineering and production manpower to do the job.

Allen went to the board, recommending a go-ahead. They concurred without a single dissenting vote.

Soon, interest began to focus on a plywood, walled-off area in the factory at Renton, where the new airplane, known as the 367-80 prototype, was taking shape. Incorporating a bold new feature, a completely sealed wing, the 367-80 was thousands of pounds lighter as a result of eliminating the old rubber fuel cells. The metal wing became the fuel tank.

The air force made no commitments, nor did the airline industry. The cost of the program increased to $16 million.

On May 14, 1954, at the shift change, precisely at 4:00 P.M., the hangar doors rolled open at the Renton factory and the new brown and yellow bird emerged from its secret nest to face the newsreel cameras. William E. Boeing was there. At age 72, he was witnessing the results of his vision—*Let no improvement in flying and flying equipment pass you by.* He could feel the enthusiasm in the electric atmosphere.

Trouble lurked in the background. When Alvin M. "Tex" Johnston, the test pilot, taxied the airplane a week later, he put her through some tough stops and turns. While wheeling into a final turn preparatory to takeoff, the left wing suddenly dropped, the left landing gear collapsing into the wing, and the left outboard engine pod coming to rest on the taxiway.

The rear spar trunnion attachment for the main landing gear had fractured. In retrospect, the timing was fortunate. Had Tex not given the airplane that last severe maneuver, he would have taken off, with a near certain failure of the gear upon landing—potential disaster for the airplane.

The *Dash 80* was repaired and back in flight status in less than two months, and on July 15, 1954, commercial aviation witnessed an historic milestone—the maiden flight of the prototype of America's first commercial jet airplane.

Quiet happiness pervaded the scene. When Tex Johnston landed the plane at Boeing Field, and taxied up to the flight test hangar, chief engineer George Martin was waiting in shirt sleeves, hands in his pockets, a broad smile on his face. For today, his work was done.

A field car drove up behind Allen, and someone pulled him out of its path. "If it had hit me now I wouldn't have felt it," Allen said.[4]

Fallout from the trunnion fracture remained. Hogged out of a large steel block, representing the state-of-art of the steel industry, it had failed to measure up to the new requirements of the dawning jet age, showing zero ductility in the short transverse direction.

John "Jack" Sweet, chief metallurgist, another graduate of the University of Washington, put his staff to work to develop an entirely new set of material specifications—based on exhaustive research—for specially processed, ultra high-strength steel forgings.

When the steel companies read the requirements, they laughed. The reality of the marketplace did not square with the idea of producing a few hundred tons of special steel in an industry which operated in terms of 100 million tons a year.

Boeing persisted, gaining support from the rest of the aircraft industry—and the Defense Department. Ultimately successful, the resulting vacuum-melted steel exhibited excellent ductility in all directions, even when heat treated to tensile strengths 50 percent

Model 367-80 Prototype Jet Transport—1954

History recorded this airplane as the Boeing *$15 million dollar gamble*. Built entirely on company funds, the airplane ushered in the jet age of commercial air transportation.

higher than that used in the original *Dash 80* forging, and became the industry standard.

The giant B-52 was becoming a tremendous production effort, and air force interest in a jet tanker to refuel them accelerated. Sensing the inevitability of an order, in the summer of 1954 Allen authorized the start of engineering and tooling for a production tanker—at company expense—promising the air force to deliver the initial unit in fifteen months.

In March 1955, the Secretary of the Air Force announced that Boeing's new jet—designated the KC-135—would become the standard tanker.

The Lockheed Constellation, leader in commercial sales in the early fifties, was running out of options for improvements in range and capacity then being demanded by the airlines. The first generation of Constellations had pioneered transatlantic flights with a refueling stop at Gander, Newfoundland. The latest stretched version with more powerful engines, was able to dispense with the Gander stop on the eastbound leg, and by 1953, the Super-Connies were flying from New York to Amsterdam without refueling at Shannon, Ireland. But the westbound leg was another matter. Flying into the teeth of the prevailing winds proved to be beyond even the Super-Connies' capability.

As early as 1948, Lockheed had considered that a jet airplane was needed for the North Atlantic. However, by 1952, the Gross brothers decided the investment would be too great, and failing to get a favorable nod for aid from the United States government, they dropped the program.

Douglas delivered 753 DC-6 series airplanes between 1947 and 1955, far outdistancing Lockheed on numbers of airplanes in commercial service. Then, in 1956, Douglas shaded the glamorous Connies when the DC-7 was introduced. A total of 121 of the DC-7 models were purchased by the airlines, and Douglas again appeared to be firmly in control of the market. Jet airplanes had been relegated to the study category.

Lockheed was busy redesigning the Super-Connies with turboprop engines and a completely new wing. Delays in engine availability resulted in returning to piston power, with concurrent airframe and wing modifications. Rollout of the prototype—known as the Model L-1649A *Starliner*—was delayed until September 1956, with first delivery to TWA in April 1957. By that time the DC-7C had captured most of the market, and only forty-three production airplanes were built.

In July 1955, when Boeing gave the go-ahead for production of *Model 707*—the commercial version of the prototype—Lockheed, wary about airline acceptance of such a giant step as the jets offered, was already heavily committed in engineering and tooling for their entry into the race, the all-new turboprop L-188 *Electra*. The deadly pace of competition did not allow for second thoughts.

By the time the Electra prototype flew in late 1957, the jet race between Boeing and Douglas was well under way. After about a year of working out design and production bugs, the Electra began commercial service with American Airlines early in 1959.

Even though the Electra came on the scene later than Lockheed had hoped, and offered far less than the jets in terms of new technology, it had the advantage of significantly lower fuel usage.

Soon after the *Dash 80* flew, Juan Trippe sent Franklin Gledhill, his purchasing agent, along with Sanford Kauffman, from his engineering staff, to Seattle to look the prototype over. Of all the airlines, Pan American was the only one who had decided to bypass the turboprop technology entirely.

In Seattle, Beall took them up for a demonstration. In spite of the bare airplane—no soundproofing inside the fuselage—both men felt it was a fantastic improvement over piston planes. Nevertheless, jet technology was still short of what Trippe wanted. The plane, as configured, was not a truly nonstop transatlantic machine, requiring one stop westbound.

A crucial decision was imminent. The Pratt & Whitney J-57, although more powerful by one-third than any previous engine, still lacked the capability for a nonstop crossing. However, they were working on an advanced version, designated the J-75, which immediately riveted Trippe's attention.

Keeping his options secret, Trippe sent his team to the Douglas factory in Santa Monica to talk to Donald Douglas, and then to Lockheed to see Courtland Gross. He wanted them to know of his decision to switch to jets as soon as a viable design appeared, and he wanted them to compete with Boeing to drive the price down.

"Donald Douglas at first refused. His DC-7 series was selling briskly. It would be the last major four-engined propeller airliner ever built, but Douglas did not know this, and he had orders for it carrying well into the future. The newest derivative, the DC-7C, was the result of a Pan American idea. Pressure from Pan Am had forced Douglas only a year before to lengthen the DC-7 wings by ten feet and to stretch the fuselage four feet in length. The result was a 20 percent increase in fuel capacity, plus engines placed five feet further outboard on each side, thereby producing less noise and vibration in the cabin. The DC-7C could accommodate ninety-one tourist-class passengers, and was the first plane that could cross the Atlantic nonstop in all weather. Donald Douglas knew he had something good in this plane. Why should he allow himself to be pressured into a race for jet orders? He told Kauffman and Gledhill that a jet program would not be economic, and he mentioned a new study by the Rand Corporation which seemed to prove that jet engines burned too much fuel.

"'I've had an analysis made of that,' Kauffman told him, and he handed over some documents. 'Why don't you have your engineers make their own analysis.'

"Douglas found that his own engineers were anxious to build the plane and that their data coincided with Pan Am's. And so the Douglas Company, though far behind Boeing in development, decided to compete. The DC-8 program, little more than an intellectual exercise until now, would move forward with all prudent speed.

"Kauffman and Gledhill went to Lockheed, where they informed President Gross of the status of their negotiations with Boeing and with Douglas. Would Gross like to build a jet also? Gross declined. Two factories competing was enough, he said. He could not take the risk.

"At this stage, it was entirely possible that Douglas would build a prototype to match Boeing's, and most airlines would refuse to buy either one. Apart from Trippe, the aviation world was terrified of jets."[5]

The explosion of the Comets in the air had brought into question the fundamental safety of jet airplanes. Operationally, too, jets seemed to promise disaster. Airports simply did not exist to handle this new type of plane. The engines burned kerosene instead of gasoline, and an entire new fueling infrastructure was required. Further, new hangars would be needed, as well as starting carts, and loading and servicing equipment—plus unknowns that had yet to surface.

With Boeing committed to the 707, and Douglas scrambling to complete the engineering for the DC-8, Pan Am was the only customer on the horizon, and Trippe decided he would purchase nothing less than a machine with true transatlantic capability and at least equivalent profitability to the DC-7C. His marketing studies told him he needed four more rows than the designs offered—at six abreast, equivalent to twenty-four more passengers. The bottom line was clear. Neither the 707 nor the DC-8 was large enough, and the engines were not powerful enough. Trippe decided to force the issue by playing the two manufacturers against one another by dangling the prospect of a large order.

By the spring of 1955, Douglas completed its DC-8 design— essentially the same plane that Boeing was already flying. The Douglas Board of Directors had authorized a production go-ahead with a minimum order of fifty planes. No orders came.

Trippe proposed building the bigger airplane in spite of the underpowered engine. He had confidence in the new J-75.

Boeing, having already invested $16 million, was totally committed. To change the size was beyond consideration.

Ralph Bell, Boeing sales director, lamented: "Our prototype is our biggest asset, but it's also our biggest obstacle. Douglas has a rubber airplane. It's easy to stretch on paper."[6]

For the moment, Trippe decided to concentrate on Douglas. Using the DC-2/DC-3 analogy, he coaxed Douglas to make the decision to redesign the DC-8 around the untested J-75. Douglas responded with a polite but firm no.

Trippe took his case to Fred Rentschler, chairman of Pratt & Whitney, and also a stockholder and member of the Pan Am board. A commitment to produce the J-75—and guarantee performance—would be the ace that he needed. Rentschler was adamantly opposed, pointing out that Pratt & Whitney had a perfectly acceptable production engine in the J-57 which matched the 707. Trippe responded by going to Rolls Royce, expanding his poker game to the international arena.

Trippe hardly hesitated in continuing to escalate the stakes. The Boeing prototype decision, which had gained the moniker "$15 million dollar gamble", paled in comparison to the less publicized actions of the Pan Am chairman.

After an arm-twisting, pleading, promising campaign, arrestingly detailed by Daley,[7] Rentschler caved in, offering to have the J-75 ready by the summer of 1959—with the appropriate guarantees that Trippe had insisted upon. For that commitment, Trippe signed for around $40 million in engines. He would own the engines with no planes to put them on.

Taking his case to Boeing first, he announced: "If you won't build the plane I want, then I will find someone who will."[8] Allen, deciding that Trippe was bluffing, refused to budge. The 707-120 was there and he could take it or leave it. After all, Allen had another ace. With the KC-135 committed, the program was already guaranteed to be successful. It would be unnecessary to gamble further capital on a new fuselage and perhaps a new wing.

Playing the game to the hilt, Trippe went to Douglas—suggesting a turndown would force him to take his business overseas. The DC-8 was still on paper—no expensive tooling had been built. Douglas capitulated, agreeing to redesign a larger DC-8 around the J-75 engine. Trippe wrote an order for twenty-five planes, but requested the deal to be kept secret for a while longer, presumably to allow him a clearer field in dealing with Boeing. He wanted to be first with both so as to be guaranteed first in the air.

Then, he ordered twenty of the smaller planes, leaving Boeing with the impression that it was the first order. This order was also kept secret, and Trippe signed both contracts on the same day.

Following an IATA executive meeting in New York on October 13, 1955, Trippe threw a party for the nation's airline executives, where he let it be known that Pan Am had just purchased $269 million worth of jets; $160 million to Douglas, and $100 million to Boeing.

In Seattle, Allen read about Trippe's deal in the newspapers. As it stood, Douglas would corner the foreign market with its big, longer-range planes, and would carve out a huge piece of the domestic market as well. Commercially speaking, the current 707-120 design was doomed before it ever entered service.

Allen phoned Trippe, offering to redesign the 707, and it was agreed that the Boeing-Pan Am contract would be renegotiated. Trippe would take six of the smaller 707s, inasmuch as Boeing was tooled up to turn them out reasonably quickly. These would suffice—with refueling stops—to open service on the North Atlantic months before anyone else did, and afterwards, they could serve Latin America. In addition, Boeing would build seventeen units of a bigger model, powered by the J-75.[9] The airplane was eight feet longer, with fifteen feet added to the span, and could carry up to twenty-four more passengers than the 120. The new design was designated the 707-320 Intercontinental.

Gaining the extra span was not equivalent to starting over on the wing design. It was accomplished by moving the zero wing station outboard from the airplane centerline, to positions on each side of the body, and designing a new center wing stub. Other changes to the wing were relatively minor.

Some industry pundits not only called Trippe a gambler, they branded him as downright reckless. He had placed orders totaling $269 million on a net income for the previous year of $10.4 million.

Airline delegations followed in lockstep to Seattle to fly in the prototype. Douglas won the second round when United Airlines ordered thirty DC-8s. It began to look as if Boeing had taken all the risks to prove the technology and Douglas was going to win the lion's share of orders simply by promising the improved version.

American Airlines ordered thirty 707-320s. Eastern chose the DC-8; Continental and Braniff, the 707. And so it went, frantic, pell-mell into a new age of transportation. Airplanes would soon provide a doubling in capacity, with nearly twice the speed of propeller machines—promising to change the shape and size of the world.

In 1957, Donald W. Douglas, then sixty-five years old, moved to chairman of the board and Donald W. Douglas Jr. succeeded to the presidency. However, more than a change in president took place. A new team became responsible for the activities and the corporate conscience of the Douglas Aircraft Company. It would never be the same.

The first of the smaller Boeing model was delivered to Pan Am in mid-1958, and the inaugural VIP flight was made on October 19—from New York to Brussels. The plane was fitted out like a club car, with eighty-four seats.

The jets were an immediate financial success. During the first quarter of 1959, 33,400 passengers were carried on Pan Am jets, with a 90.8 percent seat occupancy, an all-time high. In the first five years of the Jet Age, overseas traffic doubled, and in 1963, Pan Am's net income after taxes was $33,568,000 on operating revenues of over a half billion dollars. Later, Pan Am sold their DC-8s and standardized the fleet with 707s.

Early in 1956, Convair, then part of General Dynamics, a new, loosely organized nine-division conglomerate—of which Convair was the largest—saw themselves as a third contender in the great jet race. Reuben Fleet had long since sold his stock and left the company, and after the war, Convair enjoyed continued success with military airplanes, most notably the B-58, the first supersonic bomber. The company also developed successful twin piston-engined commercial transports; the 240, 340, and 440 series; of which over 1,000 were sold.

Encouraged by Howard Hughes, then still the controlling shareholder in TWA, Convair perceived market possibilities of as many as 250 jet transports of their own design, over a period of ten years—and predicted a rosy breakeven point at 68 aircraft. After securing letters of intent from TWA, Delta and KLM, and an engine guarantee from General Electric, the GD executive committee gave the go ahead for the Model 880, a sleek new jet similar in many respects to the 707/DC8s, but smaller and faster.

When KLM dropped out, Convair forged ahead, targeting United, who had expressed interest in a plane somewhat smaller than the DC-8s they had ordered, to handle their shorter domestic routes. They liked the 880—except for the five abreast seating.

President Allen, determined to do whatever it took to maintain leadership in the new field of commercial jets, directed his engineers to develop a model specifically to meet United's requirements. The result was the Model 720, utilizing the 120 wing, with a body shortened by eight feet and with the same width—retaining the six abreast seating—which became the standard for the entire 707 series.

Convair and United had already agreed on eighteen of nineteen articles in a sales contract for the 880, when Boeing offered the 720. United chose the Boeing machine.

When the 880 rolled out on Christmas Day in 1958, it was already doomed. American Airlines, the last hope, decided to go for the 720. Convair, in desperation, offered to build a new model, the 990, with a new GE fan engine—the first fan to go on any airliner. The 990 was to be the fastest jet liner in the world, cruising at 640 mph. American agreed to buy it—with suitable guarantees on speed, noise, payload and range, but insisted on trading in their old DC-7 airplanes. For Convair it was a double or nothing game, and they went forward on the 990. The first American 990 flew four months late, in January 1961. Since it was designed "straight to production," without a prototype, every airplane required major rework, and the guaranteed cruising speed was never achieved. A total of thirty airplanes were sold.

Boeing's response to the 990 was to put fans on the 720, which became the 720B, an airplane which developed a life of its own, eventually being purchased by nearly a score of domestic and foreign airlines.

On February 3, 1959, disaster loomed for the Lockheed Electra when one crashed on landing in New York. Eight months later, a second Electra crashed at Buffalo, Texas, and the following year, still a third fell out of the air near Camelton, Indiana. In two of the crashes, engine separation had occurred in flight. All of the planes were called back to the factory for a radical restructuring of the wing and engine mounts.

The Electra was dead. Lockheed dropped out of the commercial airplane business after selling 176 machines. A redesigned version was sold to the navy as a patrol plane.

The enthusiasm with which the public accepted the new jet airplanes was unprecedented—and well earned. They brought a new dimension of vibrationless flight and a noticeably quieter cabin. It also became apparent that the jet engines were more reliable and trouble free than their predecessors. Flight crews were quick to discover the new ease of operation. The 707 gained a reputation of being able to fly by itself—nearly dooming the program.

In February 1959, four months after the 707 began service over the Atlantic with Pan American, N712PA, the sixth airplane off the line, ran into trouble.[10]

Flying at 32,000 feet in quiet air, the flight was routine. The captain left his seat and strolled back into the cabin, chatting with the passengers. Suddenly, the airplane started nosing down. Losing altitude rapidly and increasing speed, its dive steepened. The captain, recognizing the problem, struggled to get back into the cockpit. He barely made it. With both he and the copilot straining at the controls, they pulled the plane out of the dive about 6,000 feet above the Atlantic Ocean. The loads on the wings were so great that the metal structure had surpassed its yield strength—and a few seconds more would have been too late. The only thing that saved the plane—and the commercial jet age—was the integrity that Boeing had built into the airframe.

When the airplane was returned to the factory for a complete structural and alignment check, it was found to be airworthy and fully qualified for continued flight. The report read in part, "The relative positions of the front and rear spar and the nacelles show that the wings are permanently twisted...."[11]

Pan Am flew N712PA many more years, eventually selling it to a foreign carrier, where it continued in revenue service until October 30, 1984.

With President Allen having unequivocally committed Boeing to sail on the new ocean of commercial jet airplanes, the Transport Division was formed in 1956, to devote its entire energies to that task. But by the end of 1959, the cutthroat competition with Douglas produced a financial crisis for the new division. The 707 program projected a massive loss of $200 million by the end of the year. Much of the increased cost could be attributed to the strict manufacturing quality standards that Boeing had established.

The production runs for the B-52 at Wichita, the BOMARC in the new missile production center, and the KC-135 at Renton were still creating sufficient profits to keep the company afloat. However, new investment was needed to maintain the viability of the fragile entry into commercial jets.

Overall employment, which had reached an all-time peak at over 100,000 in 1957, was drastically reduced, and stood at 80,000 in 1959.

To meet the situation, Allen listed the principles that he felt must guide the effort ahead:

"In order to obtain business," he said, "we must earn the opportunity to compete for it. In order to compete we must have a better product to sell. In order to develop and offer a better product, we must have superior conception, design capability, and a demonstrated cost performance.

"In order to be superior in those fields, we must invest capital to sustain the people who will accomplish product and design, and we must put capital into research and development facilities and efforts. In order to have that capital we must either earn it through our profits, or attract it in the money markets."[12]

Those principles were being applied by putting 80 percent of earnings back into research and new facilities, latest of which was a Mach 20 hypersonic wind tunnel, the most advanced in the country.

1. Harold Mansfield, *Vision*, (New York: Popular Library, 1966), 191.
2. Ibid., 194.
3. Ibid., 196.
4. Ibid., 200.
5. Robert Daley, *An American Saga*, (New York: Random House, 1980), 403/404.
6. Private Communication.
7. Daley, *An American Saga*, 410.
8. Ibid., 411.
9. Ibid., 414.
10. *Aviation Week & Space Technology*, 9 February, 1959, 39.
11. W.F. Minkler, *Alignment Check—Airplane N712PA*, Internal Boeing Communication, CSPR-18, 10 February, 1959.
12. Private Communication.

20

Military and Space

Speed remained the key to the future, be it commercial airplanes or weapon delivery systems.

After Convair won the competition for an advanced medium-range bomber—known as the B-58—a machine that could make a supersonic dash over the target area, the air force set its sights on a more ambitious goal—the capability of supersonic flight for the entire mission.

In 1953, Boeing won a study contract from the air force to brainstorm far-out ideas: a futuristic vehicle boosted to extreme altitudes by rocket and then allowed to glide to its target; nuclear-powered aircraft; ballistic missiles; and a supersonic bomber with speeds in the Mach 2 to Mach 3 range.

The supersonic bomber was given the top priority, and Thornton A. "T." Wilson, a rapidly rising young engineer from Iowa State University, was put in charge.

Wilson held an advanced degree in aeronautical engineering, and had just returned from a year's study at MIT as a Sloan Fellow in industrial management—a course that was then firmly embedded in Boeing's executive development plan.

By November 1955, competition had narrowed to Boeing and North American Aviation. North American, a war-spawned giant, manufacturing primarily military airplanes, was best known for its P-51 *Mustang*—the premium fighter of World War II—with a range capable of escorting B-17 and B-24 bombers deep into Europe. Both firms were awarded contracts to complete their design studies for a new strategic bomber designated as Weapon System 110-A by the air force.

Bill Allen spotlighted the effort. "This is a contract that Boeing must win," he said.[1]

To support the bid, research went forward on the combined effects of high pressure, friction, and heat; supersonic control; and manufacturing techniques. Proposing a giant step, Boeing chose titanium for the primary metal of construction. North American took a more conservative approach, choosing PH 15-7MO, a precipitation-hardenable stainless steel—cousin of the 17-7PH used in the BOMARC oxidizer tanks.

Specifically for the supersonic bomber program, Boeing constructed a $30 million Developmental Center near Plant II. The new, six-building complex, completed in 1957, provided for research and engineering, as well as the assembly of a complete prototype.

By the fall of 1957, the cards were on the table for the 110-A contract award. Ed Wells was noticeably nervous.

"What would we do if we lost?" Schairer asked him.

"There'll be hell to pay."[2]

On December 17, 1957, Convair fired the *Atlas*, first successful U.S. launch of a liquid-fueled ICBM. Schairer and Wells felt that another round of ICBM development was still to come—using solid propellant—which promised a major reduction in cost. Studies continued.

In May 1952, when Dr. Wernher von Braun, world's premier rocket scientist, suggested that it was not too early to begin the design of a space vehicle that could transport men to Mars, most of the world was not listening, and other experts in the field viewed his remarks with deep skepticism. No one had yet come close to orbiting a satellite around the earth.

Incredibly, only five years later, on October 4, 1957, the Soviet Union astonished the world, successfully launching the first man made satellite. *Sputnik*, at 184 pounds, caught the U.S.—planning its own satellite the following year—completely by surprise.

A month later, *Sputnik II*, weighing 1,100 pounds, carried a dog into space. When the U.S. finally launched its first satellite with an army Jupiter-C booster on February 1, 1958, it paled in comparison—weighing in at 30.8 pounds.

In response to the Soviet achievements—with a touch of panic—the U.S. began to expand its space efforts, passing the National Aeronautics and Space Act the same year, and creating the National Aeronautics and Space Administration (NASA).

On December 23, 1957, the 110-A competition decision was announced. North American would build the supersonic bomber. The use of titanium as the primary metal of construction was considered to be too great a step into the unknown.

Dismayed, but not disheartened by the air force decision, which seemed to be a step backward in technology, Boeing executives gathered in Allen's office. George Schairer presented the results of the solid propellant ICBM study to the assembled group. The case was impressive. However, there was as yet no air force definition—

nor timetable—for a solid-fuel ballistic missile, so it was agreed to seek the impending contract for a boost-glide vehicle.

Allen formed an advanced projects team, with top priority, giving it authority to draft key people from the other divisions in the company.

George Stoner, weapon systems manager on BOMARC, who had joined Boeing in 1941, was picked to head the team. Stoner had gained honors while working for his degree in chemistry at Westminister College in Pennsylvania, followed by several years of graduate study at MIT. He was eager to challenge the new frontier at the edge of the earth's atmosphere.

While Stoner was gathering his team, on January 1, 1958, the air force sent a request for proposal for a dynamic soaring vehicle, with a Madison Avenue name—*Dyna-Soar.*

Stoner was quick to realize—and admit—that many companies were already well into critical aspects of the complex array of materials, manufacturing processes, guidance systems, and other key parameters. He set out to marshal an industry-wide team; finalizing on General Electric, Ramo-Wooldridge, Chance Vought, Aerojet General, and North American. His active imagination soon pictured a network of Dyna-Soar flights around the earth, with multiple military uses, particularly global surveillance.

The greatest technological challenge was cooling the vehicle upon its return from the fringes of the atmosphere as it penetrated the oxygen-rich zone near the earth. Stoner was quick to note that the proposed speed of 24,000 feet per second would need to be increased by only 8 percent to reach orbital velocity, giving the system a vastly expanded operational capability.

Weight would be more critical than ever. No boosters were even in the design stage that were large enough to produce orbiting velocity.

By the law of conservation, the energy expended in the boost phase would have to be dissipated as heat during reentry. The nose and leading edge of the wing would reach temperatures in excess of

4,000 degrees Fahrenheit. Most metals melt at lower temperatures. Only ceramics and refractory metals—tungsten, molybdenum, tantalum, and columbium—remained as candidates. Ceramics were far too brittle for structural applications, and the refractory metals oxidized rapidly, requiring protective coatings to avoid burning up.

There were other choices. Active cooling, a concept chosen by the Bell-Martin team—the primary competitor—was only a matter of engineering. However, the resultant increase in weight demanded an even larger booster system. A third alternative was the use of ablative materials for the hottest surfaces. Nonmetallic in nature, ablative materials sublimed when heated, absorbing huge quantities of energy as they slowly gave up their mass. However, extensive refurbishment would be required after each flight.

Boldly, the decision was made to design the vehicle with refractory alloys, and go to orbit—Stoner opting for the system with the highest potential payoff—and the most difficult unsolved problems. The metallurgical community would have to invent new alloys, as well as coatings to protect them.

Working with the Wah Chang Company in Oregon, a primary producer of refractory alloys, the Boeing staff won a NASA contract to develop new columbium-based alloys. Ronald Torgerson, a University of Washington graduate in metallurgical engineering, was responsible for the program—resulting in the invention, development, and patenting of alloy C-103. With mechanical properties adequate to handle the structural requirements of a major portion of the hot regions of the Dyna-Soar vehicle, C-103 became the prime candidate. Development of coatings was addressed by Dr. Willi A. Baginski, a German metallurgist who had immigrated to the U.S. following World War II.

The problem of reducing the temperature gradients in the substructure remained. A certain amount of active cooling still appeared to be necessary. Max Braun, an honor graduate from the University of Illinois in structures engineering, saw it differently.

"You don't have to equalize the temperatures," he said, "if you change the vehicle to a triangular pattern. You can expand any side of a triangle without affecting the others." The principle went into the design, and the cooling system was eliminated.[3]

Equally difficult problems in many other disciplines were being confronted—and solved.

On June 23, 1958, the competition for Dyna-Soar was narrowed to the Boeing and Bell-Martin teams, each awarded contracts to develop their particular concepts.

Bill Allen was exuberant, intent on taking the final heat of the race. "We will undertake it with all the vigor and ingenuity at our command," he told the air force.[4]

Meanwhile, it became clear that *Minuteman*, the new solid propellant ballistic missile, would have a great business potential. Allen decided to enlarge the advanced projects proposal team into a Systems Management Office, headed by Ed Wells. For Boeing, this concept represented a landmark decision, emphasizing program management as the most important element in the complex world of missiles and space.

Dyna-Soar and Minuteman became the twin objectives of the newly formed group. T. Wilson, fresh from the 110-A effort, was chosen to head Minuteman—a huge national program—and preparations for a proposal required a new approach. The basic design had already been fixed, and the air force had divided the multi-billion dollar program into several packages: first stage booster, second stage booster, third stage booster, guidance and control section, warhead section, and finally, assembly and test. All but the last had already been committed to companies specializing in particular fields.

Many felt that the assembly and test portion alone would not provide enough work to be a worthwhile endeavor, but George Schairer disagreed.

"'If we're willing to go in and assist the Air Force in managing this,' he said, '...if we're willing to take the viewpoint that it's their program, not ours, and just help them do the job, I think there'll be plenty of business in it for us.'

"Industry people had been complaining that 'outsiders' were directing the air force programs; the Space Technology Laboratories, an outgrowth of Ramo-Wooldridge, had been picked to provide engineering supervision of Minuteman.

"'I don't see why we should fight them,' Schairer maintained, in a discussion with Wells. 'They're part of the scenery. We can work with them. We've got to get our people to quit this 'not invented here' complex.

"Wells agreed completely. 'The thing we've got to get across to our people is that we have to be responsive to the requirements. That means being responsive to the customer's view as to what the system should accomplish. They want to overcome the shortcomings of the liquid systems, Atlas and Titan, in terms of readiness, reliability, reaction time, and ability to be maintained over a long period without constant attention. Our job will be to bring an understanding of these needs, and how we can help to meet them.'"[5]

The result of that conceptual approach was the implementation of an effort that analyzed every aspect of the system—with even more emphasis on the management side than on the technical side. A 1/20-scale model was constructed and fired from an underground silo at the north end of Boeing Field. The Boeing proposal covered plans for hardened silos; underground control cubicles with their automatic equipment; a launch site installation system with missile handling devices; checkout and maintenance gear; the integration of the missile itself; a plan for management of the assembly and test plant; construction of installations; and plans for the research required to support each aspect of the program.

On October 10, 1958, Wells was working late—as usual—when he received a teletype from the commander of the Air Force Ballistics Missiles Division of the Air Research and Development Command, indicating the Boeing proposal had been evaluated as the best submitted.

Four days later, in Los Angeles, Bill Allen signed the contract.

The dimensions of the assembly and test portion continued to grow as it became evident that major aspects of the Boeing study were as yet unassigned by the air force, and the company was the logical contractor to inherit them. The final result was that Boeing was assigned overall responsibility for making Minuteman work as an effective strategic weapons system.

With Dyna-Soar increasing its demands for the invention of new materials and technologies, Boeing created the Scientific Research Laboratories in January 1958. Conceptually similar to the Bell Telephone Laboratories, where the transistor was born, it employed 100 scientists—with an open charter. There were no fixed working hours—assuming that ideas were not captive to any particular time of the day or night.

In a further move to benefit from research and development efforts within the company, the Boeing Associated Products (BAP) group was formed in August 1960. Strictly a marketing organization, its purpose was the exploitation of byproducts from aerospace R&D efforts—for commercial applications. The initial venture was subsidized, with the intent that it would eventually become profitable, actually achieved in its fifth year.

A survey of major industrial companies—including those in France, West Germany, Italy, Holland, England, and Japan—as well as the U.S., revealed that internally generated research developments were not widely utilized beyond the original project scope. Of the 181 companies surveyed, only 28—all in the U.S.— had created formal "spin-off" programs, and only 7, one of which was Boeing, resulted in profitable ventures.[6]

As Dyna-Soar languished at the decision level, becoming more and more tentative, Boeing felt additional efforts should be made to assure a piece of the impending space business.

With study contracts involving missions to the moon and Mars, exotic new systems were being visualized. Dr. Walter Hiltner, a magna cum laude civil engineering graduate from the University of Washington, masters from MIT, and doctorate from Cal Tech, who had joined the company in 1947, led a group to study rocket engines with cryogenic fuel—liquid oxygen and hydrogen. Included in their studies was an experimental station atop 14,410-foot high Mt. Rainier, to check out personnel reaction to hazardous isolation.

The delay for the Dyna-Soar was agonizingly continued, but finally, out of the blue on November 9, 1959, Bill Allen received a phone call from General Beverly Warren of the Air Materiel Command. "Congratulations," the General began, "I expect you'll be glad to know that your company has been selected as systems contractor for the Dyna-Soar program."[7]

Bill Allen was more than a little awed at the thought of the bizarre, sled-like wings of a Dyna-Soar glowing white like a meteor, as its pilot guided it down from space. Allen wrote a message to all Boeing management on the winning of the contract. "It is a project that captures the imagination. What we have won is an opportunity. What we do with the opportunity is entirely up to us."[8]

Allen's strong initiatives at the loss of the 110-A had paid off handsomely. Contracts for both the Minuteman and the Dyna-Soar had been secured. As a paradoxical footnote to history, the B-70 program was canceled before the airplane flew. North American built two units, the first making its maiden flight from Palmdale, California, on May 11, 1964.

Two months before the Dyna-Soar decision was revealed, the first silo hole, sixteen feet in diameter and eighty-six feet deep had been drilled at Edwards Air Force Base, California, in preparation for tethered Minuteman tests.

On September 15, 1959, test missile No. 1 was being counted down—with high expectations. When the countdown reached zero, a ring of white smoke pulsed out of the hole, followed by angry orange flames. The nose of the Minuteman came up, and just as the entire missile cleared the hole, it flopped over, a jet of fire pouring from the aft closure, as it ignominiously thumped down on the desert floor. In the blockhouse, spirits fell.

Examination of the missile revealed a fracture in the aft closure plate, the result of a defective piece of steel.

Two weeks later, the second tethered test went off without a hitch, and the program was back on course. The Ballistic Missile Command, responding to the political powers who had declared a "missile gap" with the Soviets, called for operational readiness to be moved up from mid-1963 into 1962.

When the question reached Seattle, T. Wilson assessed the possibilities with his staff and the associate contractors. "With a mixture of perspiration and zeal, Wilson said it could be done."[9] The new schedule called for 100 missiles to be in place and operational by the middle of 1963, and 400 by 1964.

On February 1, 1961, the missile gap began to recede into history as the first operational Minuteman made a perfect flight to its planned impact point 4,200 miles down range. The air force pronounced it an unqualified success.

Boeing was faced with a production line that stretched across hundreds of sites in the north-central states of the United States, integrating the efforts and the products of a half-dozen major associate contractors. The final product was a launch complex—delivered underground—and ready to fire missiles.

Ernest H. "Tex" Boullioun, from the University of Texas, came to work at Boeing in 1940, almost by chance. Arriving in the Pacific Northwest on a motorcycle, Tex lost it in a poker game in Portland on his way to Seattle. Hitching a ride the rest of the way, he began his career at Boeing as an inspector. Tex, always seeking the heart of a problem, rose rapidly in the quality control department, and when Minuteman was ready for deployment, was in charge of installing the BOMARC missiles. Assigned to the same key role for Minuteman, Tex, along with Howard "Bud" Hurst, factory manager, a self-made man who started in the shops in 1929, devised the plan for implementation of Minuteman.

Instead of bringing the work past the workers on a traditional production line, they would bring the workers past the various installations, each special team accomplishing a specific task. That meant 8,000 men in the field, working in fifty to sixty holes at a time. Every task was broken down into eight-hour increments, so that skilled workers could put in a day or more and move on. Families lived in mobile homes, moving from base to base.

Ignoring those who said it couldn't be done, Boullioun convinced T. Wilson that it could, and they set up a control room in the Developmental Center in Seattle to track the entire operation on massive wall charts.

Busy days became the standard for the new teams—a special breed of employees called the *Outplant Crew*. They went to the plains of Montana and the Dakotas, braving the bitter arctic cold, blazing summer heat, and stinging winds.

In all, at the peak, Boeing put 33,400 employees on the program. The company's major work force was in Seattle, conducting engineering, subassembly and support activities. At Ogden, Utah, Boeing set up operations in a facility at Hill Air Force Base to assemble the missiles and dispatch them to the six air force bases stretching from Montana to Missouri. Engineering support and test launches were the responsibility of a Boeing team at Cape Canaveral, and later at Vandenberg Air Force Base in California.

Under the incentive features of the contract, Boeing consistently beat schedule and cost targets, giving the nation one of the best managed, mission-capable strategic systems in its history.

The installation of Wing I, in Montana, was completed ahead of schedule in August 1963. The final delivery of Wing II in South Dakota was made in November, installed and operational and turned over to the air force three weeks ahead of schedule. Wing III in North Dakota was delivered ahead of schedule in April 1964,

Wing IV in Missouri in June.

On September 24, 1964, Minuteman II, an improved missile with longer range and more accurate guidance, made a flawless flight from Cape Kennedy to a target in the South Atlantic.

Four days after Christmas, 1970, the first squadron of new Minuteman III missiles was turned over to the air force at Minot Air Force Base, North Dakota. A total of 550 Minuteman IIIs joined the 450 Minuteman IIs already in place.[10]

Minuteman was one of the largest and longest programs in Boeing's history. In December, 1978, the last missile rolled out of the Ogden plant, twenty years after the initial contract award.

By spring 1961, senior project engineer Harry Goldie, a magna cum laude whiz-kid from the University of Washington electrical engineering school—and later, Cal Tech—who joined Boeing in 1949, was able to report to George Stoner that most of the major structural and aerodynamic design features of Dyna-Soar had been settled. The majority of his 1,600 engineers were turning to sub-system design: control, electrical power generation, hydraulics, and electronics.

Major problems remained. For example, there was a need for wires to go to sensors in the leading edges of the wings where they would be subjected to 3,000 degrees Fahrenheit. There were no suppliers—they turned away—laughing. Goldie gave the problem back to the project group. "We'll have to invent our own," he said, without batting an eye.[11]

Many other challenges surfaced, each one requiring an extension into the unknown, while the program remained in a strait-jacket—waiting for a military mission.

The Soviets continued their lead in space, when on April 2, 1961, they startled an awed world with the announcement that a man had been launched into orbit and safely returned to earth.

Minuteman
Minuteman II firing, August 23, 1965.

Yuri Gagarin, a 27-year-old air force major, accomplished the feat in a 10,395-pound *sputnik* called *Vostok*.

The following month, on May 25, the U.S. sent Navy Commander Alan B. Shepard, Jr., into space for a fifteen minute ride, landing downrange in the Atlantic Ocean.

Twenty days later, President John F. Kennedy asked the Congress to approve a multi-billion-dollar program to send a man to the moon and return him safely to the earth. Space efforts went into overdrive around the country, to achieve that goal before the decade was over.

With Kennedy's bold new initiative, the air force went to the House of Representatives with a request to increase the Dyna-Soar appropriations, speeding up the program by a full year.

The positive response from Congress for additional funds did not produce a speedup. Instead, Robert S. McNamara, secretary of defense, decided to withhold the funds and review all the options. He believed that the more sophisticated Dyna-soar would be late for the orbiting role, and favored ballistic launching of space capsules.

On December 10, 1963, Secretary McNamara announced his decision: Dyna-Soar was canceled. The program had already consumed $400 million dollars and years of effort. Abruptly, 5,000 Boeing employees, and thousands of others around the nation, were out of a job. It seemed that bad news always came around Christmas.

History will be unable to assess whether McNamara made the correct decision. It is altogether possible that the *Space Shuttle*—first launched on April 14, 1981—might have been operational many years earlier, had the innovative Dyna-Soar technology been continued to maturity.

1. Private Communication.
2. Harold Mansfield, *Vision*, (New York: Popular Library, 1966), 227.
3. Private Communication.
4. Mansfield, *Vision*, 237.
5. Ibid., 237.
6. E.E. Bauer, *Spinoff Utilization in Research and Development*, (Seattle: University of Washington, 1971).
7. Private Communication.
8. Ibid.
9. Ibid.
10. *Boeing News*, 5 October, 1978, 3.
11. Private Communication.

21

The Impossible Airplane

Enthusiastic acceptance of the new commercial jets with their speed and quiet cabin comfort was unprecedented. Sales of 707s and DC-8s quickly spread around the world.

The Convair 880 and 990 airplane programs died an early death, and the combined cost of $425 million, written off at the end of 1961, represented the largest in corporate history.[1] The battle for dominance in the commercial jet market was left to Boeing and Douglas.

The red ink on the 707 program was not only due to the price war with Douglas. Major research and testing efforts had been mounted, and capital investment in facilities was unprecedented.

Boeing had determined to produce a machine that was structurally safe for many thousands of hours of high-altitude, pressurized cabin operation.

Early in 1956, a huge water tank had been constructed at Plant I to simulate the airplane flight environment. An entire fuselage was submerged in the 20-foot wide, 20-foot deep and 130 foot-long-tank. Continued pumping of water in and out, on a regular schedule, simulated pressure changes as well as the gust cycles expected during thousands of flights.

A complete cabin pressure cycle could be accomplished in five minutes, during which twenty-five gust cycles were simulated. As the load and material performance history was developed, the design was continually improved. Final proof of structural integrity was made with the "guillotine," a device used to slash instantaneous incisions of varying length in the pressurized structure, providing a statistical validation of the behavior of cracks with continued cycles.

To test and qualify materials for windshields, a "chicken gun" was designed to propel the bodies of chickens against the windshields at jet speeds—simulating bird strikes.

Many other specialized test setups were developed for specific components and systems.

Demand for jets on shorter routes was soon a reality. Indeed, propeller airplanes were fast becoming an anachronism in the minds of the traveling public—long before the economies of jets justified them on short routes.

In May 1958, before the first 707 was delivered to Pan American, John J. "Jack" Steiner was appointed to head a planning group for a Boeing short-range jet. At that time, Maynard Pennell—engineer extraordinary—who had cut his eyeteeth on the B-29, and headed the 707 program as senior project engineer—was in charge of preliminary design. Jack Steiner worked for Pennell as aerodynamicist. The two men had great respect for each other's ability, sharing a common vision—the growth and proliferation of the commercial jet airplane business.

Both had graduated from the University of Washington; Pennell with a degree in aeronautical engineering in 1940, and Steiner majoring in both law and engineering. Ultimately turning exclusively to engineering, he graduated at the top of his class, and with borrowed money, headed for MIT with plans for a doctorate. In New York, at a meeting of the Institute of Aeronautical Sciences, he met and sought career advice from George Schairer. Schairer put him to work writing a thesis on the hydrodynamic stability of flying boats while he earned his master's credits. In 1941, Steiner began his life-long career at Boeing.

It was a fortunate coincidence that Steiner and Pennell had come together at a propitious moment in history. It was Pennell, perhaps more than other, who led the thrust to the commercial jet age.

When Steiner was given the short-range jet assignment in 1958, the plane had a number—the 727—but not much more. Thirty-eight design variations had been tried, and it was beginning to look like an endless journey. To keep the airplane as small as possible, they had concentrated on two-engine versions, but two engines under the wings posed a serious load-and-balance situation, and two on the back added excessive structural weight to the fuselage.

The world market was judged to be 500 airplanes in the short-haul category; however in 1958, the Lockheed Electra was still a strong competitor, with a short-field capability that looked impossible to match with jets, and Douglas was working hard on a short-range jet called the DC-9. As a further complication, there were no jet engines available of the right size.

"If we're serious about offering a short range jet," said Harry Carter, chief of market research, "we're going to have to come up with one that can operate as economically as the turboprops—and into the same short fields."

"That's O.K.," said Jack. "If we don't have a few problems we'll die of comfort."[2]

Steiner viewed all of those negatives as simply problems to solve.

Before the year was out, Douglas was discussing the DC-9 with airlines in Europe. The concept was a scaled down DC-8 with two engines in pods under the wing—a configuration Boeing had already rejected. The Boeing strategy remained to design a still smaller airplane, so as not to interfere with the sales of the 720, smallest of the existing family.

The public, enamored with jets, still had an aversion to anything less than four engines, perceiving them to have greater safety.

Discussions with the airlines did not provide much to go on. Uncertainty as to what the next step should be was predominant. United, a bellwether of the industry, used Denver as a hub on its transcontinental flights, and a one-stop airplane would have to be good for mile-high Denver. Performance requirements for a twin, with one engine out, would be very difficult to meet. With United favoring four engines, and hedging its bets with turboprops, it was apparent the Electra was the horse to beat.

Boeing found TWA receptive to a twin—but only lukewarm. In a phone conversation with Bob Rummel, TWA engineering vice president, Steiner listened intently, when Rummel, half joking, said, "Why don't you compromise on three engines and make a good airplane?"[3]

Boeing's interest in a three-engine airplane stood at zero. There were more problems than with the twin. Where to put the third engine—if indeed the right-sized engines were available—or even on the drawing boards?

With so many unknowns, a prototype seemed imperative. The finance department put a thundering no on the suggestion.

Even without the added expense of a prototype, the necessary price of a 727 appeared to be in the $3.25 million to $3.5 million range—with production of 200 units needed to break even. There was no such market in sight. United and TWA together might be good for 80—still a big if with Electras selling for $2.1 million, and British Viscounts for $1.27 million. A market analysis showed a price between $2 million and $2.5 million would be required for a 727 to be competitive. The project seemed to be clearly impossible.

The team studied a preproduction airplane in lieu of a true prototype, with sufficient lead time ahead of the first production unit to avoid investment in two sets of hard tooling. Dave Breuninger of manufacturing estimated a cost of $6 million for such a machine.

"What's the alternative?" Jack asked. "Build the first airplane with the regular production tooling? Flight test it concurrent with production?"

"That's right."

"It will cost more if we have to make changes then; that's exactly what you want to avoid."

Breuninger smiled. "You have to get it right the first time."[4]

After still another review, engineering could not find anything that made sense, and was beginning to harden on the four-engine concept, a machine slightly smaller than the 720. It was reported that Douglas had reached the same conclusion on their proposed DC-9. The sales department balked, insisting on a truly small airplane. Bob Rummel of TWA was still pushing for three engines.

By 1959, the marketing department presented a depressing outlook. "The market is not yet ripe for exploitation," their report read. They added that whether the airplane was built by Boeing or Douglas, it would probably have to be priced well above the figures used in the study, and close to the price of the 720. "In short, it appears that a small jet is not economically possible."[5]

Sales engineer Art Curren, genuinely disturbed, brought Steiner a factory workload forecast. "It drops off too damned abruptly for comfort the end of '62,' he moaned. "We're in a really bad hole in '63 and '64. If we're going to sit in on the poker game, we've got to put up or shut up."[6]

After discussions with Joe Sutter, head aerodynamicist, Steiner concluded that what was needed was an entirely new design formula—discard all the warmed-over variations and start fresh—in the Boeing tradition.

Sutter, described by his department head in the University of Washington school of aeronautical engineering, as "my brightest student,"[7] had been digging into boundary-layer control and other ways to increase lift, exactly what was needed to provide superior performance on short, high-altitude landing fields.

William H. "Bill" Cook, with a master of science from MIT, and chief of the technical staff, agreed. He devised a research plan to test a series of alternatives in the wind tunnel and fly the most promising concepts on the 707 prototype. A particularly provocative idea was the use of multiple flaps.

With new urgency, Steiner and Pennell got Bill Allen's approval for a two-month, all-out evaluation program, culminating in a go-no-go recommendation to the corporate offices.

Abruptly, Ed Wells reported that United Airlines was prepared to sign a letter of understanding with Douglas by the first of July—only thirty days away.

Wells—quiet, thoughtful, competent—seemed always to have the correct advice. "Don't panic," he said.

"Let's project the potential through the next ten to fifteen years," Wells told Steiner. "We have to realize that the important thing is how many we can sell altogether. The profit comes from staying in the market, not with the first ones you build....We have to look beyond the present. We ought to be in a position to sell whatever is in the best interest of the customer. Try to get there by just cutting costs, and you may not get there at all."

"You aren't concerned about the cost problem?"

"Of course. My point is let's not compromise on getting the product we can sell."[8]

In late June, the puzzle was complicated further when Eastern indicated their preference for three engines. American was adamant on two, and Douglas publicly announced its decision to build a four-engined DC-9.

Taking stock, Steiner concluded that Douglas was ahead with their four-engined version, with a tie-up with Pratt & Whitney for engines. In England, de Havilland was ahead on a three-engined design. The field was left for a two-engined airplane—but it meant losing United.

A three-engined airplane seemed to be common ground that just might get all the major airlines together. But there were no engines of the right size. Schairer proposed that Boeing write its own specification for an engine, rather than wait for something to come along.

Rolls Royce was building the engines for the newly announced three-engined de Havilland *Trident*. Steiner needed more power, urging Rolls to design a larger one. Desiring to get into the U.S. market, Rolls agreed.

The team considered a three-engined airplane with two mounted on the wings and one in the tail. A breakthrough on the lift problem had been achieved, and when the test results were all digested, the aft-mounted engine design looked surprisingly good.

With no time to work out an exotic boundary-layer control, the technical staff had concentrated on multiple slotted flaps, finalizing on a triple-slotted trailing edge flap system, with a flap on the leading edge. The combination provided a small, efficient wing for high speed, but also with high lift for short runways.

Just when it appeared that the technical problems were yielding to solution, the tooling estimate of 1.5 million man-hours shot up to 5 million. A 727 production decision was still on hold.

When British European Airways signed a contract for twenty-four three-engined Tridents at the end of August 1959, with all mounted aft, and a "T" tail, Pennell decided that the Trident was the competition to beat. All efforts were directed to designing a

better machine. Location of the horizontal tail was the crucial parameter.

Teaming with European partners was reviewed and rejected—
and time ran. Engines mounted on the tail called for still another
extensive wind tunnel testing program.

By May 1960, Joe Sutter had the results. The low tail came out
negative and the "T" tail was in. Finally, the 727 had a configuration. The "T" tail, with sweepback, provided an unforeseen benefit, having the effect of lengthening the airplane, which increased
the latitude for load-and-balance. Concurrently, the horizontal
stabilizer was smaller, trading off for the heavier structure required
for the aft-mounted engines.

Sales and marketing fretted that the public would view the airplane as simply a copy of the Trident. However, with the British
plane already committed to the factory, Boeing had a unique advantage. Sitting in the catbird seat with a "paper airplane," it was
no great task to design a superior product. That's exactly what
happened. Engineering design for production—no prototype—
was committed on June 10, 1960.

The Rolls engine looked good to Steiner and the company had
willingly worked with Boeing at their own expense, but Eastern
wanted to switch to a new, larger, Pratt & Whitney engine which
they viewed as a more rugged design, with more opportunity for
growth. Steiner worried about the modifications required for the
airframe—and the increased cost.

Eddie Rickenbacker, president of Eastern made the final decision—choosing the Pratt & Whitney. With this change, plus a
loading stairway in the tail, and other additions requested by the
customers, the price was set at $4.2 million, a price that once
seemed inconceivable from a sales point of view. But the latest design was a far different machine, with much greater earning potential.

Cash requirements were estimated to build up to $130 million
prior to the first delivery. Now, the very survival of the Boeing

Airplane Company was again on the line.

Allen went to the board in late August with a recommendation to go ahead with the 727 if orders could be achieved for 100 airplanes. The board approved.

Steiner took to the road to try to gain a commonality compromise among the airlines. United and Eastern agreed to the latest configuration. Allen proceeded to hammer out contracts. The best he could do was forty planes for Eastern and forty for United—twenty of which were subject to cancellation—with a deadline of December 1.

As the deadline approached, the order list was stuck at eighty, with twenty still subject to cancellation. Allen fretted. The board left the decision to him. *Act—get things done—move forward*. The buck could not be passed.

Deciding there was no turning back, Allen pushed the button, and on November 30, 1960, one day before the deadline, he signed contracts with United and Eastern, for a total of $420 million—then the largest single transaction in commercial aviation history.

Five hundred engineers were now on the program and more were being added at the rate of 120 per month. Manufacturing had to gear up a completely new production line, with hard tooling. Everything was aimed at the rollout, scheduled—and achieved—on November 27, 1962. The impossible airplane was a reality.

Wells and Schairer wanted to be doubly certain of the structural integrity of the 727. They recommended the testing of two complete airframes, rather than the traditional, single static test unit. The second airframe would be subjected to fatigue testing, simulating flight conditions for the complete life of the airplane—considered at the time to be twenty years.

"With all the investment we're putting into it the only way we can come out on the program is by having enough sales," Wells told division manager John Yeasting, in advocating the admittedly expensive precautionary steps. "We'll be in a much better position to get these, if we're on the soundest possible foundation. We'll get our money back in the long run, if we get our changes in early."[9]

The extra testing meant painful additions to the budget, but Yeasting approved them, as did Allen. The whole case for the airplane rested on it being right.

Prior to first flight, the company had invested over $150 million, and five customer airlines were committed to a total of $700 million.

After the airplane completed its test flights, its performance was the harbinger to its outstanding commercial success. It was simply a far better airplane than any offered by the competition.

Mansfield captures the mood at Boeing after the proving flights. "Jack Steiner and Joe Sutter went to Dick Rouzie, director of engineering. 'We're in trouble. We've made a mistake,' Jack said.

"Rouzie was accustomed to trouble, having been with Boeing since 1928—fresh out of Purdue University in mechanical engineering—but he was worried, until he saw Jack's grin.

"'We've got a lot better performance than we're supposed to have.'"[10]

The airplane was achieving more than 10 percent better fuel mileage, promising millions of dollars in fuel savings.

As demonstrated throughout Boeing's history, its strong, patient, intense engineering efforts had once more been the key. The triple slotted flap system devised by Bill Cook and his staff, stood out as a technological breakthrough.

The first 727-100 was delivered to Eastern airlines on October 29, 1963, entering service on February 1, 1964. The 727 spawned a family of airplanes, responding to the customers needs. The -100, first off the line, an all-passenger configuration, had a typical capacity of 28 first class and 66 economy seats. It was soon followed by a -100C convertible, and a -100QC quick change convertible. The plane grew to a typical capacity of 20 first class and 114 economy seats, with the first delivery of the -200 to Northeast

Airlines on December 11, 1967. An advanced -200, incorporating many engineering innovations, rolled out of the factory on September 23, 1971. Finally a -200F freighter was produced for Federal Express, the last unit—and last of the 727 family—delivered on September 18, 1984.

A total of 1,831 units were sold, a record for commercial jet airplanes—a record which was not destined to last—exceeded by still another Boeing model in February 1990.

Model 727—1963–1984

The "Impossible Airplane," which became a best seller. Here, the final airplane of the 727 series rolls out of the factory.

The 727 found a niche of size and performance in the commercial transport world with no worthy competitor, becoming a "cash cow" for Boeing for many years. The airplane is expected to remain in service into the twenty-first century.

One day, when Jack Steiner visited the production line at the Renton factory, a big sign, always there, caught his eye. "STOP. Do not enter unless you are interested in making a QUALITY PRODUCT in a SAFE MANNER."[11] Steiner stopped. And entered.

1. *Fortune*, January, 1962, 65.
2. Harold Mansfield, *Billion Dollar Battle*, (New York: Arno Press, 1980), 8.
3. Ibid., 19.
4. Ibid., 24.
5. Ibid., 29.
6. Harold Mansfield, *Vision*, (New York: Popular Library, 1966), 248.
7. Private Communication.
8. Mansfield, *Vision*, 251.
9. Ibid., 297.
10. Harold Mansfield, *Billion Dollar Battle*, 140.
11. Ibid., 174.

22

Supersonic Airplanes

A commercial supersonic airplane was a certain economic impossibility for any private company. At a minimum, developmental costs would have to be borne by the government. Nevertheless, industry's goal was speed—and the economic realities were only vaguely defined—as enthusiasm for this new frontier grew.

Technical problems of staggering proportions remained. Aerodynamically, a supersonic wing fell far short of the desired lift-over-drag ratio of the subsonics, translating to a requirement for vastly more powerful engines. Severe sweep-back helped in the L-over-D ratio, but the resultant delta wing left no good place to locate the landing gear or the engines—and produced an unacceptably high landing speed.

Titanium, the best candidate for construction of an airplane traveling three times the speed of sound—because of the 600 degree Fahrenheit operating skin temperature—had barely passed the pure metal stage in the necessary forms: sheet, plate, extrusions, and forgings. High strength alloys, still in the laboratory, remained to be proven.

One square inch of finished 0.040-inch-thick sheet of commercially pure titanium cost five cents in 1964, compared to one-fifth of a cent for clad aluminum alloys of the same thickness. The new titanium alloys would cost considerably more, and scrap—unlike aluminum—was not reclaimable.

Following the failure to win the B-70 supersonic bomber business, Boeing accelerated its research efforts toward future supersonic vehicles. Maynard Pennell felt an intuitive optimism that a commercial supersonic transport (SST) would materialize, certainly during the decade of the sixties.

However, in spite of new enthusiasm in preliminary design, Bill Allen worried that a supersonic effort would drag Boeing down. With the 707 deeply in the red, and the 727 only a gleam in John Steiner's eye at the time, a supersonic transport seemed to be pure fiscal insanity. Nevertheless, Allen saw the inevitability of the next wave of technology, and he shifted top corporate executives into positions to create the managerial posture necessary to step up to this new challenge. The time seemed to be right for a Mach 3 machine; and North American, Douglas, Lockheed, and Convair all began moving in the same direction.

Companies in both Britain and France were also studying supersonic transports, clamoring for government subsidies.

At the Paris Air Show in 1961, Sud-Dassault of France displayed a model of a Super Cavarelle designed to convince the world that the French were in a position to produce a four-engined seventy-passenger supersonic plane with a range of up to 2,000 miles.

The French revelation put added urgency on the British efforts, and after some sparring to set up a joint program—with no progress—the two governments intervened, and in March 1962, an agreement was formalized and approved.

On the engine side, there was remarkably little conflict, with Bristol-Siddeley holding the upper hand with its already proven Olympus. Further development was agreed as a joint effort with France's SNECMA.

The airframe and systems were another matter, with little visible common ground. Again, the governments intervened, the two companies agreeing to work out design problems as they went along. A blizzard of technical proposals were traded back and forth, and by 1965, both firms were ready to cut metal on two identical *Concorde* prototypes—one assembled in France and the other in England. The airplane would be a more conservative design—all aluminum—for Mach 2 speeds.[1]

Researchers at NASA's Langely Field laboratories had been working on ideas to solve the wing problem. In early 1959, John Stack, director of research at Langely, called Schairer. "We have a new invention we're showing to industry. Can you send someone back?"

"Sure, what is it John?"

"We have some new ideas on variable sweep."[2]

The idea of changing the sweep of the wings in flight had been tried, when Bell, under an air force contract, had built and flown a fighter. Changing the sweep proved to be only part of the solution. To preserve stability, the Bell machine's wings were not only hinged, but also mounted on tracks, moving backward and forward along the fuselage. After demonstration of that complex mechanism, industry interest cooled considerably, but Stack refused to abandon the idea. With additional wind tunnel tests, he demonstrated that there was indeed a correct place for a fixed hinge point.

At Boeing, efforts focused on a pivot mechanism—linchpin of any family of variable-sweep airplanes—military or civilian. The result was a unique bearing design capable of transmitting heavy loads for thousands of cycles.

Part of Boeing's work in preliminary design studies in 1959 had been directed toward tactical fighters. Vaughn Blumenthal, another of the legions of engineering graduates from the University of Washington—in charge of the fighter effort—was invited to a briefing at Wright Field in early 1960, to discuss the design of a variable sweep fighter. When the companies in attendance were asked if they were ready to take on such a project, the only one to volunteer was Boeing. Blumenthal expressed an eagerness to begin. "We can start immediately," he said.[3]

Recognizing that the wing pivot design could also apply to an SST, and sensing the opportunity for capturing the crucial edge in the expected fighter competition, Wells authorized construction of a full scale-mockup. The new technology would make all existing fighter airplanes obsolete.

The company was confident and growing, and in Morton, Pennsylvania, on March 31, 1960, the Vertol Aircraft Corporation, with 2,300 employees, was acquired, becoming a Boeing division, adding helicopters to its line of products. There, three new models were showing promise; the big *Chinook*, of which the army had ordered ten; the *Sea Knight*, that had just won the Marine Corps competition; and a civilian version called the *Model 107*, that had been sold to New York Airways.

In recognition of the increasing diversity of the product line, the Boeing Airplane Company became The Boeing Company on May 3, 1961.

When Wright Field released a request to study a proposed experimental tactical fighter—to be called the *TFX*—and to utilize variable sweep wings, Boeing was already ahead of the industry in the technology.

Election years were the worst possible times for fast government action on pending government programs. Thus, the formal competition decision for the TFX hung in the balance all during 1960. Finally, Secretary of Defense Gates decided to leave the decision to Robert McNamara, new secretary of defense under President John F. Kennedy.

McNamara ordered a study to find out if the navy and the air force requirements for a fighter could be integrated.

More than a year later, on October 1, 1961, the Defense Department requested formal proposals on the TFX, calling for a design which would satisfy both the navy and the air force. For Boeing the delay was deadly, their technological lead quickly evaporating. Bill Allen linked the outcome of the TFX to the company's future viability. Efforts were redoubled, and in February 1962, Boeing was chosen as one of the finalists—along with a team headed by General Dynamics.

A source selection expected in May was postponed until June—pending further study. The net result of all the delays was to make the two airplanes almost identical, throwing the decision into the political arena.

In early November, with still no decision, rumors drifted out of the Pentagon that Boeing had won—in all probability the largest single defense program of all time. With four years of dedicated effort behind them, Boeing expectations were still understandably high. On November 24, Secretary McNamara announced the decision. The General Dynamics team was the winner. Boeing—and Seattle—were stunned.

Henry M. Jackson, Senator from the State of Washington, called President Allen, highly concerned. He had learned that the Boeing bid was lower by $100 million, and that all the evaluating groups had recommended Boeing. Jackson wanted to call these facts to the attention of Senator John McClellan's Senate investigating committee, of which he was a member. Allen hesitated, fearing the request would be attributed to Boeing and would color future relations with the Department of Defense. He cautioned his staff not to become involved, leaving the hearings to the political process.

The hearings did not reveal any irregularity or evidence of influence. However, they did reveal sharp differences of opinion. The operational people favored the Boeing proposal, but the secretaries reported that the evaluation scores were so close that either product was considered acceptable. In sum, the final decision rested on one man—Secretary McNamara—who professed to have two criteria: commonality and cost. According to his analysis, Boeing had shown 60 percent commonality, and General Dynamics, 85 percent. Nevertheless, Boeing had proposed to do the job for $100 million less—on a fixed price contract.

Paradoxically, the technological innovations incorporated in the Boeing design—resulting in superior performance—were considered by McNamara to be too risky, and he simply did not believe the cost figures would hold for follow-on requirements. The General Dynamics design had avoided such new features as in-flight reversible thrust and the incorporation of significant amounts of titanium in place of heavier steel parts. It was an unusual turn of events—where superior technology, so crucial to military superiority—failed to win.

Bill Allen was called to testify. He was reluctant, but Ed Wells felt the technical questions needed clarifying. They both testified on April 24, 1963; Allen stressing Boeing's low cost bid, which he pointed out was based on jet bomber and transport experience as well as the BOMARC, itself a complex supersonic interceptor, and Wells explaining the extensive testing of the advanced features.

"When large steps can clearly be taken in military capability, will the enemy permit us the luxury of taking a smaller step?" Wells asked.[4]

The committee solicited Allen's comments on two possible courses of action: a reversal of the decision, or twin awards of identical contracts, with both constructing an airplane for a flyoff competition.

"We did not seek this investigation," Allen replied. "Nor do we seek redress in the halls of Congress. As between the two alternatives, however, the second course of action offers the best possibility of meeting the objectives of the committee."[5]

No further action was taken. For the second time in its history, Boeing dropped out of the fighter business.

Juan Trippe, looking for the next step in air transport was eager to take on something new. He was aware of the discussions for a supersonic transport, a project so expensive that only the government could afford to finance it. Daley relates the next series of events, so typical of the operating philosophy of Trippe.

"President Kennedy, who had received conflicting advice on the project, was trying to decide whether to back it or not, and he sent a man named Najeeb Halaby to tell Trippe not to buy the foreign supersonic until he had made up his mind. Halaby, as head of the Federal Aviation Administration (FAA), held virtual Cabinet rank.

"Trippe, too, had received conflicting advice. Lindbergh, for one, was strongly against supersonic jets on environmental grounds. Their noise figured to turn airport environs into wastelands, and for all anyone knew, they might destroy the ozone layer above the earth. Lindbergh was opposed on economic grounds also.

"But to Trippe, even as he approached what ordinary men considered retirement age, nothing was impracticable, and if the SST was to be the next step, then he wanted to be the man who would bring it on. He knew President Kennedy was wavering and might withdraw funding from the American SST, and so he decided to force the President's hand. When Kennedy promised a decision for the Monday following Memorial Day 1963, Trippe optioned six Concordes, and arranged for this news to be made public the day before."[6]

Thus, Kennedy felt pressed to announce that the United States, too, would build a supersonic transport, and called for a joint government-industry program. On August 15, 1963, the FAA invited industry to submit proposals for an airplane "superior to the European Concorde." The leap to titanium technology in the manufacture of perhaps the most complex of all machines, was committed.

At the briefing, Douglas, now led by Donald Douglas, Jr., announced that his company would not enter the race. Boeing, Lockheed, and North American were left in the SST arena.

NASA had worked out four possible configurations for a supersonic transport, and both Boeing and Lockheed were already under contract to evaluate them. The so-called SCAT-16, for Supersonic Commercial Air Transport, with a variable-sweep wing; and SCAT-17, with a delta wing and a canard up forward, were the two believed to have the most commercial promise.

With years of intensive study and testing behind them, engineers at Boeing were convinced that the variable-sweep, pivoting wing was the best approach. Pennell, still not satisfied, decided one more hard look was needed. He formed a separate team within the project to come up with the most competitive delta wing possible.

When the results were in, the variable sweep design promised to save 50,000 pounds. Wells took a look at the figures. "We'll submit the variable," he said.[7]

Lockheed and North American both decided to submit proposals with a delta wing, making the competition one of clear choices in technology.

Maynard Pennell explained the Boeing position in an oral presentation in Washington, D.C., on January 21, 1964.

"The NASA research on the variable-sweep arrow wing, along with our own, has proved that aerodynamic compromise is no longer necessary," he said. "With the variable sweep principle we can achieve superior supersonic performance in terms of payload-range and at the same time, low-speed flying qualities better than present commercial transports."[8]

The FAA began evaluation of the proposals, and it was soon clear that the effects of the sonic boom and the airplane's economics were both very serious problems.

In 1965, the SST competition completed Phase II-A, and Boeing again reported to the FAA. The body had been reshaped, the passenger capacity increased, and the aerodynamics improved.

"A 30 percent reduction in seat-mile costs has been achieved and substantiated by wind tunnel test results," Pennell reported. "The airplane will have lower seat-mile costs than subsonic transports on all but the shorter routes."[9]

The development costs were still the big hurdle, and they were mounting steadily. The government had decided to pay 75 percent, and to reimburse the contractor's 25 percent investment in the event of cancellation. Financing for a prototype had yet to be faced.

With a giant new logistics transport design in the competitive phase for the air force, a plane known as the C-5A, speculation increased in Washington about the need for a supersonic airplane. Perhaps a 750-seat commercial version of that airplane should be the next step, they reasoned.

With undiminished confidence, the FAA recommended a continuation of the SST competition into a Phase II-B. North American was dropped. Boeing and Lockheed remained.

In August 1965, President Lyndon B. Johnson approved the plan to continue—short of a prototype—for a period of eighteen months, with industry still bearing 25 percent of the cost.

In Seattle, confidence never wavered. To give the SST the strongest possible emphasis, a supersonic transport branch of the Commercial Airplane Division was formed. Maynard Pennell moved up to vice-president of engineering and product development. T. Wilson, corporate vice-president for operations and planning, was assigned to give overall direction. Heading the program directly as branch manager, and newly appointed as a vice-president, was H. W. "Bob" Withington, an MIT graduate in aeronautical engineering, who had joined Boeing in 1941.

The Soviets were also known to be working on an SST, and Najeeb Halaby, pushing hard for an American go-ahead to the prototype stage, suggested that the Russians might be first.

Defense Secretary McNamara expressed little faith in the ability of the FAA, under Halaby, to manage the program. Feeling that their estimates on developmental cost and purchase price were too conservative, he urged continued studies.

Wielding enormous influence over any decision, McNamara's opinions prevailed, and economic considerations became the primary concern.

The American SST decision quickly became a testing of the wills between two powerful men in the government, Najeeb Halaby and Robert McNamara. Halaby postured the effort in terms of "a life and death struggle, so far as commercial airframe manufacturers were concerned, with the British, French, and Russians. To the winner, the guy who produces the first commercially profitable, safe, and efficient aircraft, goes a $3 billion to $4 billion market."[10] McNamara remained unmoved.

Concerned with the fragmentation of direction, President Johnson replaced Halaby as head of the FAA with Air Force General William F. McKee, instructing him to assume direct control of the SST program. The appointment did not end the pulling and tugging in the various branches of the government, and the SST bogged down in government edicted studies.

A study emerged in 1965, concluding that an economic basis for a supersonic transport no longer existed.

Negative factors continued to pile up when the effects of the sonic boom, heretofore on the periphery of SST decision making, moved to center stage.

Subsequent testing resulted in the conclusion that overland supersonic operations would not be publicly acceptable.

Thus, the sonic boom was brushed from the table of contention by the simple decision not to fly overland—except at subsonic speeds—worsening the economic equation.

Competition between Boeing and Lockheed tightened. Lockheed, originally viewed as the weaker competitor—with its fixed wing—improved its design. Boeing responded in kind. Its swingwing design, now with a very large horizontal tail, integrated with the fully sweptback wing, was looking better than ever. Weight had increased from 500,000 to 750,000 pounds.

Promotional efforts of the two manufacturers were in sharp contrast. Horwitch had this to say about the approaches of the two competitors: "Boeing was surprisingly subdued, merely trying to relate its SST effort to its obvious success in developing commercial jet aircraft. Lockheed's promotional behavior, on the other hand, was flamboyant, public, and aggressive." In August, a two-page Lockheed advertisement appeared in the *New York Times*, claiming that the firm's double delta configuration would be virtually stall-proof and would create a cushion of air under a landing plane.[11]

The manufacturer's proposals were submitted in early September 1966, and technical evaluations began immediately, with approximately 235 government experts participating. In December, the Boeing-General Electric design was selected. In Seattle, reaction was restrained—exhaustion and skepticism had taken their toll.

In mid-January 1967, Pan American offered the FAA an important proposal for airline prototype financing; the airlines would deposit $1 million per airplane position, and in return would receive a $3 million credit against the purchase price. The $1 million would be at risk, i.e., not returnable if the SST program

Supersonic Transport Mock-up—1971

After years of research and development, funds for the construction of two SST prototypes were authorized in 1968.

was terminated, and could be used, if lost, as an income tax deduction. By mid-February, ten of the twelve U.S. airlines holding delivery positions, had agreed to participate.

A headcount of United States senators revealed sixty-three were favorable to the SST, twelve leaned toward it, fifteen were uncertain, and ten opposed. President Johnson hesitated, hoping for greater support.

In April 1967, McNamara, the most skeptical of Johnson's advisors, urged a go-ahead, and the president requested fiscal 1968 funding of $198 million. Development phase contracts were awarded to Boeing and General Electric, calling for the construction of two SST prototypes and 100 hours of flight testing at an estimated total cost of $1.44 billion, over a period of about four years.

By June, 113 delivery positions had been allocated to twenty-six airlines, fifty-seven domestic, and fifty-six foreign.

Bill Allen enthusiastically predicted that at its peak, the two SST prototypes would generate 9,000 new jobs in the company.

In December 1967, the Concorde reached its first milestone, when the French-assembled prototype 001 was rolled out of its hangar at Toulouse. Shortly thereafter, at Filton, the British-assembled 002 followed.[12]

The SST story had not yet reached its final chapter.

1. Geoffrey Knight, *Concorde, The Real Story*, (New York: Stein and Day, 1978), 23-25.
2. Harold Mansfield, *Vision*, (New York: Popular Library, 1966), 264.
3. Private Communication.
4. Ibid.
5. Ibid.
6. Robert Daley, *An American Saga*, (New York: Random House, 1980), 430/431.
7. Private Communication.
8. Ibid.
9. Ibid.
10. Mel Horwitch, *Clipped Wings*, (Cambridge, Massachusetts, 1982), 40.
11. Ibid., 163.
12. Knight, Concorde, *The Real Story*, 62.

23

The Seventeen-
inch Decision

Competition with the 707 nearly drove
the Douglas Aircraft Company to bankruptcy. The initial advantage of a "paper airplane," allowing promises of improvements in
size and range, were more than overcome by subsequent problems.
Major retooling was required after the DC-8 was in production,
and other deficiencies discovered during flight testing resulted in
costly corrective action. Boeing, even with its heavy losses, was
nevertheless winning the sales battle.

During the competition with the 727, lack of a Douglas jet
prototype was again painfully evident. New innovations were cap-
tives of the wind tunnel; whereas Boeing was free to flight test.

The four-engined DC-9 offered to United, simply a small version of the DC-8, was never able to compete, and Douglas was
forced back to the drawing boards.

The short-haul market was opening rapidly, and with speed still the pacing criterion, Douglas opted for a narrower body, with five abreast seating. Boeing was busy on the 727, and in no position to think about still another model.

In the spring of 1962, Douglas revealed specifications for their Model 2086, a new, short-haul twinjet transport with aft, body-mounted engines, designed to operate economically on route segments of 250 to 300 miles. The airplane was configured to carry fifty-six to seventy-four passengers.[1]

While still in preliminary design, the Model 2086 became the forerunner of the DC-9-10. However, following close behind, was a larger, improved model with longer range—the DC-9-30—which flew less than six months later, on August 6, 1966. Douglas moved briskly into the short-haul market, and the DC-9 evolved into a family of airplanes. (Once again, to the consternation of historians, a -20 flew about a year after the -30.)

The public was clamoring to get everywhere faster, and the increased speed made possible by the reduced drag of the smaller cross section, was an attractive attribute. Soon the DC-9-30, with a nominal capacity of ninety-seven passengers, along with the French Caravelle and the newly announced British BAC 111 twinjets, had captured most of the market for short-haul equipment. By April 1964, of the large U.S. customers, only United and Eastern remained uncommitted to a twinjet machine.

At Boeing, the 727 was absorbing all available resources, but the possibility of the DC-9 growing to threaten its market loomed large, and a study was launched to ascertain whether a twin should be considered.

"'We'd have to start immediately to get ahead of a United Airlines decision on the DC-9.' Steiner told Yeasting in a meeting on April 21, 1964.

"Yeasting was skeptical, but agreed to go to Bill Allen with a proposal. 'I think it would be worth putting up a half million to take a ninety-day look at it,' he recommended. 'I don't believe there is one chance in ten that we can come up with anything that makes sense, but I think we ought to do this to make sure. The DC-9 doesn't have leading edge flaps; we may be able to pick up some other advantages by reason of our later start.' Allen concurred, and the Model 737 program study was begun on May 8, 1964."[2]

With the competition already fixed on five abreast seating, Boeing chose to go to six, providing significant commonality with the 707 and 727 fuselage. Having the same cross section also provided for standardization of cargo containers, including compatibility with the DC-8.

However, in the airplane business, no advantage comes without a price. The seventeen-inch wider cross section, with its increased drag, resulted in a fifteen-mile-per-hour penalty in cruising speed, compared to the DC-9. No one could predict the consequences of that difference.

Location of the engines was open to the option of wing or body mounting. Sutter wanted to take another look at the wing mounted design. In theory, the larger engines should not produce the same interference effects with the airflow that forced the 707 to go to pods. Testing proved the concept to be sound, and 1,200 pounds of weight was saved—equivalent to six passengers.

In Europe, international sales manager Ken Luplow had been discussing a 737 with Lufthansa. The airplane appeared to be ideally suited to serving the multiple major cities in Germany.

With Lufthansa moving favorably toward the 737, Allen was in a dilemma—worse than on the 727. There, he had orders for eighty airplanes in hand with no competitor in the field. On the 737, there was strong competition, and only a single potential customer. Allen went to the board in November to present the 737 status, but had no basis for a go-ahead recommendation. Instead, he launched an intensive sales campaign to line up Lufthansa, United and Eastern.

Model 737—1967

Originally named "Fat Albert" because of its short, stubby look, the little airplane quickly became known as the "Little Giant,"—a tribute to its capability from short, high, hot runways.

By January 1965, a crisis had developed. Neither Eastern nor United made any commitments. Lufthansa insisted on a Boeing yes or no—ready and willing to buy DC-9s.

In February, the Boeing board was forced to face the problem head-on, with no new movement on the part of the U.S. prospects. Although the market looked bleak, several members argued for a go-ahead, if only because holding off posed a still bigger risk. Fortunately, airline traffic was booming—and so they decided to proceed.

In Germany, at the Lufthansa Board meeting on February 19, 1965, chief executive Gerhard Hoeltje was reluctant—as the only airline customer—to recommend the 737. It would be easy for Boeing to drop the program. With board members already arriving for the meeting, Hoeltje phoned to pin Boeing down. He wanted personal assurance from Bruce Connelly, vice-president of the Transport Division.

Ken Luplow made an urgent call to Seattle. It was 10:00 A.M. in Cologne, 1:00 A.M. in Seattle. Rubbing sleep from his eyes,

Connelly gave the green light, and the Lufthansa board continued to deliberate. After breaking for a late lunch, they approved an order for twenty-one airplanes.

Within a week, Eastern announced their decision for the DC-9. Success for the 737 was hanging by the United Airlines thread. Production with only Lufthansa as a customer appeared to be financial suicide.

The 737, in an all-tourist configuration, offered 103 seats, 6 more than the DC-9 sold to Eastern. Douglas featured its greater speed and five abreast seating. Seat-mile cost was becoming the major criterion for equipment selection where traffic was heavy, and the wider body was beginning to look like a good decision.

The competitive battle centered around the perception of market growth and market share; as to whether the airplane with the greatest number of seats, *ceteris paribus*, was the best revenue earner. Nobody wanted to fly empty seats. Thus, airplane-mile cost was the other predominant parameter.

With United involved in a major fleet planning program to go all jet by 1970, Boeing concentrated on a long-range program of a 737/727 mix which would meet the airline's combined requirements. The advantage of already having the 727 in the United fleet was significant. To make up for the delay in getting the 737 into service, Boeing offered additional 727 airplanes at attractive terms, with the right to turn back the extra 727s when the 737s became available. The strategy worked.

In April, United announced a gargantuan order: forty 737s, twenty 727 passenger and six 727QC airplanes. They leased an additional twenty-five 727 passenger airplanes, and signed options for thirty more 737s and nine more 727QCs.

On April 9, 1967, Brien S. Wygle took the 737-100 up for its first flight. Wygle, a career test pilot, had many first flights to his credit. Although a native of Seattle, his family moved to Canada, and he enlisted in the Royal Canadian Air Force in 1942. After serving in combat cargo operations in England, India, and Burma, he returned to peacetime ventures in 1946, graduating from the University of British Columbia with a degree in mechanical engineering in 1951.

Wygle joined Boeing the same year, as a test pilot for the B-47 bomber program, and worked on Boeing flight test programs for more than forty years. As vice-president of flight operations, he led the simultaneous certification of the 757/767 twins, a first in aviation history.

The initial delivery to Lufthansa was made on December 28, 1967. United wanted a larger airplane, and the 737 received a six-foot body stretch to add two seat rows, accommodating 115 all-tourist passengers. The new derivative was designated the -200, the first unit delivered the day after Lufthansa received their first -100 airplane. Douglas had already delivered 228 DC-9s.

Undaunted, Boeing offered a convertible model—which could be changed from a passenger to a cargo configuration in a few hours. The first delivery went to Wien Consolidated Airlines in October 1968.

The stubby little airplane, with the same body cross section as the 707 and 727, quickly gained the nickname "Fat Albert," however more in admiration than derision. Early sales were encouraging. During the first two years following its initial service with Lufthansa, 223 airplanes were delivered.

After the Airline Pilots Association took issue with the two-man crew of the 737, even though it had been certified by the FAA, a labor management arbitration panel ruled that United must operate the 737 with a crew of three; the damper was put on domestic sales. Deliveries dropped precipitously in 1970—to thirty-seven airplanes.

A struggle developed within Boeing to decide the fate of the 737. An objective analysis indicated the airplane would never recover its developmental costs. Airlines could still purchase the DC-9 with a two-man crew, and Douglas' two-year lead seemed insurmountable.

However, foreign carriers were not constrained by the domestic, three-man rule for the 737, giving an argument for those pushing to continue. The optimists eventually won out, and it was decided to offer still more improvements to the airplane and concentrate on the overseas market. The leading edge flap system was redesigned to provide more lift, and more powerful engines were offered, giving the airplane unchallenged superiority in short field operation. For passenger appeal, it was fitted with a new interior—"the wide body look." The improved machine was designated the 737-200 ADVANCED, with first delivery to All Nippon in Japan on May 20, 1971.

Sales almost hit bottom in 1972. Only fourteen airplanes were sold. The production level was barely adequate to operate a profitable line. The program limped along for the next several years, with the specter of phase-out hanging over it. In retrospect, perhaps Douglas was a little complacent at this juncture—the 737 had all but received a knockout blow. In any event, Boeing simply tried harder, and hidden in the long period of slow sales, was the steady increase in customers.

The airplane found a home in Africa, where its performance from short, high-altitude fields, even on hot days, was unmatched. To further increase its capability, a kit was designed to allow operation from unimproved runways, and soon it was being utilized on grass, dirt, gravel, or coral—almost any type of level surface.

From a disappointing beginning in 1969, when only two 737s were in service in the entire continent of Africa, the increase was dramatic. By 1978, more than fifty airplanes were flying for airlines blanketing the continent—Air Algerie, Air Madagascar, Air Zaire, Angola, Cameroon, D.E.T.A., Egyptair, Nigeria, Royal Air Maroc, South Africa, Sudan, and Zambia.

Airlines in Asia, Australia, and Central and South America also placed a string of orders, with VASP, a domestic Brazilian carrier purchasing twenty-two, becoming the largest 737 operator outside of the United States.

Operation From Unimproved Airfields

The 737 operated from grass, dirt, gravel, and coral runways—from most any level surface. Here, a 737-200 takes off from a grass field in Hope, B.C., Canada

Fat Albert was dead. Satisfied customers had renamed the versatile plane the "Little Giant." By 1978, the order total stood at 543 units. Even more significant was the number of operators—which reached seventy—surpassing Douglas.

In 1978, sales took off. A record total of 146 units were ordered, and the production line was accelerated from three to seven airplanes a month, with a further increase to eight and one-half by the end of 1979.

The drive to further improve the 737 intensified. To make the airplane an even better community neighbor, noise reduction research was a continuing effort, in collaboration with Pratt &

Whitney. Following the introduction of quiet nacelles in 1975, a new exhaust gas mixer was developed in 1978 that reduced the level of low frequency noise. The same year, Boeing provided an improved cockpit, featuring an integrated automatic flight control system, allowing landings during low weather minimum flight conditions. Not long after, British Airways was the first to receive a 737 with a technologically advanced flight deck. The new deck was equipped with digital instruments throughout and featured an automatic engine thrust control system, which achieved substantial fuel savings.

Douglas responded with their own technology improvements, increasing capacity in a series of fuselage stretches in their DC-9-50 and -80 models.

After years of controversy over a three-man versus a two-man cockpit crew, a presidential panel was created to settle the issue. In July 1981, the task force released its findings. Although the issue focused on the new, larger, DC-9-80 derivative, which was just entering airline service, the ruling to allow a two-man crew set the precedent for reducing the cockpit complement in future airplanes.

In late 1980, Boeing offered its customers an even more productive 737; a reengined, lengthened version, which would accommodate sixteen more passengers. Designated as the -300, its General Electric CFM-56 advanced technology engines were more powerful, more fuel efficient, and significantly quieter. First delivery was to USAir in November 1984.

Orders ballooned. By October 1985, sales of all 737 derivative models totalled 1,418, passing the DC-9 series, which stood at 1,400. Every other working day, a 737 rolled out of the Boeing factory at Renton.

In 1985, the 737-300 led the world in commercial airplane orders of any category, with 252—chosen by twenty-six airlines.

A year later, Piedmont Airlines launched the 737-400, a stretched version of the -300, accommodating up to 169 passengers in an all

The 5,000ᵗʰ Commercial Jet Transport Rolls Out

On August 17, 1986, a 737-300 airplane became the 5,000ᵗʰ commercial jet transport to roll out of the Boeing factories since the first 707 was delivered in 1958.

economy configuration, with first delivery in September 1988.

The 737 family was now broad and deep, but new attention was directed to the small end, incorporating all the technology, materials, and manufacturing processes proven on other Boeing models. Designated the -500, it was offered in 1987. Southwest Airlines in the U.S., and Braathens in Norway, kicked off the program with combined orders of forty-five planes. About the same size as the old -200, the -500 consumed 25 percent less fuel, representing the latest airframe and engine technologies.

In February 1990, with sales of all 737 models nearing 2,800 airplanes, number 1,833 off the line—a 737-300—surpassed the record of 1,832 set by the 727. (The first 727 was never sold, re-tained as a test bed for Boeing.)

Somewhere along the way—the exact unit not disclosed by Boeing—the 737 turned the corner into profitability, succeeding the 727 as the company's "cash cow."[3] Only the "old timers" re-membered the days when the airplane was nearly relegated to oblivion.

The continuing improvement in airplane performance, cost of operation, and service in the field were the factors that allowed the 737 to beat the DC-9—in spite of its two-year lead in airline ser-vice.

However, in the final analysis, one single attribute—the wider body—was the underlying foundation for the competitive differ-ence, providing a seat-mile cost that Douglas could never over-come. The higher speed of the DC-9, reducing flying time by ten to fifteen minutes on close city pairs, was never a factor.

Clearly, a major benchmark in Boeing's climb to world leader-ship in the commercial jet transport business was the seventeen-inch decision.

1. Crosby Maynard, *Flight Plan for Tomorrow*, Douglas Aircraft Company, 1962.
2. Harold Mansfield, *Vision*, (New York: Popular Library, 1966), 335.
3. Private Communication.

24

Going to
the Moon

John F. Kennedy's call to his countrymen
to go to the moon challenged every American. Never before in the
history of nations had such a formidable goal been set before
mankind.

Responding to the call, a tide of research and development
contracts issued from the NASA centers at Ames, Goddard, Langley, Lewis, and Marshall, later joined by the Manned Space Flight
Center at Houston.

The race to space was on. America's cards were on the table.
The military had not yet justified a role in space, and civilian efforts under NASA quickly took the lead.

NASA was doing advance planning for a direct lunar flight
even before the president's declaration of a timetable. There were

two major elements to the program—the Saturn launch system consisting of the booster stages to power the flight—and the Apollo spacecraft to carry the astronauts.

In a top management meeting, Boeing officials weighed the choices, deciding that the booster system had the best chance of providing business beyond the moon landing.

In the beginning, Saturn was being developed by the NASA Marshall Space Flight Center at Huntsville, Alabama. Formerly known as the Redstone Arsenal, where the first American satellite had incubated, the center was headed by Dr. Wernher von Braun. The design, construction, and testing of the prototype Saturn C-1 was being done there, but industry was invited to compete for the production contracts. The C-1 first stage booster was designed to deliver 1,500,000 pounds of thrust, four times that of Atlas, and nineteen times that of the Redstone vehicle that launched the first Mercury capsule.

There was also an opportunity to bid on the next increment of booster size; the C-3, or Advanced Saturn, which would employ two of the C-1 engines. The C-1 would put twenty-five tons into orbit, and the C-3 would lift fifty tons.

Boeing had been familiarizing itself with the Saturn since its inception in 1958, and an office was opened in Huntsville to keep abreast of developments. After several unsuccessful bids on parts of the Saturn system, Boeing won a contract to study the merits of solid versus liquid rocket engines in July 1961. The study concluded that liquid propellants would be superior for the large boosters envisioned.

Even before the Dyna-Soar was canceled, George Stoner was named to head the Saturn proposal, reporting to Lysle Wood, head of the big and growing Aerospace Division. Wood had risen rapidly since beginning his Boeing career after graduating from Montana State College in 1926.

Saturn-Apollo *Moon Rocket*—1967

Producing a thrust of 7.5 million pounds, the 36-story Apollo-Saturn lifts off from Cape Kennedy on its successful first flight of November 9, 1967.

The government had an empty facility at Michoud, Louisiana, an old ordnance plant from World War II days, which NASA designated as the manufacturing center for the Saturn booster stages. The first stage would be 138 feet long and 33 feet in diameter, built entirely of aluminum alloys. No forgings had ever been made approaching the size of those needed for the Saturn. The completed boosters, too large for land transport, were scheduled to be barged to the Canaveral launch facility.

Stoner knew how difficult it was to convince personnel to pull up stakes and move, particularly to the Deep South. When the proposal team was formed, he laid down the ground rules.

"You're going to have to move down there to the southland and see that it is done," he said. "If you don't want to make that commitment, tell us now."[1]

The man Stoner picked as his assistant was Richard "Dick" Nelson, an engineering graduate of the University of Minnesota who had been project manager on BOMARC. Nelson took on the task of manufacturing the boosters at Michoud.

Dr. Wernher von Braun, outlining the requirements for the C-1 first stage booster, indicated the Advanced Saturn should be quoted on the basis of two rocket engines, but there was a possibility of going to four or more.

Sensing an opportunity to leap ahead, Stoner wanted to go big.

"I think we should recommend the biggest one we can make," he told his proposal team. "The spacecraft people will have a hard enough time getting Apollo light enough for a direct launch to the moon. Let's make their job easier."[2]

To posture the size, they checked the heaviest single piece that was being hauled by ship, train, truck, and airplane. Ship compartments were limited to 100,000 pounds, trains about the same, with trucks capable of 70,000. Air transport was also capable of nearly 100,000 pounds, and Stoner decided to aim for launching a payload in that weight range. Studies confirmed that a cluster of five engines, each with the 1.5 million pounds thrust of the Saturn

C-1, could lift 240,000 pounds into earth orbit, or 90,000 pounds to escape velocity. The five-engine cluster, with one in the center and four on the corners, made an ideal geometry. Coincidentally, the thirty-three-foot diameter tanks would just clear the roof trusses of the Michoud plant.

In response to the request for bids, a two-engined version was submitted for the Advanced Saturn, but a five-engined version was strongly recommended—and submitted as an alternate bid.

Chrysler won the C-1 competition, but the major task was still to be awarded. NASA, confident and with full presidential and congressional backing, moved rapidly.

On December 14, 1961, the Marshall Space Flight Center at Huntsville notified Boeing that they had won the contract to build twenty-four Advanced Saturn first stage boosters. A call from von Braun confirmed that NASA was going straight to the alternate proposal—the 7,500,000-pound thrust booster. It would be called *Saturn V,* capable of lifting the equivalent of a Mississippi River steamboat, fully loaded, straight up into orbit of the earth.

The appetite of NASA was unquenchable, and opportunities abounded for work related to the moon project. With BOMARC winding down, Boeing had engineering expertise that welcomed new horizons. It appeared that photographic preparations for the moon landing was still a fertile field. Perhaps a comprehensive photo-mapping was needed to assure a manned landing success.

Lysle Wood assigned Robert "Bob" Helberg, BOMARC program manager, to look into the possibilities, and make an assessment whether Boeing could win a competition.

Helberg had come to Boeing in 1935, starting on the YB-17, after graduating from the University of Washington in aeronautical engineering.

Learning that NASA was planning to request proposals for an advanced photographic spacecraft to orbit the moon, and thinking about the expertise that Boeing had gained in managing large systems during Minuteman, Helberg went to Wood with a positive recommendation. "If we can bring together the companies that have the specific technologies, I think we can win this," Helberg reported.[3]

Working with Eastman Kodak and RCA, Boeing was well along in planning before the formal request for proposal was released on August 31, 1963. The short-fused request for a lunar orbiter, with a five week turn-around for response, thus worked to Boeing's advantage.

Eastman would design the cameras for a double lens system, taking both wide-angle, and high resolution pictures, the latter capable of distinguishing features the size of a card table. RCA would design the solar panels and batteries for onboard power. A miniature computer was proposed, capable of storing 2,700 bits of information, and serving in place of the camera crew, flight crew, and laboratory crew. The ten-by-ten-by-nine-inch electronic wizard would give commands to the various pieces of equipment. In fourteen days, a minimum of 200 pictures would be taken at close range. The proposal was submitted on October 4, 1963.

Two weeks after the Dyna-Soar was canceled, Boeing was notified that they had won the *Lunar Orbiter* contract. The bid price was $80 million dollars. For that sum, on a fixed price incentive basis, Boeing would deliver five spacecraft for flight missions, plus three more for testing purposes.

Space, in spite of previous study contracts, was a vast unexplored ocean. Boeing would require hundreds of millions of dollars of specialized facilities and testing equipment, capitalization which had to be committed based on faith in the future. No less than a completely new facility was demanded. Stoner urged the construction of a single facility to house all the space oriented laboratories separately located around the plant—and to add new ones.

Lysle Wood took the plan to Bill Allen, who agreed that such a facility was an essential step in preparing for space ventures, and

Facilities for Space Testing—Kent Space Center—1965

This 50 foot-high, 39 foot-diameter vacuum chamber, largest of the 11 in the Center, is *man-rated*. Here, the Boeing designed Lunar Orbiter is being loaded into the chamber for space simulated testing.

more specifically for a Manned Orbiting Laboratory, the MOL, on which the company was bidding.

Late in 1963, Boeing acquired 320 acres of truck gardening land in the Duwamish valley south of Seattle for a space center. The first two major laboratory buildings were only a start for a facility which eventually covered most of the huge site. The main building was devoted to equipment for simulating navigating and maneuvering aspects of space flight as well as housing a space environmental chamber. The space chamber, thirty-nine feet in diameter and fifty feet high, was exceeded in size only by the NASA Goddard facility at Greenbelt, Maryland. The Boeing chamber was capable of an internal vacuum of 10^{-9}mm of mercury, simulating an altitude of 400 miles. The lunar orbiter spacecraft was placed in the chamber via a giant cover that rolled to one side.

The second building was designed to house the materials and processes staff with its nearly $3 million worth of testing and evaluation equipment, and a new microelectronics research laboratory.

Nate Krisberg, as chief of the technical staff, was given responsibility to activate the new, fully equipped microelectronics laboratory, designed to study and develop integrated semiconductor circuits, progeny of an infant science that proposed to put a complete radio set on a tiny chip of solid matter. Krisberg, a West Point graduate and retired air force colonel with a Ph.D. in nuclear physics, had joined Boeing in 1961.

Allen was quick to recognize that an entirely new manufacturing capability was necessary to produce the new devices, and he directed Lysle Wood to go out to the industry and find an expert to head up such a program.

At General Motors, Malcolm T. "Mal" Stamper, a fourteen-year veteran who had worked in its new technology center from its beginning, and was responsible for electronics manufacturing at its AC Spark Plug Division in Milwaukee, was also seeking new horizons. Stamper's name surfaced when Admiral Raborn, in charge of the Polaris missile program, mentioned his significant contributions to the new field.

Stamper was invited to Boeing and interviewed directly by Allen and his vice-president of administration and corporate secretary, James E. "Jim" Prince. They decided it was a match, and Stamper was hired in 1962. Stamper recalls that about 5,000 people, split off from several organizations, were put together to form Electronics Operations, a new unit, over he which he was named manager.[4]

Graduating from Georgia Tech in 1944, with a degree in electrical engineering, Stamper served as a naval officer during World War II. He was always a team player, harking back to his days as a guard on the Georgia Tech football squad, which played in the Orange Bowl in 1945. Prior to joining General Motors, he studied law at the University of Michigan.

Following his successful development of electronic production, Stamper was named as operations manager for the MOL proposal team.

Plant expansion continued to accelerate. During 1965, an additional $165 million was authorized, six times the average level for preceding years, and the 1966 expenditure was still higher. In the span of scarcely more than two years, plant facilities had doubled.

In May 1967, NASA selected Boeing as the Technical Integration and Evaluation (TIE) contractor for the Saturn-Apollo program. Under TIE, Boeing had the responsibility to certify that the Apollo spacecraft and launch vehicles were compatible and ready for flight. The organization consisted of slightly more than 3,000 employees, supplementing NASA and its other contractors. Before NASA pushed the buttons, Boeing was required to provide assurance of the desired result. Thus, prime responsibility for decisions in America's pioneering voyage to the moon was shared between Boeing and NASA.

In August 1966, the Boeing-built spacecraft, NASA's Lunar Orbiter I, was hurled into space and placed in orbit around the moon. A talented robot, it obediently photographed the surface, transmitting more than 400 pictures back to earth. The moon had bared its secrets, and the map was in place.

When Neil A. Armstrong and Edwin E. Aldrin, Jr., piloted their Apollo lunar module, *Eagle*, to a landing on the moon's Sea of Tranquility, on July 20, 1969, the main chapter in Boeing's space efforts was rapidly drawing to a close. The moon landing climaxed a program in which the company had been involved for nearly ten years.

Even before the astronauts landed, concern emerged over what should be the logical follow-on to the massive Apollo program.

The Lunar Rover *Moon Buggy*—1971–1972

Astronaut preparing to explore the surface of the moon in one of the two Lunar Rovers built by Boeing.

Industry presidents were invited to recommend projects which could stand the klieg lights of an increasingly restive Congress, and an administration bogged down in the Vietnam War.

Everything from the mundane of weather forecasting to the exotic of missions to Mars, was suggested. Secretly, however, a small voice in every individual whispered that the nation was on a roll, cautioning against false optimism for any major new program. Both guns and butter for America, the slogan of President Johnson, simply could not endure.

For the technological community, the decade of the sixties had received its baptism for greatness. A glorious page had been turned, and a new decade lay ahead.

1. Private Communication.
2. Ibid.
3. Ibid.
4. Malcolm T. Stamper, interview by Donald S. Schmechel, 1 November, 1986.

Malcolm T. Stamper 1925–
President 1972–1985, Vice Chairman 1985–1988.

25

The Jumbos

The Communists were on the move in Southeast Asia. In March 1961, President Kennedy authorized increasing aid to Laos, where rebel forces were attempting to overthrow the government. In neighboring Vietnam, the Viet Cong were killing more South Vietnamese every day in their drive to reunify their divided country as a monolithic Communistic nation. The area was no longer a geographical nonentity. Uneasy details splashed over the front pages of American newspapers.

The domino theory became the prevalent wisdom. One by one, all of the countries of Southeast Asia would fall to the Communists.

The U.S. Department of Defense began thinking about ways to move troops and equipment rapidly to forward areas. The idea of a super-size logistics transport was gaining force.

As director of engineering for the Airplane Division of Boeing in 1961, Maynard Pennell assigned William L. Hamilton, a young engineer and operations analyst, to study the factors involved in the movement of an entire army division by air.

Hamilton had come to Boeing in 1950, after graduating from the University of Washington with a degree in electrical engineering, and later earning a master of science degree in industrial management at MIT, as a Sloan Fellow.

"Bill, I want you to do a comprehensive job of analyzing the airlift requirements for the U.S. Armed Forces over the next couple of decades," Pennell said. Hamilton, a quiet, thoughtful man, only nodded.

"Break it down to the fundamentals," Pennell continued. "We need a rock-solid base to build from."[1]

Hamilton started from scratch, gathering about a dozen other engineers, and went to work building scale models of army vehicles to load onto the floor plan of an advanced heavy aircraft layout. Boeing had developed a computer program for simulating the loading of aircraft with military cargo.

As the analysis progressed, the team was surprised to find that army vehicles were not as dense in pounds per square foot as commonly assumed. The central consideration became the maximizing of the floor area.

Next, specific concepts were studied by Kenneth F. Holtby and his product development staff. Holtby, a mechanical engineer from CalTech and also a subsequent Sloan Fellow, had joined Boeing in 1947 on the B-47 bomber program. Working with Hamilton's group, in a dramatic departure from convention, they moved the cockpit up and over the body. The resulting configuration not only maximized the floor area on the main deck—the design allowed the entire nose of the airplane to be hinged—opening the giant maw of the fuselage.

The nature of operations—fast loading and unloading at unimproved runways in forward areas by an unarmed plane—further dictated the design parameters. With a high wing to clear the fuselage, and a low landing gear, the plane would sit close to the ground, facilitating ramp loading.

The final proposed design of over a half million pounds, looked big even in comparison to the eight-jet B-52 bombers, the largest aircraft of any type in service.

By the time the 4,272-page proposal was submitted to the air force in September 1964, Boeing engineers had been working on the concept for four years and the investment of company funds exceeded $10 million.

Originally referred to as the CX heavy logistics transport by the air force, it was officially designated the C-5A. Lockheed and Douglas were also in the competition.

By 1965, some tough questions faced Bill Allen as to where the priorities should go. In addition to the C-5A, there were two other huge programs in the hopper—both of which the company was heavily involved in—the SST and the MOL. Allen directed Harold "Hal" Haynes, vice-president of finance, to review the money problems. Haynes had to keep the company in a position to move into any one of those programs, and all three if possible, at least as far as capital was concerned.

Haynes, one of Boeing's most respected executives, served under four presidents. Sometimes referred to in both awe and respect as the great white sphinx, in deference to his shock of prematurely snow white hair, Haynes managed the financial world of the company almost from the day he arrived as assistant to the controller. Before coming to Boeing in 1954, he had been a certified accountant with Touche Ross, Inc.—company accountants—following his graduation from the University of Washington school of finance in 1948.

On August 25, 1965, MOL, the Manned Orbiting Laboratory, was awarded to Douglas. The keen disappointment at Boeing was only partially offset by the expectation that a C-5A decision would favor Boeing.

Word leaked from Washington that Boeing was receiving the highest technical rating on the C-5A, but that Lockheed was low on cost. T. Wilson, executive vice-president, expressed confidence that the cost effectiveness of the Boeing proposed design in saving military dollars in future years, would offset the higher purchase price.

An uneasy optimism prevailed. Then, on September 15, 1965, the International Machinists Union called a strike. The old sore—seniority—was opened. Boeing continued to hold that promotions—and layoffs—should be primarily based on the merit system. Mercifully, the strike only lasted eighteen days, settled by an agreement to make a joint study of the company merit rating system.

Jolting news came during the strike. The air force announced the results of the competition for the C-5A. In an emotional message over the public address system, the measured cadence of T. Wilson's voice spelled it out:

"I regret to report that Boeing has lost the C-5A competition. The award was made to Lockheed. It is an understatement to say we are disappointed; however, we are not disappointed in our people. What we learned will be applied to our other business efforts."[2]

In the early sixties, with the "military-industrial complex" under attack, President Kennedy had ordered Robert McNamara to do something about the poor image of the Defense Department, for military procurement. McNamara responded by changing the rules. The resultant philosophy could not have been conceived any better to fit the Lockheed method of operation.

Termed *Total Package Procurement* (TPP), the major innovation of the new philosophy was the requirement for each manufacturer to present a single bid for the entire program. The bid must not only include research and development, but the production phase as well—in short, a total price for the finished hardware.

The bid for 115 planes submitted by Boeing was $2.3 billion. Douglas asked $2 billion, and Lockheed, feeling that renegotiation would be a certain option at a later date, simply presented a bid low enough to be assured of winning. Their bid was $1.9 billion, $400 million less than Boeing, and even $300 million less than the Pentagon's own estimate.

The question of whether the Lockheed bid was realistic, which was McNamara's criterion on the TFX competition, did not emerge. TPP had become the new darling at the Pentagon.

The C-5A was to be built at the Marietta, Georgia plant. At the time, no one knew exactly how badly the program had been underbid.

There was little doubt that the award to Lockheed was a political decision, steered by Georgia's Senator Richard Russell, then chairman of the Armed Services Committee.[3] For Boeing, fat with commercial orders, the loss could be borne, but for the Georgia Marietta plant, it would be a mortal blow.

At Marietta, shortly after World War II, the C-130 Hercules troop transport, was conceived under the tutelage of Daniel "Dan" Jeremiah Haughton. A shrewd man with numbers, Haughton had majored in accounting and business administration at the University of Alabama. Starting as a systems analyst at Lockheed's Burbank headquarters in 1933, he rose rapidly, quickly coming to the attention of the Gross brothers. They spotted him as a man cut from the same cloth as themselves.

By 1949, Haughton was president of two Lockheed subsidiaries. He proved himself a capable salesman, personally covering the entire United States, all the while promising nearly impossible delivery dates and undercutting his competitors on every hand. It was an attribute which endeared him to the hearts of the Gross brothers, and indeed, continued the crystallization of the Lockheed image as a slick operator—playing the promise—and worrying about delivering the goods later.

Within a year, the Haughton-managed subsidiaries were in the black, and Dan Haughton was on his way to the top. In 1952, he was rewarded with the presidency of the Marietta operation.

The Hercules was a well designed airplane, admirably suited to the task for which it was intended. After the Korean War was over, the air force continued to back the project, even though the prototype had not yet made its first flight.

This happy scenario presented only one problem, and it was major. In order to win contracts, Lockheed had practically patented their tactic of promising impossible delivery dates, with unrealistic costs, a practice referred to as "buying in." Pure Haughton. With his Alabama-inherited, plain-as-hominy-grits manner, he charmed his way to signed contracts, sometimes on not much more than pure personality.

As the Hercules cost overrun quicksand began to close around him, Haughton cast his eyes on even bigger prizes to bail out the failing program. With the breakeven point moving into the future, he had to find a formula to sell more and more airplanes. He not only succeeded, but made an estimated $300 million in profit to Lockheed on sales of 1,400 of the C-130s to thirty-seven countries.

What Boulton termed the "Grease Machine,"[4] worked in many modes, but the result was always to get cash into the hands of middlemen.

In Indonesia, generous contributions were being made to a widows and orphans fund, front for a consultant who assigned the money to the head of the Indonesian Air Force.

Marketing expenses, which in Japan grew to proportions alarming even to Lockheed's accountants, had been receipted simply as: "received one hundred peanuts," or received a number of "pieces." Peanuts and pieces represented $3,300 each.[5]

In the Netherlands, the connection was to Prince Bernhard himself; in West Germany, to the Defense Minister, Franz Josef Strauss.

In the case of the F-104 Starfighter, an advanced interceptor developed after the Korean War, the multi-modified plane met virtually none of the air force's original specifications, and was canceled after the delivery of 170 machines. That left Lockheed with 2,830 planes short of it minimum target of 3,000 planes. Modifying the airplane still further, they went after the export market.

Robert Gross was still at the tiller, but close behind was sweet-talking Dan Haughton. Gross picked Japan as the initial target. The Japanese military had already chosen the Grumman F-11A Super Tiger, and traditionally, approval by the National Defense Council was no more than a rubber stamp.

Incredibly, Lockheed turned the decision around in Japan, selling 230 airplanes.

According to Boulton, "By the end of January, John Hull, the Lockheed salesman, had found his way to the fringe of an extraordinary underworld of fixers and string-pullers whose methods would have scandalized the embassy cocktail set, but whose value to Lockheed was to prove virtually incalculable."[6]

When the smoke had cleared, it appeared that Lockheed had subverted the political process in Japan. The details remained secret until 1975.

With victory in Japan, the next target was Western Europe. After campaigns in Germany, Belgium, and Italy that stretch the imagination, and in spite of the fact that the F-104 had earned the name of "The Flying Coffin," Lockheed sales passed 3,000 machines worldwide. However, it is doubtful that any of the overseas sales could have been accomplished without the passing of millions in questionable payments.

In 1961, Dan Haughton was named president of Lockheed, and in 1967, he became chairman.

At Boeing the booming space and missile business of the sixties was being augmented by accelerating sales of the 707 and the 727.

Vertol, too, was moving ahead aggressively on the Sea Knight and Chinook helicopters. Nevertheless, with the MOL gone, the C-5A loss created a giant spike of anxiety.

As airline traffic continued a steep rise around the world, the Europeans began talking about an airbus, and Boeing began looking into plans to stretch the 707. However, with Douglas already in the market with a stretched DC-8, the idea for a higher capacity 707 was abandoned.

The worldwide need for a larger capacity airplane seemed to be staring the company in the face.

Joe Sutter, now chief of technology, was bullish. "The happy thing is, we do have something to sell," he reported to engineering director Dick Rouzie.[7]

Whatever the new machine was, it would have to come fast. With the supersonic airplane several years in the future, the long-body DC-8s were threatening to gobble the long-range market, stopping the 707 in its tracks.

The giant C-5A aroused the imagination, but its size was intimidating for a commercial version. Not so for Ed Wells, staring in silence at pictures of the 707 in one of the early review meetings.

"If there is one thing we have learned it's that our airplanes are always too small," he said, breaking his silence. "Let's at least double it."[8]

The C-5A technology at Boeing was both wide and deep, and extensive market studies had already been completed on commercial derivatives.

Sutter was certain the elements were there. The most difficult decision was selection of body cross section. Passenger accommodation was not the main consideration, as passengers would flock to the SST—very real at the time. The goal was to produce an efficient commercial freight carrier, employing containers. The width of the container was finally chosen as the highway maximum of eight feet, and the airplane was designed for two eight-by-eight containers, side by side.

Extrapolation of historical passenger traffic growth to 1970 set the probable required capacity at about 375, and the 747 was born.

To John Yeasting, vice president of the Commercial Airplane Division, the project was a frightening one. It would take an investment of more than $500 million, dwarfing the investments on the 707, 727, and 737 combined.

Sutter maintained his confident air. "The 747 or something like it has to happen," he said.[9]

Bill Allen, secretly eager in response to the new enthusiasm in the engineering department, turned on Yeasting in his office the morning after the October 1965 board meeting.

"I woke up this morning in a cold sweat. That 747 of yours! Here I've been going all over the country saying how impossible it would be to undertake the supersonic transport without government support. This 747 will cost us half of what the SST development will cost."[10]

The time for betting the Company—which showed a net worth of $762 million[11]—was again at hand. Allen prepared for the inevitable.

Setting the stage to undertake the 747, the company tripled its authorized capital stock.

Juan Trippe was among the first to realize that the next step was perhaps not the SST after all, but rather a giant jet that would carry at least double the passenger loads of the 707s and DC-8s. A major breakthrough in jet engine design, the bypass fan, had been made, promising ample power.

When the C-5A was awarded, Trippe immediately called Gross, attempting to start negotiations for a civilian version. Gross said he had enough problems building the C-5A. Douglas was satisfied with their stretched DC-8, and not interested in a larger airplane. Trippe turned to Boeing.

On December 22, 1965, after a number of conferences among Boeing, Pratt & Whitney, and Pan American; Trippe and Allen signed a statement of their intentions. Boeing would build the 747, and Pan American would buy and operate twenty-five of the giant airplanes.

In spite of its cost—$22 million per copy—more than four times that of a 707-320, the world's airlines rushed to gain delivery positions. Including the Pan Am order, sales to fifteen airlines reached ninety-three within five months after the decision to go ahead was announced, and Boeing had a $1.8 billion commitment to produce. Both Boeing and Pan American had put their corporate existence on the line.

Problems abounded. The maximum empty weight of the airframe, pegged at 274,094 pounds in the Pan Am contract, was climbing alarmingly, and after the first year of engineering gestation, stood at 308,924 pounds, threatening a payload reduction of more than 10 percent. The only remedy was to increase the gross takeoff weight, which was raised from 550,000 to 710,000 pounds.

Engine power came into focus. A still more powerful engine was needed, requiring larger nacelles and, indeed, major modifications to the wing.

To produce such a plane in the quantities contemplated—seven airplanes a month at peak production—an assembly building, encompassing 160 million cubic feet would be required, larger in volume than any existing building in the world.

Mal Stamper was moving rapidly in the company, having been appointed as special assistant to the general manager of the Aerospace Division when Boeing lost the MOL opportunity, and his achievements at both General Motors and Boeing were not lost to head hunters. Harold Geenen, chairman of ITT, decided privately that Stamper was a man he wanted. Stamper suggested outrageous terms—which only made Geenen more determined—ultimately offering an annual salary of $100,000, and reporting directly. Stamper made a quick trip East to accept Geenen's offer. Back at

Boeing, President Allen was dismayed but not surprised—Stamper was making $28,000 a year at the time.

After a rapid assessment, Allen offered the choice of five different positions, all at vice-president level.

The offer touched a nerve somewhere in Stamper's complex makeup, and he accepted, sending his regrets to Harold Geenen. The increase in salary was only $12,000, but the new position included stock options. Thus, in June 1965, after only three years with the company, Mal Stamper became vice-president and general manager of the Boeing Turbine Division.

As Stamper recalls, Allen didn't mince words. "I want you to make our turbine division the best in the world, or get rid of it," he said.

When Stamper reported back, he told President Allen it would cost $75,000,000.

"Sell it." Allen directed.

"Who in corporate will be helping me with the selling details?"

"You're the boss, you sell it."

The board of directors approved the sale and Stamper was out of a job. Allen called him in.

"What would you like to do next?" he inquired.

"How about working on your toughest problem?"

Allen chuckled. He had observed this brilliant, impatient, decisive engineering manager at close range during the gas turbine review period. The gargantuan 747 undertaking was now in sharp focus in his mind, and he knew it would require a giant of a man to make it happen.

After thinking about his options, Allen said, "How would you like to build the world's largest airplane?"

Stamper *smarted off.* "The only airplane I ever built had rubber bands on it."

Not accustomed to nonsense, Allen reared back in his chair. "Do you want to build it or don't you?" he demanded.

Of course, Stamper jumped at the chance.

Allen pointed to an aerial photograph of Paine Field, a former World War II military base near Everett, Washington, which had nothing much to offer except a 9,000-foot, little-used runway.

"We'll need an entirely new plant adjacent to the field, to build the 747," Allen said. "I want you to take responsibility for directing the program from start-up to fleet deliveries. The first airplane has been committed to Pan Am in September 1969."

Stamper stared at the photograph. All he could see was a forest. It was January 1966.

Years later, Stamper told friends, "I haven't seen daylight since."[12]

Beginning with 780 hilly acres of undeveloped and heavily forested land in the early summer of 1966, contractors cleared and leveled 250 acres and laid a two-mile-long railroad spur with a 5.6 percent gradient to serve the factory site.

The first locomotive, pulling outsized rail cars, was moving over the new spur by November. Working around the clock, contractors completed the first increment by January 1967—a low bay manufacturing and mockup building—allowing initial occupancy by Boeing workers. The huge mockup, completed at the main plant, was immediately moved into place.

Only four months later, in May 1967, work was started on the first 747 in the main assembly building—still under construction—and by year end, with the building nearly complete, 5,000 employees were on the job.

The work force, eventually growing to 20,000, was named *The Incredibles* by Mal Stamper. "I remember escorting workers to their cars, telling them to go home, that they'd put in enough hours," he recalls. "But they'd be back in the plant before I was."[13] For himself, he recalls that he practically lived at Everett, and "probably only had Christmases off over a three-year period."[14]

The Everett 747 facility was essentially an assembly plant, with more than 65 percent of the airplane subcontracted. Only the wing and the thirty-three-foot-long forward body section, enclosing the flight deck, were manufactured in Boeing plants. This commitment to spread the work throughout the United States was maximized on the 747, a continuing Boeing tradition, beginning early in the company's history. At the time, $2.1 billion in subcontracts were in effect, shared by approximately 20,000 companies residing in all fifty States and several foreign countries.

In spite of major problems on every hand, production moved apace, and the first 747 rolled out of the Everett factory in September 1968, and flew on February 9, 1969.

Bill Allen masked his anxiety in a hearty handshake with test pilot Jack Waddell on that gray day at Paine Field, but his stark words left nothing unsaid: "Jack I hope you know The Boeing Company flies with you today."[15]

Jack Waddell was no ordinary test pilot. In the tradition of Eddie Allen, he was also an aeronautical engineer, obtaining a masters degree from Cornell University in 1952.

Waddell served as a U.S. Navy pilot in the South Pacific during World War II, and was a test pilot for North American before coming to Boeing in 1957.

Astonishing onlookers by its quietness, the plane used only half of the runway for takeoff and flew like the queen of the skies she was to become. At first flight, 196 airplanes had been sold to thirty-one airlines, and Boeing had committed to increase the production rate from seven to eight and one-half airplanes a month.

The situation for Douglas was crucial in 1966 as they attempted to configure the correct plane to challenge the 747. With sales of over $1 billion, the company reported a loss in excess of $27 million. On the verge of a financial crisis, they began exploring the possibility of a merger.

North American and General Dynamics were involved in early discussions, but the McDonnell Aircraft Company quickly moved to the fore as the most likely candidate. McDonnell, a strongly based manufacturer of military airplanes, had never built a commercial airplane. The merger of the two capabilities seemed ideal.

Talks led to terms, and on a cold, rainy morning in April 1967, the stockholders gathered at Beverly Hills to vote the Douglas Aircraft Company out of existence. Donald Douglas, Sr., then seventy-five years old, moved to semi-retirement, stepping down from chairman, and becoming a board member of the new company, the McDonnell Douglas Corporation.

The headquarters of the newly merged company was established in St. Louis, with James S. McDonnell, Jr., "Mr. Mac" as its chairman.

A relative newcomer to the community of aviation pioneers who started their own companies, Mr. Mac had become one of its giants.

Educated at Princeton University with a degree in physics, McDonnell first worked with airplanes at the Army Air Corps Flying School in 1923, where he was a test pilot. After obtaining a masters degree in aeronautical engineering at MIT, he established the McDonnell Aircraft Company in St. Louis on July 6, 1939.

McDonnell expanded quickly, devoting early efforts to subcontracting for larger manufacturers. Before the end of the war, McDonnell designed one of the earliest jet fighters for the navy, and never looking back, became one of the largest producers of jet fighters in the world. At the time of the merger, McDonnell had completed a very successful year, showing a $43 million profit on sales of just over $1 billion.

McDonnell Douglas finalized on an airplane with three engines, smaller than the 747, believing that U.S. airports would never be ready for the "jumbo" that Boeing had announced. The capacity would be in the 250-to 300-passenger range.

Lockheed, after dropping out of commercial competition when the ill-fated Electra ended production—with the C-5A safely in their pocket—was thought to have an advantage in entering the jumbo competition. Haughton, the eternal optimist, saw what appeared to be a new opportunity, and in the fall of 1967, publicly announced that Lockheed was prepared to take orders for the L-1011, also a 250-to 300-passenger capacity trijet, to be known as the Tristar. Two months later, McDonnell Douglas followed, taking orders for the DC-10.

With Boeing targeting for the global market and the longer routes, the early cutthroat competition was between McDonnell Douglas and Lockheed. For the trijets, the sale of each plane meant minus one to its competitor.

American Airlines was first to announce. The decision had been agonizingly close. There was hardly a day when there was not either a Lockheed or a McDonnell Douglas man in the head office. At the end of the evaluation, an American Airlines official called Mr. Haughton in to inform him that Lockheed had lost the order. Dan Haughton, as intensely emotional as he was loyal to Lockheed, sat down and cried.

The American Airlines order, made public on February 16, 1968, was for twenty-five airplanes, amounting to a contract price of $382 million, or about $15.3 million per plane. American also took options on twenty-five more airplanes, raising the potential of the order to over $800 million.

With his two-month sales lead having evaporated, Haughton decided to mortgage Lockeed's future a little deeper, slashing the price of each Tristar by $1 million.

By the end of March, Lockheed had orders for 118 Tristars from Eastern, Delta, and TWA. A fourth order for fifty machines by Air Holdings, Ltd., a hastily conceived consortium launched by Lockheed itself, with Rolls Royce of England as a partner, was achieved. Thus, Haughton had tightened the loyalty of Rolls, the engine manufacturer. They were in the venture together—win or lose.

The score was suddenly 168 to 25, and McDonnell Douglas gave pause to consider. David Lewis, new president of the Douglas operations, convinced Mr. Mac they had to stay in the race. To show their determination, they chopped one-half million dollars from the price of each DC-10.

On April 25, 1968, United Airlines, the largest United States customer, and last to decide, ordered sixty DC-10s.

To tighten the screws for Lockheed still further, the depth and bread of the C-5A (Galaxy) problems were becoming apparent, threatening to drag down the Tristar—and the company—with it. There was no way that Lockheed could build the airplane at the prices quoted. The Pentagon, feeling a shared responsibility, and fearful of a public outcry, quietly agreed to make progress payments before they were due.

Flying the first four airplanes off the line in an integrated plan, Boeing compressed the certification program to ten months—by far the most ambitious in aviation history.

The apparent smoothness of the certification program masked serious delays in delivery of the new JT9D series high bypass engines, powerplant for the 747s.

Those were scary times, with the massive program running well over its cost target. Nevertheless, confidence prevailed because of the integrity of the airframe, which had sustained a wing loading of 116 percent of its ultimate design load during its structural test to failure. Those results guaranteed a significant improvement in airline performance, translating to either more fuel for extended range, or an increased passenger load.

The arrival of engines in sufficient quantities in late 1969 led to the "year of the 747" in 1970. The airplane went into service for Pan Am on January 22. Twelve months later, in January 1971, the operational statistics numbed the mind. Ninety-eight 747s, flying the colors of eighteen airlines, carried seven million passengers a distance of more than 71 million miles. The 30,000 revenue flights represented 15.5 billion passenger-miles, five times that logged by the 707 at an equal point in service.

1. Private Communication.
2. Ibid.
3. Berkeley Rice, *The C-5A Scandal*, (Boston: Houghton Mifflin Co., 1971).
4. David Boulton, *The Grease Machine*, (New York: Harper & Row, 1978).
5. Ibid., 5.
6. Ibid., 44.
7. Private Communication.
8. Ibid.
9. Ibid.
10. Ibid.
11. *Annual Report*, The Boeing Company, 1965, 25.
12. Malcolm T. Stamper interview by Donald S. Schmechel, 17 October, 1986.
13. *Boeing News*, 30 September, 1988, 1.
14. Stamper/Schmechel interview, 1 November 1986.
15. Private Communication.

Thornton A. "T" Wilson 1921–
President 1968–1972, Chairman 1972–1988.

26

Disaster Averted

There were no roses for the herculean 747 efforts. In fact, storm clouds swept over the skies of the market. The unprecedented pace of delivery to the 747-hungry airlines of the world in 1969 was a harbinger of trouble ahead. The frenzied competition between the DC-10 and the L-1011 added to the over-capacity.

The heady Boeing sales of $3.3 billion in 1968, then an all-time high, faded quickly into history, as the stark realities of 1969 forced the company to bite the bullet once again—harder than ever before.

The year of 1968 also represented a climax of another sort. On April 29, President William M. Allen moved up to chairman of the board, and T. Wilson—an Allen protege—was appointed to the presidency, signalling the end of the "Allen Era."

The office of chairman had been vacant since the end of 1965, when Claire L. Egtvedt requested that his name not be submitted for reelection. Egtvedt had served continuously for forty-nine years, nurturing the ethical corporate conscience and integrity of product endowed by William E. Boeing. As president for twenty-three years, Bill Allen had carried the tradition forward to a degree unmatched in the industry. This formidable task now fell on the shoulders of T. Wilson, at what proved to be a major testing phase in the history of the company.

Employment had ballooned, averaging 142,400 in 1968, also a record. Some observers accused Boeing of becoming fat and sloppy. *Time*, looking back from a 1980 vantage point reported that Seattle's nickname for the company was "The Lazy B."[1]

The sudden downdraft in the business climate was not limited to commercial airplanes. The last phase of the moon program was being focused in Huntsville, where Boeing was busy designing the Lunar Rover. When the decade of the seventies dawned, most of the $25 billion devoted to the manned moon program had been spent. Anticipating the end, NASA announced in January that 50,000 jobs would be cut.

The SST was still a going concern, and late in 1969, Congress authorized an appropriation of $85 million for the 1970 fiscal year to continue design and construction of the two prototypes. However, the SST was not yet making a significant contribution to the employment picture—with rollout planned for late in 1972—and proponents in Congress were facing an increasingly difficult battle for funding.

On the national scene, the U.S. economy was sliding into recession. On July 12, 1970, President Nixon signed the first public employment legislation since the WPA in the 1930s, and a year later, in August, imposed a wage and price freeze.

Who knew better than the people at Boeing that change did not just happen—it had to be forced—and welcomed. The company had always embraced the Heraclitean axiom that neither man nor corporation could step into the same river twice.

Job cutting became the order of the day at Boeing in 1969. Wilson was matter-of-fact, dismissing any other notion than to overhaul the company from top to bottom. At the time, he remarked: "The logic is simple. If I don't do it, the board will bring in some ice water guy from the outside who will. I decided I might as well be the ice water guy."[2]

By far the largest entity was the Boeing Commercial Airplane Company, one of several companies in a new corporate structure created in 1961, with The Boeing Company as the headquarters operation.

Wilson called in his close friend and protege, Tex Boullioun, head of the Commercial Airplane Company. "Tex, we're not getting anywhere. I'm going to get fired in six months if we don't make some kind of a turnaround. I just want you to know there's only one guy that I know of for sure that's going to go before I do, and that's you."[3]

With Boullioun a believer, Wilson embarked on a plan to reduce employees proportionately at every level—from vice-president to floor sweeper. In 1969 alone, 25,576 persons were laid off.[4] Then in 1970, the bloodletting became a river. An additional 41,000 people hit the streets, leveling off at an average employment for the year of 79,100.[5]

The reductions in force were accompanied by reduction in plant capacity, and in 1970 alone, four million square feet were eliminated.

There was more bad news still to come. On March 23, 1971, the U.S. Senate voted to cut off all further funding for the SST. The American supersonic airplane was dead, leaving the Concorde with no competition outside of the Soviet Union.

During 1971, total employment was again drastically reduced, reaching a low of 56,300. The "Boeing Bust" had consumed the jobs of over 86,000 employees in the span of three years.

When the second Lunar Rover landed on December 11, 1972, with the Apollo 17 mission, the moon program was completed.

Seattle, and the Puget Sound region—where most of the people were employed—became a disaster area; and statewide, Washington unemployment hit 14 percent, highest in the nation. Someone placed a huge billboard sign adjacent to Interstate Highway 5, with the grim admonition: "Will the last person leaving Seattle, turn out the lights."[6]

With NASA reducing drastically, the small research contracts coming out of their laboratories began drying up, and company-funded R&D was also slashed. Indeed, the Boeing Scientific Research Laboratory was swept away in the massive layoff campaign.

The year of 1970 had been the harbinger of the role that overseas sales were destined to play in the fortunes of the company. That year, $716 million in sales of commercial airplanes to foreign carriers was booked, while not a single sale was made in the United States domestic market.

Diversification became the new watchword, with the goal of adding less cyclic—or counter-cyclic—programs to the product line. The enthusiasm for new ventures reached a crescendo in the operating units of the company, and Wilson established the Office of Corporate Business Development (OCBD), to aid in focusing these efforts.

The OCBD, a small think tank with a staff of eleven—each aimed at a specific aspect of the multiple product line—had a two-pronged charter. First, to develop a ten-year business plan, updating it annually for presentation to the Executive Council; and second, to make independent assessments of the projects being developed by the operating divisions. Incredibly, this was the first time in the company's history that such a plan had been formalized.

The diversification wave included light rail transportation, small automated people movers, commercial hydrofoils, energy systems, urban planning, service industries, waste water purification, desalination systems, and even real property development, to name only the most significant projects.

OCBD was headed by Henry K. "Bud" Hebeler, reporting directly to Wilson. Hebeler, with a masters degree in aeronautical engineering from MIT—and unlimited energy—brought a fresh outlook to the group. Having returned to MIT as a Sloan Fellow in business management in 1969, he was highly qualified to objectively view Boeing's new posture.

On September 29, 1972, William M. Allen retired after forty-seven years of association with the company. *In a company that was known for team efforts, if one were obliged to select the single most outstanding leader since William E. Boeing himself, it would have to be Bill Allen.*

T. Wilson was elevated to chairman of the board, and Mal Stamper was elected to president.

Early in 1973, with business and financial cooperation appearing to be a certain requirement for international competition, Wilson turned to Hebeler.

"Bud, we need to know more about the capabilities of the rest of the world in aerospace."[7]

The company had launched a cooperative design study with an Italian firm in 1972, initially looking at a quiet, short-haul machine, and now Wilson wanted to define and broaden the international fraction.

"Our deal with the Italians—how do we know we are teaming up with the best people—the most capable from a competitive standpoint? We need to wring that out."

Hebeler nodded. "I can get two or three guys on it right away."

"One more thing," Wilson emphasized, as Hebeler was turning away. "I want you to boil down the world—to about a dozen countries. Then we need to look more closely at the finalists."[8]

After the task force had reduced the world to twelve country-candidates, Wilson requested that numerical scores be assigned to each. Then, to spread the risk, two were chosen.

It was decided to continue with the Italians as one of the partners, even though they finished seventh in the numerical scoring. Japan came out in the top five—all bunched within four points—and was chosen as the second partner.

During 1973, a memorandum of understanding was signed between Boeing and the Japanese Civil Transport Development Corporation, calling for a one-year exploration of marketing, schedule, and financial feasibility of a joint development and production program for a new commercial jet aircraft. The agreement recognized Boeing's on-going efforts, known as the 7x7, and a proposed Japanese YX jetliner program.

With most of the economy still weak in recession, Boeing began to show signs of new health. Wilson's Draconian actions in setting the company on a *lean-and-mean* path had pulled it out of its dive. Subsequent performance testified to success. In 1969 it took 25,000 employees to turn out seven 747s per month, and by 1980, 11,000 were able to do the same job.

In May 1970, Boeing Computer Services (BCS) was incorporated as a new subsidiary of the company, and Boeing committed itself to the marketing of software. Vested with the charter to do the computing for its parent, BCS instantly became one of the three or four largest of all such companies in the United States, with a base of twenty years of experience. The new subsidiary embarked on commercial sales, and in its first seven months, signed contracts with more than 250 customers located in twenty-seven States, the District of Columbia, Canada, and Australia.

Another major business objective was achieved in July 1970, when the air force announced that Boeing had been chosen as the prime contractor for the Airborne Warning and Control System (AWACS).

Then in January 1971, the Short Range Attack Missile (SRAM), on which Boeing had invested substantial developmental funds, was ordered into production. Eventually, 1,500 SRAMs were built and deployed with the Strategic Air Command's B-52 and FB-111 fleets.

Luck and timing were on Boeing's side in 1972, when McDonnell Douglas decided to close its DC-8 production line. Mr. Mac—with continuing success in producing fighters for the air force—was reluctant to pour excessive resources into the failing Douglas Aircraft Company. He expected the DC-10 to mature to a profitable program on its own after the initial infusion of capital to kick it off. The continuation of DC-8 production was viewed as a diversion of critical resources. He reasoned that the first-generation jets would soon disappear from the sales columns.

For McDonnell Douglas, it was a regrettable decision, as demand soon began increasing for a plane to handle the long thin routes that were unprofitable for the jumbos—and the 185 passenger DC-8-62 offered a good capacity match.

Boeing was facing the tough decision of what to do with the 707 production line. With only seven airplanes added to the order books in 1971, the program was not breaking even. Thus, Mr. Mac's decision provided the incentive to keep the line in operation. A production rate of one airplane a month would turn a small profit, and there was a possibility that AWACS, utilizing a modified 707 fuselage, would grow into a sizeable program.

Subsequent events proved the significance of the DC-8/707 decisions in contributing to Boeing's growing dominance of the commercial airplane market. In the years that followed, the company sold eighty-one additional commercial 707 airplanes, a gross value of approximately $1.5 billion. Of special significance, was the acquisition of new customers. Noteworthy among those were Tarom of Rumania, the first airline customer in an Eastern Bloc nation; Iraq in Asia; Egypt and Sudan in Africa; and of extraordinary importance—The People's Republic of China, (PRC)—purchasing ten airplanes in 1972.

The PRC became a major customer for Boeing airplanes, buying 737, 747, 757, and 767 machines in subsequent years. The 707, with its proven performance, had opened the door.

In 1973, with the first five 707s delivered to the PRC, a customer-support field office was opened in Beijing—a major milestone in worldwide support, considering the country was tightly closed to the outside world. The office was one of more than sixty such offices that Boeing was maintaining around the world to support its customer airlines. Indeed, field support had matured to be viewed as one of the linchpins in the Boeing image of product integrity, contributing significantly to airline purchasing decisions.

With the DC-8-62 out of the competition, Boeing decided in 1973 to produce a 747 derivative known as the SP—for Special Performance—a smaller airplane aimed at the long thin routes. The fuselage was reduced by forty-seven feet, while retaining the identical wing and lift devices. Only the tail required modification—to accommodate for the shorter body. The airplane offered extended range, higher cruising altitude, superior takeoff and landing characteristics, lower noise, and improved fuel economy, along with the four-engine reliability which the public preferred on long flights, particularly over water.

The first SP rolled out of the factory on May 19, 1975, making its maiden flight on July 4. In the autumn of 1975, prior to its delivery to Pan American on March 15, 1976, the airplane was committed to an intensive marketing campaign. The month-long, worldwide sales demonstration tour took the 747SP to eighteen countries, including three dramatic long distance flights: New York to Tokyo, Sydney to Santiago, and Mexico City to Belgrade. Each of the flights covered some 7,000 statute miles.

The 747SP made further history when Pan American, in commemoration of its fiftieth anniversary, flew one of its planes on a record breaking flight around the world over both the North and South poles. The SP covered the 26,383 mile distance in just over fifty-four hours, making only three stops for refueling. Actual flight time was forty-eight hours and three minutes.

Commercial airplane sales, which hit a low of 97 in 1972—down from a peak of 376 in 1968—rose steadily, reaching 189 in 1974. Then after a slight dip, they grew to a new record in 1978. In that year, 461 new jet transport orders, valued at $11 billion were announced by 85 customers—more than 50 percent of them foreign.

Employment, too, had climbed steadily from the 1971 low, and in 1980, again passed the 100,000 mark, averaging 106,300 for the year.

Ten years had wrought a storybook recovery. In 1970, the company was teetering on the edge of a precipice, and by 1980 had rocketed to a record sales performance, with a backlog of over $20 billion. The turnaround had been accomplished by tough-minded management and dedicated people.

The concentrated drive for excellence paid handsome dividends in other than commercial airplanes. In 1980, the company won the fly-off competition for the Air Launched Cruise Missile (ALCM), starting a production run for some 3,400 units—the largest single air force contract since the Vietnam War.

Also in 1980, AWACS came to maturity worldwide, when Boeing signed contracts for $2.2 billion for eighteen AWACS aircraft for the North Atlantic Treaty Organization (NATO). Major contracts were also received from the army and the air force to update and improve the CH-47 helicopters, B-52s and KC-135 tankers. The B-52 bomber fleet, still a vital force after nearly thirty years in the Strategic Air Command, was scheduled to be equipped with new electronic equipment. More powerful and fuel efficient engines were being installed on KC-135s, leading to a complete retrofit of the 732 airplanes in the fleet.

However, commercial airplanes continued to capture the public interest. *Time*, which featured T. Wilson on its April 7, 1980, cover, was expansive in its salute to Boeing, citing only a few of the many praises from pleased customers.

"More than just state-of-art and solid engineering sets Boeing apart in the eyes of its customers, says Derek Davison, managing director of Britannia Airways, a small Luton, England-based charter operator that owns twenty-two Boeing 737s and plans to add three more later this year; 'In the end, a large measure of the thinking in our decision to go ahead with the 737 rested on the confidence we had in the people at Boeing. The most important thing about them is that you can trust them. They take the long view: never try to pull off a deal on information that could lead to misunderstanding. They are better salesmen because they are better professionals.'"

"Explains Donald Lloyd Jones, American Airlines senior operational vice president: 'Technically, Boeing is very competent, but so are Lockheed and McDonnell Douglas. The major distinction is the excellent sales force. They have salesmen assigned to customers who represent the customer's needs to Boeing as much as sell Boeing planes to the customers. The result is that people develop a great deal of faith that Boeing will do what it says and is leveling with them.'"[9]

T. Wilson was not resting on his laurels. His remark, "I wake up in the middle of the night and do logic problems,"[10] was a measure of his intensity.

1. *Time*, 7 April, 1980, 54.
2. Private Communication.
3. *Seattle Times*, 3 June, 1984, Pacific Section, 12.
4. *Annual Report*, The Boeing Company, 1969.
5. *Annual Report*, The Boeing Company, 1970.
6. *Seattle Post-Intelligencer*, 1 January, 1980, D11.
7. Private Communication.
8. Ibid.
9. *Time*, 7 April, 1980, 57.
10. Private Communication.

27

Bribery Overseas

"As long as Boeing builds the best airplanes, it will be sufficient. The world will recognize the superior product and buy it." Those words, credited to William M. Allen, embodied his corporate business philosophy.

Payments of any kind to middlemen were very suspect at Boeing in the early days of the commercial airplane sales campaigns. Ralph Bell, who was director of aircraft sales operations during the fifties when the battle was raging between the 707 and the DC-8, recalls, "There were two or three instances in which it was suggested that Boeing hire a local representative in Europe or South America. I was negative, and Bill Allen was adamant that we not do it."[1]

As Allen would not make payments to middlemen, neither would he accept gifts from customers. One day a beautiful handmade fly-fishing rod was delivered to him. It was from C.R. Smith, president of American Airlines. Allen returned it, explaining that a Boeing rule forbade an employee to accept a gift from a company with which Boeing did business.

Two weeks later the rod came back—addressed this time to "Miss Nancy Allen," Bill's daughter, with a note from Smith. "This is for Nancy," read the note, "and your damn company rules don't apply to her."[2]

However, in the late fifties, two Englishmen, including one former official of British Overseas Airways (BOAC), now British Airways, were hired as consultants to help sell airplanes to BOAC. Despite the reluctance of Bill Allen and those close around him, it appeared to be an increasingly necessary practice.

Early in the 707 program, selling was sometimes no more complex than writing up the order, with the airline executive coming to Boeing to sign the final papers, and airlines waiting their turn at the Seattle plant to obtain coveted final assembly positions and delivery dates.

When the initial wave of market demand was satisfied, it became necessary for the sales force to range farther afield. The intensity of the technological battle demanded a parallel effort on the sales front. New services were offered to the airlines; including traffic analyses, route feasibility studies, performance criteria for airports, runway evaluations, economic expectations, and even help in making financial arrangements. Competition increased and model derivatives proliferated.

The same morality that had served the company in the United States seemed outmoded—perhaps even an impediment to overseas sales. Many foreign accounts depended to some extent on the advice and aid of consultants. The conventional wisdom became: *when in doubt, seek help.*

Consultants were retained, and paid regular commissions, which were legitimate sales costs. Commissions were paid on a contingency basis. If there was no sale, there was no commission.

T. Wilson interceded directly on the issue of consultants, approving each one individually after a rigorous screening program. He demanded compelling reasons for retaining them, often suggesting that "maybe Boeing had too many."[3]

Some Boeing salesmen felt frustrated about the company's scruples when Boeing would not take the extra step—matching payments that they knew were being made by competitors.

Mr. Herbert Grueter, manager of Boeing's Far Eastern airplane sales between 1968 and 1973, believed that Boeing needlessly lost business by failing to fill a few outstretched hands. He cited the All Nippon decision to buy Tristars. Grueter claimed to be very aware of the payments that Lockheed was promising to the Japanese. He felt certain that one million dollars in bribes would have landed the order.[4]

In the summer of 1975, echoes of the "Lockheed Scandal" reverberated through the boardrooms of corporate America. The Securities Exchange Commission (SEC) had disclosed that Lockheed was conducting massive bribery campaigns in overseas markets, and the U.S. Senate Subcommittee on Multinational Operations, under Senator Frank Church, began hearings on their business practices.

Other U.S. firms, including all of the major aerospace companies, came under scrutiny of the Church Subcommittee, the SEC, the Federal trade Commission (FTC), and the Internal Revenue Service (IRS). Many of those companies were eventually investigated by the Justice Department as well.

Responding to the SEC accusations in the summer of 1975, after months of denial, Lockheed acknowledged "that it had made $22 million in payoffs to foreign countries since 1970 to get lucrative aircraft contracts—a practice it termed necessary to meet the competition."[5]

The Lockheed dispute took twenty-one months to resolve, and in May 1977, pursuant to a negotiated court order, a special committee of Lockheed directors filed a report specifying how the company "secretly generated as much as $38 million for questionable foreign marketing practices."[6]

The corporation was attempting to recover from huge losses incurred on the Tristar program, clinging to solvency by a slender thread. Only a few years before, they had been rescued from certain bankruptcy by a one-vote margin in the United States Senate, who approved a governmentally guaranteed loan of $250 million to keep the company afloat.

To aid in bringing his company back, Dan Haughton presided over one of the biggest bribing operations of all time. President A. Carl Kotchian acted as top salesman for the company on many occasions, jet-hopping around the world to press the flesh and wave greenbacks before uncommitted airline executives. That story is told in painful detail by David Boulton.[7]

Boulton reports that on one occasion, Kotchian holed up in a Tokyo hotel room for an excruciating seventy days, waiting to see if $3.5 million in bribes would land a crucial sale of twenty-one Tristars to All Nippon Airways—who had already taken options on DC-10s. Incredibly, he turned the sale around.

Lockheed's woes did not end with the completion of the SEC probe, they still had the Justice Department to reckon with. In mid-1979, the Lockheed Corporation pleaded guilty to having concealed payments to Japanese government officials, including a $1.8 million payment that allegedly went to the office of Kakuei Tanaka, then prime minister.[8]

Lockheed pleaded guilty to a Justice Department charge of four felony counts of wire fraud, four felony counts of having made false statements to the government, and two misdemeanor violations of customs law.[9]

When the government made its case, Haughton and Kotchian bore the brunt of the responsibility. Both of these men, forced to resign early in 1976, expressed a mixture of relief and bitterness over the episode that had consumed their careers. In commenting on Lockheed's sales practices, Kotchian remarked: "Some call it gratuities, some call them questionable payments. Some call it extortion, some call it grease. Some call it bribery. I look at these payments as necessary to sell a product."[10]

The company could not be charged with bribery because Public Law 95-213 (which became known as the Corrupt Practices Act), did not take effect until December 1977. Instead, the Justice Department accused the company of violating criminal laws in attempting to conceal payments from the Export-Import Bank (Ex-Im), a government agency that makes and guarantees loans for overseas sales—and was involved in the All Nippon transactions.

Ex-Im regulations require American firms to sign statements certifying their company has not made any unusual payments, rebates, commissions, or other fees to sell planes.

Interest quickly focused on the practices of Lockheed's main rivals—giant Boeing and its most tenacious competitor, McDonnell Douglas.

At the time, McDonnell Douglas reported that between 1970 and 1975, approximately $2.5 million in foreign fees, commissions, and consultants payments were made to promote sales of commercial aircraft.[11]

Almost three years later, the SEC filed suit in a district court in Washington, D.C., charging the St. Louis-based manufacturer of violating federal securities laws in connection with $15.6 million in payments since 1969, to secure foreign sales. They said the company failed to disclose the payments, made to government officials and airline executives.[12]

In January 1979, the SEC completed its case against McDonnell Douglas. The charge that $15.6 million in improper payments were made in fifteen countries, remained. McDonnell Douglas agreed to a negotiated settlement in which it neither admitted nor denied the allegations, but agreed to suspend such payments and to appoint a three-member investigative panel and to issue a report within six months.[13]

The special panel reported on July 20, 1980, that McDonnell Douglas had made $21.57 million in questionable payments to sales agents in eighteen countries between 1969 and 1976. The company justified its action, saying, "Company management became involved in questionable payments because of a motivation to operate the affairs of the corporation in what was perceived to be in the best interests of the shareholders and employees. Management's participation in questionable payments was reluctant and spare and occurred with the conviction the payments comported with local practice and with U.S. law."[14]

In a further action, the Justice Department indicted McDonnell Douglas, as well as four top executives, on criminal charges of mail fraud, conspiracy, and making false statements to a federal agency. This was the first time in the payments investigations, that corporate individuals had been charged with illegal practices. Trial was set for January 1981.

In a surprise move, James McDonnell, frail at eighty-one years, but still active as chairman, rejected plea bargaining and demanded a court trial. Mr. Mac, true to his straight-laced, no-nonsense, behavior, indicated he would never have condoned the sales practices of the California-based Douglas commercial airplane operations, had he been aware of them. Against the advice of both his lawyers and his doctors, he insisted that the government prosecutors proceed with their case.

"If this company that I have led, is as rotten as you say, then I want to see it in court and all McDonnell Douglas people will have to take the consequences," he told four young prosecutors.[15]

Again, as in the Lockheed case, bribery charges could not be brought, since the alleged actions had preceded the Corrupt Practices Act.

The trial was never held. Following the old man's death the same year, McDonnell Douglas took the plea bargaining path, and in September 1981, the Justice Department agreed to drop criminal charges in return for guilty pleas and payment of fines to settle the civil suit.[16]

The company pleaded guilty to charges related to payments on aircraft sales in Pakistan, Zaire, South Korea, the Phillipines, and Venezuela.

In its 1975 report to the stockholders, Boeing presented its sales practices in regard to consultants:

"The company has used sales representatives and consultants on a contingent fee basis where such arrangements appeared to be advisable for the conduct of business in the foreign countries involved. A limited number of the sales representatives and consultants held a position with their governments, but management believes none had the authority to purchase or approve the purchase of the company's products or services. All payments made with respect to foreign business have been clearly identified in the company's accounting records, and no funds have been diverted, either directly or indirectly, to so-called slush funds."[17]

A year later, after a complete review of consultant practices in foreign business transactions, T. Wilson reported:

"In August 1976, the Board of Directors approved an updated policy statement and implementation instructions relating to sales consultants, political contributions, and financial records, formalizing requirements and procedures designed to assure the company that in conducting its business it will continue at all times to be in compliance with applicable laws, and that the nature and extent of all payments made by the company with respect to foreign sales will continue to be accurately recorded in the accounts of the company."[18]

Top Boeing officials also denied any knowledge of the Lockheed payments at the time the scandal broke. Mr. James E. "Jim" Prince, a quiet, sensitive man, for many years the corporate secretary and personal confidant of both Bill Allen and T. Wilson, always cautioned against illegal action of any kind.

After receiving a law degree from Harvard, Prince had joined the Seattle law firm of Todd, Holman and Sprague, devoting most of his time to the Boeing account. Prince too, had local roots, graduating from the University of Washington in 1930 with a bachelor of arts degree. He joined Boeing full time in 1952 as vice-president for administration.

When Jim Prince was asked to comment on those payments, he shrugged, saying "We may have had some rumors, but nothing at all precise."[19]

As the SEC investigations proceeded, Boeing submitted what it termed to be a complete disclosure in July 1978. In an out-of-court settlement, the company agreed to provide details of its foreign transactions, without admitting or denying guilt, and to abide by the terms of an injunction barring it from participating in fraudulent activities or filing false reports.

Boeing revealed that it had made payments of $54 million in connection with $943 million worth of airplane sales in at least eighteen countries, which it considered to be legitimate commissions or consulting fees.[20]

• Following the settlement with the SEC, a special committee of three outside directors was created by the Boeing Board of Directors to review the company's procedures for policing questionable payments.

On February 16, 1979, the Boeing review committee of outside directors completed its task, reporting to the SEC that "The Boeing Company has made a complete disclosure of payments to foreign officials, and no further investigations are required."[21]

In spite of those findings, the Justice Department continued to pursue the case.

Although time and sensation had dulled the senses, it was no less startling when it was reported in July 1982, that Boeing had withheld certain facts concerning commissions.

Boeing pleaded guilty to the charge of concealing from the U.S. Ex-Im Bank $7.38 million in irregular commissions, paid to agents in airplane sales in Spain, Honduras, the Dominican Republic, and Lebanon. Payments in Spain and Lebanon accounted for 95 percent of the total.[22]

In spite of a clearly defined corporate policy, a few middle managers in the Boeing sales force had promoted questionable practices. Even though the preponderance of Boeing's total sales commissions were found to be legal business practices, the company was nevertheless accountable.

Adding columns of figures and citing numbers of countries in which consultants were used, sometimes improperly, does not illuminate nor focus the issue. Indeed, it is necessary to consider the total fabric of a corporation's history. There is a profound difference between isolated cases of errant judgement on the part of a few individuals on the one hand, and deliberate and enduring corporate policies on the other. Every company develops a corporate behavior according to the personalities and practices of its senior officers—indeed tracing back to the founders.

Easily overlooked when comparing total payments for commissions and consulting fees among the big three of U.S. commercial airplane manufacturers, was Boeing's dominance of the market. In the world car market in the decade of the seventies, General Motors held a 20 to 25 percent share. In the world computer market, IBM had about 30 percent. In the world market for commercial jets, Boeing had 50 to 55 percent.

But history is harsh. Omar Khayyam provides a reminder:

> *The Moving Finger writes; and having writ,*
> *Moves on: nor all thy Piety nor Wit*
> *Shall lure it back to cancel half a Line,*
> *Nor all thy Tears wash out a Word of it.*[23]

Over the centuries, governments have grappled with the problem of bribery and its twin brother, extortion, vainly trying to establish a line where legitimate fees end and illegal payments begin.

In a recent comprehensive work, Professors Jacoby, Nehemkis, and Eells of the Graduate School of Business at Columbia University, conclude that political payments are institutionalized facts of international business. They find that in almost every country in which American businessmen have ventured as investors or traders, they have encountered the phenomenon of the payoff—the practice of bribing government officials as a condition of doing business, of government employees expecting—in fact, demanding—kickbacks on contracts in pursuance of their discretionary power.[24]

In a free enterprise economy such as the United States, where sales commissions are a legal practice—indeed an essential method of stimulating competition—the difficulty arises in transplanting those practices to the overseas environment.

Latin America, Africa, and parts of Asia proved to be areas where bribery was rampant and accepted—if not officially condoned—as a part of normal business practices. It was viewed by the indigenous population as simply dealing among friends. In almost every part of the world, it had a name. In Africa, it was *cumshaw*; in the Middle East, *baksheesh*; in Korea, *chongtok*; in Trinidad, *boobol*; and in Spanish-speaking Latin America, *mordida*.

Boeing salesmen attempted to engage honest men who had legitimate contacts in places of influence, but on the other hand, felt an intense pressure to make sales.

Consultants worked as independent contractors in all respects, with no authority to obligate Boeing in any manner whatsoever. The consultant was also required to assume all expenses and pay all costs in relation to carrying out his duties, receiving no compensation whatsoever until the airplane was sold.

Many consultants worked through two or more years of one-year contracts, spending much of their time, and potentially considerably of their own money, betting on the favorable outcome of a sales campaign, only to find an empty pot at the end of the rainbow. No commissions were offered for the sale of used airplanes, which made up the total fleets of many small operators.

Reports of multimillion-dollar commissions earned by a few legitimate consultants around the world were highly publicized. Nothing was ever said about the dozens of others who never made a penny, and in some cases lost their life's savings on one wrong perception.

Although the aerospace industry was the most visible, attracting extensive media attention during the SEC probes, when the investigations were completed, a total of $412 million was reported to have been given away in questionable overseas payments by 288 United States corporations.[25]

Until the time the Lockheed scandal broke into the news, the United States regulatory agencies seemed to stand idly by, with no visible policy, taking little note of the difficult equation that was developing. This inaction gave a sense of security to Lockheed, who had already embodied bribery into its sales policy, and were forced to further excesses in order to survive as a business entity. Moreover, the lack of government regulations encouraged companies to view certain sales activities with their backs turned.

The Watergate revelations in 1972 had introduced a national concern over illegal activities in government, and the climate quickly developed into universal suspicion.

American news media, fresh from their Watergate bonanza, welcomed the revelations, exploiting and sensationalizing each new disclosure. *Time* announced on the cover of its February 23, 1976, issue: "The Big Payoff, Lockheed Scandal, Graft Around the Globe." *Newsweek* printed a special feature story. Many newspapers, including the *Washington Post* and the *New York Times*, embarked on a series of overblown editorial comments which influenced many Americans.

Not until 1977 was a law considered which specifically addressed itself to the problem of bribes. That law was drafted in the unrealistic atmosphere of suspicion that pervaded the times, and thus represented a severe overreaction. On December 19, 1977,

President Carter signed into law (Public Law 95-213), the Foreign Corrupt Practices Act of 1977.

The Act was intended to put an end to bribery overseas, imposing heavy fines and/or prison sentences of up to five years on the officers of offending companies. However, the ink was scarcely dry before many responsible people in government began to feel uncomfortable about the Act's long-range effects.

Early in 1977, even the *New York Times* concluded in an editorial that "——qualified discretion is preferable to unqualified morality. In a volatile world, the need for flexibility is great."[26]

Nowhere was the effect of the Act more dramatic than in the aerospace industry. In the early seventies, exports of aerospace hardware provided the single highest net fraction to the positive side of the United States balance of payments of any category of manufactured goods, and was second only to agricultural products on an overall basis. United States products not only lost market share as a result of the Act, but more importantly, the precious momentum built up in the decade of the sixties was seriously blunted.

Airbus Industries, the West European consortium, gained encouragement. Many European governments, already with partial or even total ownership of aircraft production facilities, began more active stimulation of trade through hidden subsidies to enhance their products in the world marketplace.

The European airplane manufacturers had no inhibitions concerning bribes, and their governments seemed unconcerned. The sales campaign in Peru in 1974 provides a graphic example of the realities of some foreign markets.

In spite of intensive sales efforts, including a costly series of demonstration flights of a 737 airplane in Peru, proving its unique performance from short, high elevation airfields, in a hot climate, AeroPeru—the national airline—announced the purchase of Fokker F-28s from the Netherlands.

Later, it was learned that the decision had been "cast in concrete" even before the 737 airplane arrived in Peru, as a result of passing *mordida* of $1.5 million on the $12 million order for three airplanes. The money was reported to have been funneled directly to the *Ministro da Aeronautica*.[27]

Many countries, particularly in Latin America and Africa, conducted the procurement of airplanes, both military and commercial, via the Ministry of Aeronautics. Ministers might change on an annual basis, the new minister appointing his own man as president of the airline. More serious still, normal business was occasionally upset by coups.

The completion of an airplane sale was the result of a two-to-five year process of incubation; route analyses, economic forecasts, financial studies, and constant technical updating. Many sales campaigns were brought to the very threshold of signing before quietly expiring as a result of a nose dive of the country's economy or a change in key personnel.

Although American airplane manufacturers are still caught in the uneven position of competing with foreign government subsidies in the case of Airbus Industries, at least the Corrupt Practices Act—in spite of its faults—provided an even field for U.S. companies to compete against one another.

1. *Wall Street Journal*, 7 May, 1976, 1.
2. *Washington*, The Evergreen State Magazine, November, 1988, 17.
3. Private Communication.
4. *Wall Street Journal*, 7 May, 1976, 1.
5. Ibid., 4 December, 1975, 1.
6. Ibid., 20 February, 1979, 13.
7. David Boulton, *The Grease Machine*, (New York: Harper & Row, 1978).
8. *New York Times*, 2 June, 1979, 29.
9. Ibid.
10. *New York Times*, 15 February, 1979, A1.

11. *Aviation Week & Space Technology*, 8 December, 1975, 15.
12. Ibid., 18 December, 1978, 18.
13. Ibid., 8 January, 1979, 25.
14. Ibid., 4 August, 1980, 21.
15. *Wall Street Journal*, 9 October, 1980.
16. *Asian Wall Street Journal*, 11 September, 1981.
17. *Annual Report*, The Boeing Company, 1975, 5.
18. *Annual Report*, The Boeing Company, 1976, 4.
19. *Wall Street Journal*, 7 May, 1976, 1.
20. *New York Times*, 16 February, 1979, D5.
21. Ibid.
22. *Wall Street Journal*, 1 July, 1982, 40.
23. *Rubaiyat of Omar Khayyam*, (London: George G. Harrap, 1940), 42.
24. N.H. Jacoby, P. Nehemkis, and R. Eells, *Bribery and Extortion in World Business*, (New York: MacMillan, 1977).
25. Charles E. Simon Company.
26. *New York Times*, 23 February, 1977, A22.
27. Private Communication.

28

The New
Technology
Twinjets

By 1978, Boeing was on a roll. Behind
was the 1977 strike by the Machinists Union—at forty-five days,
the second longest—but only the third in its history. The year set
a new record for commercial airplanes sold, when 461 orders were
booked—more than twice that of all other producers combined.

Profits of 5.9 percent of sales were the second highest in history, topping the Fortune 500 companies in total returns, and exceeded only by the 6.3 percent record established in 1941.

There were other positive factors for Boeing. Both Lockheed
and McDonnell Douglas were in trouble, with neither the Tristar

nor the DC-10 making a profit. The 747 was approaching break-even and orders were booked for eighty-three airplanes, having increased from the low of twenty-one in 1975, when the production line was running at a rate less than two airplanes per month. At the end of 1978, the line was humming along at seven—near capacity.

At year end, *Dun's Review* named Boeing as one of the five best managed United States companies, with an expansive prediction:

"It is clear that Boeing will be the only American company producing planes (McDonnell Douglas has almost officially withdrawn from the race, and Lockheed simply does not have the financial resources), and it will compete probably with just one company, the French-English Airbus Industrie."[1]

T. Wilson decided it was time to act. The new technology twinjets had been incubating longer by far than any previous commercial airplane, and no new model had appeared in the industry for ten years. Airline interest had been building for a 180-to 200-passenger airplane to take advantage of the operational economies promised by new engines, and incorporating new technologies all along the line, including materials of construction.

Exhaustive efforts to sell derivatives of the 737 and 727 had come up empty when the prime candidate, an additionally stretched version of the 727 failed the market test. Edward Beamish, senior vice-president of planning for United Airlines, after studying the proposed 727-300, told Boeing: "We looked at what it would do for earnings potential and said no, this is not what we want."[2]

Besides economies of operation, there was a wave of airline interest in improving passenger comfort, resulting in an almost universal desire for a twin aisle, wide body interior for a medium-range airplane.

Boeing studies, which included traveling mockups with various seating arrangements—which were evaluated by thousands of passengers—finalized on twin aisle, seven abreast seating at 2-3-2.

The Model 767, maturation of the 7X7 design studies, was ready for kickoff.

Nevertheless, the new airplane, as promising as it seemed to be, could not cover the total potential medium-range market. It was too large to be considered as a 727 replacement, and with 1,482 of those sold at the end of 1977, it was essential to consider that market as a separate opportunity. To replace the 727, Boeing designed the Model 757, a six abreast, single aisle airplane.

When Wilson gave the green light to the twin programs in the summer of 1978, they represented the boldest and most costly commitment in Boeing's history, nearly twice the net worth of the Company.

Forbes, in a complimentary review of some of Boeing's previous ventures, had this to say:

"Nothing in the past, though, compares with the multi-billion-dollar gamble the 757 and 767 programs represent."[3]

"T." did not consider it a gamble. "I don't agonize over that kind of a decision," he said later in an interview. "We seemed to be ready to take on something new. We had the disciplines and the organization in place that could handle that.... I don't stew and fret too much about the market. That's something over which we don't have any direct control. What I agonize over is whether we're doing a productive job on what we've got, and whether we're meeting our commitments."[4]

The threat of European competition had never been taken seriously by U.S. airplane manufacturers. Several European airplane models had made a brief entry into the United States, but soon disappeared. The French Caravelle and the British Viscount were notable examples. The British BAC-111 held out a while longer. The Concorde failed to make any sales.

However, a new energy and a new purpose began to appear in the industry of Western Europe in the early seventies. J.J. Servan-Schreiber, an impetuous Frenchman, first issued the call to arms in 1968. He abraded his European compatriots for their lack of tenacity and desire in failing to weld together a coherent regional plan to produce equipment which could compete with—and even beat the Americans. Servan-Schreiber worried that by the early eighties, the world's third greatest industrial power—after the U.S. and the Soviets, would not be Western Europe, but United States industry in Western Europe. He correctly perceived the problem not to be a torrent of American riches, but rather a more intelligent use of skills.

Servan-Schreiber challenged his countrymen in the European Economic Community (EEC) to find a way to reverse the trend. He yearned for a concerted, cooperative effort with imaginative goals that could endure. There was no paucity of ideas in the creative minds of the inventive Europeans, it was only their reluctance to turn ideas into practice, which to many was viewed as mundane and unsatisfying. Innovation was left to the ugly Americans—"a nation of tinkerers."[5]

Servan-Schreiber named a number of candidates: space, atomic energy, and supersonic airplanes. The wide acceptance of *The American Challenge*—no book in France since World War II had sold so many copies—testified to a deep-seated frustration felt by many Europeans.

When two of the EEC members, France and Great Britain, undertook the first supersonic commercial transport, they provided a modicum of an answer to the Sirvan-Schreiber challenge. However, Airbus Industries, a multinational consortium, was the first venture with a broad base of participating EEC countries. The initial product, the A300 Airbus, proved to be as good as technically planned, however, its impact as a world market contender was still viewed with skepticism by U.S. producers. In 1973, the round-the-world appearances, which included a fly-in at the First International Air Show in Brazil, were written off as last gasp efforts to bolster a sagging program. Only eleven firm orders were in hand at the end of 1974.

There was widespread concern about the cohesiveness and after-sales support of an aerospace facility that straddled several national frontiers, as Singapore Airliners assessed the A300 as late as May 1976, buying the Boeing 727 instead.

Airbus kept trying. They offered attractive financial terms. Low interest rates and no principal payments for the first year were not uncommon. The terms were backed by the host governments of the manufacturers. An industry-tested manager was hired from American Airlines to oversee the marketing campaign in the U.S. The consortium turned itself inside out to prove it was in business to stay.

The fortunes of Airbus changed abruptly in 1977 when Eastern Airlines accepted an offer too good to refuse—the lease of several A300B machines at a cost far below market. As a sweetener, free maintenance support was provided for a six-month trial period. After the trial period was over, Frank Borman, President of Eastern, was convinced. In mid-1978, he bought twenty-three of the airplanes and took options on nine more.

In actual fact, Airbus Industries provided a concession in the $778 million order—a load factor guarantee which amounted to $168 million. In effect, Eastern was compensated by Airbus for the difference in the cost of operating the 240-seat A300B and the much smaller, 170-seat 757. Airbus Industries then recovered those costs in full through a government subsidy.

Orders for the Airbus jumped to sixty-nine planes in 1978, and took off with ninety-eight in the first five months of 1979. The Eastern decision not only wedged the door open to the American market, it served notice to the rest of the world that Airbus had arrived.

When Airbus Industries announced a directly competitive airplane to the new technology Boeing 767 in mid-1978, the 211-passenger A310, the last of the doubters disappeared.

The family concept, so successfully employed by United States producers, was also offered by Airbus. The new intensity succeeded in winning over the airlines of Western Europe—previously almost exclusively American turf. By April 1979, Lufthansa, KLM, Swissair, and Air France had ordered or taken options on a total of 151 airplanes of the two models, with twenty-five other airlines in Europe and Asia ordering or taking options on an additional 210 airplanes. Notable among the latter was Singapore Airlines, who announced an order for six A300B transports with options for six more—a 180-degree reversal of its stand taken two years earlier.

The world's airlines now viewed the European technology as equivalent to the Americans, and there was no match in the financial arena. Nevertheless, Boeing still excelled in a third area—equally as crucial for a successful airline as technology and finance—customer support.

As an integral part of its concern over integrity of product, Boeing placed a high priority on following those products from the cradle to the grave.

Boeing guaranteed to put critical spare parts on board an airplane within four hours after the airline request, to be flown anywhere in the world, and even borrowed from the production line if the customer's airplane was *AOG* (Airplane on Ground). In addition, the pro forma purchase agreement provided for a full-time engineering representative, located at the airline's main base prior to delivery of the first airplane, and to remain for twelve months after the last airplane was delivered, maintaining uninterrupted technical support. In many instances, the engineering representative remained at the airline several years longer, and for large operators, the Boeing office became permanent. Many of the offices had more than one representative and included Boeing mechanics, usually with licenses in aircraft and engine maintenance.

The men in the field were charged with twin objectives: first, to assist customers to the greatest possible extent; and second, to send significant operating information back to Boeing, to assure a continuing superiority of product. By 1978, 124 representatives were located in the field, manning seventy-five bases on six continents.

In November 1970, the Boeing Commercial Airplane Company crystallized the customer support organization, with division status, appointing George D. Nible, previously manager of the 747 Division, to head it. Nible was a self made man like "Bud" Hurst and Charlie Thompson—rare in a company dominated by engineers—joining Boeing as a mechanic on the B-17 in 1941. After service in the navy during World War II, he rejoined Boeing in 1948, and two years later became a supervisor in flight operations.

The new organization reported directly to the executive vice-president. In 1979, the flight operations personnel were included. When Customer Support celebrated its fiftieth anniversary in September, 1986, the organization had nearly 2,800 people.

On July 14, 1978, United Airlines committed $1.2 billion for thirty 767s, still a "paper airplane," and a week later, T. Wilson ordered it into production. In November, American and Delta ordered the 767, bringing total orders to eighty, and TWA followed with ten a month later. The airplane sold faster than any previous model, with 135 orders on the books within a year; the three largest Canadian trunk carriers, and All Nippon adding to the four U. S. carriers.

Orders for the 757 were slow, with British Airways and Eastern Airlines contracting for a total of eighty-two firm orders and options.

"Upon those that step into the same rivers different and different waters flow.... It scatters and...gathers...it comes together and flows away...approaches and departs.

"All things are in process and nothing stays still...."[6]

If Boeing had learned one thing as it approached the promise of the eighties, it was that change was constant.

In Asia, the sleeping giant was awakening. On January 31, 1979, President Jimmy Carter and Deng Xiao Ping, Deputy Prime Minister of the PRC, signed agreements to normalize the relations between the two countries. Resumption of diplomatic relations ended three decades of estrangement of old friends. Leonard Woodcock was named as the first U.S. ambassador.

Thirteen months earlier, Boeing had announced the sale of three 747SP airplanes to the PRC, to be delivered in February 1980. The normalization became real to mainstream Americans when it was learned that Coca-Cola had contracted to build a bottling plant in Beijing. They were certain that McDonald's hamburgers could not be far behind.

On January 30, 1980, a Boeing field service office was reestablished in Beijing, having been closed in 1975 at the completion of the 707 program.

The 747SP order was one of the first steps taken by Deng in the modernization campaign to bring China into world commerce. The vast nation had been ravaged by Chairman Mao's ten-year Cultural Revolution, which debilitated an entire generation, and did not end until his death in 1976.

The significance of the 1972 decision to keep the 707 production line open was refocused by the 747SP purchase. The airplane proved to be the best ambassador that could be imagined to weld the Chinese into the Boeing family. They simply would not consider anything but Boeing planes, eventually buying a large fleet of 747s as well as the 737, 757, and 767 models, with the total sales running into billions of dollars. It was not until 1983 that the Civil Aviation Administration of China (CAAC) took delivery of its first McDonnell Douglas airplane, part of a larger program to coproduce twenty-five airplanes at the Shanghai Aircraft Factory.

In 1985, CAAC, in a herculean effort to bring modern air transportation to the far reaches of the massive country, went on a buying spree; purchasing the British BAC 146, the Russian TU-154, and the Airbus A310. By January 1990, CAAC's fleet numbered 170 planes—preponderantly Boeing—flying 300 domestic and 50 international routes. The following June, CAAC ordered thirty-six additional Boeing planes—valued at $4 billion—including 747-400s.

Models 757 & 767—1982

The new technology twins. The wide bodied, seven abreast, double aisle 767 quickly took the lead in early sales, however, the narrow bodied, six abreast, single aisle 757 overtook it in 1988.

A continuing goal of the Chinese was to modernize their own airplane manufacturing facilities, to produce a product which met all the U.S. Federal Aviation Administration requirements. To that end, in 1990, they invited both Boeing and McDonnell Douglas to compete in a major in-country manufacturing venture to produce a short-range jet to serve on China's domestic routes.

When Mr. Mac, Chairman of McDonnell Douglas, passed away in 1980, the company entered a phase of uncertainty, unmatched since the earliest years of the Douglas Aircraft Company. The investigations into questionable payments resulted in a committee of directors recommending that a majority of the board be non-management people, and the company accepted the recommendations, ending the dominance of the board by insiders.

Although the company's fighter plane business was very strong, a new commercial airplane had not been launched for ten years. The DC-10, still a long way from break-even, seemed to be a jinxed airplane. A near fatal blow came in May 1979, when an American Airlines plane lost an engine during takeoff in Chicago, killing all 273 passengers on board. The FAA promptly issued a grounding order. This was the third fatal crash involving a DC-10 in the nine years it had been production.[7]

Most damaging of all was the crash of the Turkish Airlines DC-10 near Paris, in March 1974, which was traced to a faulty design of the rear cargo door mechanism. A series of service bulletins had been released to solve the problem, which affected 135 DC-10s, flown by twenty-three carriers.[8]

The FAA had decided to ground the DC-10 fleet until modifications were completed—however, McDonnell Douglas, concerned over the loss of image and the affect on sales—persuaded the FAA to treat the modifications as routine.

Investigation revealed that the modifications had not been made to the door of the crashed Turkish airplane. More serious still was the claim by McDonnell Douglas, early in the investigation of the crash, that the modifications had been incorporated.[9] When the remains of the door were retrieved from the Paris woods, it was obvious they had not.

Accidents are no respecter of logo or origin. Indeed, the worst accident in commercial airline history was the Japan Air Lines, Boeing 747 crash on August 12, 1985, which claimed 520 lives. However, in the rare instance that workmanship or part quality was contributory, Boeing was quick to accept the responsibility. In the Japan Air Lines 747 crash, even while the investigation was continuing, Boeing agreed to share the compensation to survivors and families on a fifty-fifty basis with the airline. Boeing concurred that an incomplete repair made in error by Boeing technicians seven years earlier may have been a factor.

After the Chicago DC-10 crash, sales slowed to trickle and never again recovered. The program fell far short of breaking even. With a total of 446 airplanes sold, the last DC-10 rolled out of the Long Beach plant in November 1988.

McDonnell Douglas won the competition against a Boeing 747 tanker design for the air force with their KC-10, which helped to bridge the production line gap until a new stretched derivative of the DC-10, known as the MD-11, was ready.

The DC-9 breathed new life as the DC-9-80—a stretched version with more powerful engines—heralded a series of derivatives. After twenty DC-9-80s were leased by American Airlines in a bold new financial initiative, McDonnell Douglas leased or sold 190 units in a little more than a year. Dun's 1978 prediction of the company's demise was suddenly obsolete. In April 1983, the DC-9 designation receded into history, and the MD 80 series appeared.

Lockheed had taken some big blows. Long the largest defense contractor in the U.S., its image had been diminished by massive cost overruns on the C-5A program and a resulting $200 million write-off in 1971. Almost simultaneously, the bankruptcy of Rolls Royce caused the company to go to Washington for a $250 million bailout loan. At the same time the investigations into illegal payments were burdening the company. By 1976, Lockheed had lost the lead in defense contracting to General Dynamics, with McDonnell Douglas second, and Boeing moving to fourth from its 1970 twelfth place. By 1981, Lockheed had fallen to sixth.

On December 7, 1981, with an outlook for a continuing $150 million-a-year loss on the Tristar, the directors voted unanimously to kill the program. Lockheed's initial break-even prediction of 300 units had soared to 500—and only 244 sales were actually realized.

Taking a $400 million write-off on a plane that had lost $2.5 billion in its thirteen years of existence, Lockheed again dropped out of commercial airplane competition.[10]

Four years, one month, and five days after placing the order, United Airlines took delivery of its first 767. "It's about the most exciting day I've had the opportunity to participate in," said Richard Ferris, chief executive officer of the airline.

"Boeing promised us an airplane that would do certain things," Ferris said. "This airplane not only is on schedule, in fact, it's one day ahead of schedule, but it also has performance that exceeds the expectations of, I believe, The Boeing Company, and I know, of United Airlines."[11]

Mal Stamper, after the delivery ceremonies at which he officiated, confirmed the 767s dramatic actual performance above the design goals. "We've come up with an airplane that is better in takeoff performance, better in landing performance, has more range by some 800 miles, and has 4,600 pounds more capability in terms of carrying load, and it does it with about 8 to 10 percent more fuel efficiency.[12]

"Getting it into service, getting it under our original cost estimates and one day early—I don't know how you can improve on that. And that's due to the great team at Boeing," Stamper said.[13]

Indeed, there were many firsts, not the least of which were the twin contracts with the Italians and the Japanese, who each produced fifteen percent of the airplane in factories many thousands of miles from the assembly line in Everett, Washington.

When fatigue testing of a complete 767 airframe—first off the line—was finished, it had been put through 100,000 simulated one-hour flights. In three and one-half minutes, all segments of a typical trip were simulated: taxi out, takeoff, climb, cabin pressurization, cruise, descent, depressurization, landing and taxi in. The 100,000 flights simulated forty years of airline service.

Significantly, the equivalent of ten years of service had been completed prior to the initial revenue flight by United Airlines.

Following close on the heels of the 767 life tests, the 757 accomplished a one-upmanship performance, completing 100,001 fatigue cycles.

Sales of the new technology Boeing twins, after the large early orders, turned sluggish. In 1982, American Airlines canceled its order for fifteen 757s, citing lower earning expectations. In 1984,

Engine Size

The jet engine size grew dramatically as the airplane size increased. Here a covey of stewardesses fits into the nose cowl of a 767 engine.

the 767 booked only twenty-four sales, even dropping below the 757, which captured thirty-seven. The following year, sales for both planes sat in the doldrums; the 767 line producing only two planes a month, and the 757 outlook even bleaker, booking sales of two planes for the entire year. Break-even was nowhere in sight.

History was again proving the volatility and riskiness of the commercial airplane business. The heady predictions of 1,200 or more of each model filling the skies of the early nineties seemed very remote.

"In the aviation industry," said Mr. Wolfgang Demisch, analyst for First Boston Corporation, "you make these decisions every ten years, give or take a few. You then have to live with the consequences for the next fifty."[14]

Indeed, some industry wags were beginning to call the venture a bad decision.

1. *Dun's Review*, December, 1978, 36.
2. *Fortune*, 25 September, 1978, 46.
3. *Forbes*, 26 November, 1979, 42.
4. *Seattle Times*, 11 March, 1984, Section D.
5. J.J. Servan-Schreiber, *The American Challenge*, (New York: Atheneum, 1968).
6. Donald A. Schon, *Technology and Change*, (New York: Delacorte Press, 1967), xi.
7. *Seattle Times*, 27 May, 1979, A7.
8. John Godson, *The Rise and Fall of the DC-10*, (New York: David McKay, 1975), 174.
9. Ibid., 237.
10. *International Herald Tribune*, 21 December, 1981, 7.
11. *Boeing News*, 26 August, 1982, 1.
12. Ibid.
13. Ibid.
14. *International Herald Tribune*, 12 September 1985, 20.

Frank A. Shrontz 1931–
President 1985–1988, Chairman 1988–.

29

Challenges and Change

T he cards began to fall in a new high stakes game in the spring of 1982, when Airbus Industries bid for the lead in medium-range airplane sales. Announcing the Model A320, an all-new 150-passenger twinjet, they promised deliveries in 1988.

McDonnell Douglas, having opted to pass in 1978, was also developing a new twin—known as the Model D-3301.

Boeing had been studying a 150-passenger airplane, but the list of *unk-unks* (unknown-unknowns) was longer than ever, and the company paused to digest them. Then in March 1984—an agonizingly long wait for airline fleet planners—Boeing signed an agreement with Japan to develop a brand new competitor to the

A320. However, no announcement was forthcoming for a kickoff nor for a timetable. Boeing was playing close to the vest.

At the time, Tex Boullioun stated flatly, "The A320 is absolutely impossible economically. It's going to be tough for anybody to come up with a new, small airplane that makes any money."[1]

Setting the tone for delaying decisions by the world's airlines, Joe Sutter told the 1983 Paris Air Show attendees: "We're just sounding a note of caution for people looking at airplanes like the A320, because time marches on and technology marches on. Structures, aerodynamics, systems, and engines are constantly improving."[2]

Although T. Wilson's first love was new airplanes, he paid increasing attention to derivatives. One of the chief spokesman for wringing out all the potential of the 737 was F.A. "Frank" Shrontz, a rising star who was vice-president of sales and marketing in 1981.

On February 25, 1985—the year that the 737-300 booked its incredible sales total of 252 units—Frank Shrontz was named as president, and Mal Stamper moved up to vice-chairman, a new post created by the Boeing board of directors.

Shrontz was only the second lawyer of the eight presidents in the company's seventy-five-year history (six were engineers). A graduate of the University of Idaho College of Law in 1954, with an MBA from Harvard in 1958, he came to Boeing the same year—as a contracts coordinator. By 1967 he was assistant to the vice-president for contracts and marketing.

In 1973, Shrontz left Boeing to become Assistant Secretary of the Air Force, followed by Assistant Secretary of Defense, returning to Boeing in 1977. Those posts prepared him well for the military side of the company, which was in a rebuilding phase when he returned to Boeing in 1977 as corporate vice-president for contract administration and planning.

As president, one of the major decisions facing Shrontz was to define the nature of Boeing's business mix in a period of increasing military sales—accompanied by stiff new research and development requirements prior to contract award.

In the Boeing Aerospace Company in 1985, President Mark Miller drew up a list of five "must-win" projects: SRAM II, follow-on of the highly successful short-range air launched missile; updated avionics for the anti-submarine P-3 plane; a hard mobile launcher for small ICBMs; a remote control launching system for the ICBMs; and modules for the proposed NASA space station.

By the end of 1987 all five had been won. The NASA program included designing and building the astronauts' living quarters; the laboratory and logistics modules, as well as the node structures connecting the modules; the environmental control and life-support system; and the thermal control and audiovisual systems in the pressurized modules. This contract ensured Boeing's continued place on the space frontier, with the first elements to be launched in 1994.

Miller came to his new responsibilities with an impressive background. A mechanical engineering graduate from Oregon State University in 1948, he had been director of engineering on the Saturn V, and manager of TIE Apollo.

In 1983, Boeing won a production contract for six Inertial Upper Stages (IUS), an unmanned space tug to move satellites from the space shuttle to their final positions in orbit. The IUS was on board *Discovery* when the U.S. returned to space on September 29, 1988, thirty-two months after the tragic explosion of the *Challenger*.

Also on the military side, Boeing made a strong bid to reenter the fighter airplane field, teaming up with Lockheed and General Dynamics on an advanced machine designed to maintain U.S. superiority in the air well into the next century.

The successful development of the avionics for the B-1 bomber resulted in a similar contract for the *Stealth*, and the AWACS surveillance plane continued its success in sales to Saudi Arabia and the NATO countries.

The embryo electronics manufacturing capability originally organized by Mal Stamper had matured, and in 1985 the Boeing Electronics Company was established, with Bud Hebeler as president.

In late 1985, the Boeing High Technology Center was created as a long range, applied research facility. After the Boeing Scientific Research Laboratory experiment during the sixties, Boeing officials decided that research had to be more specifically channeled.

When the facility opened the following year, five technologies had been identified as key elements: radio frequency, microelectronics, information processing, photonics, and materials and devices— aimed at keeping Boeing on the leading edge of technical excellence. Heading the new laboratory complex was Dr. Edith W. Martin, first woman to become a Boeing vice-president. Dr. Martin had a doctorate in information and computer science from the Georgia Institute of Technology, among other credits, including graduate studies in mathematics at the Universtat Karlsruhe, Germany.

An exciting new development—the marriage of a helicopter and a turboprop—became a reality in a teaming effort with Bell when the tilt-rotor, all-composite construction, V-22 *Osprey* was rolled out in May 1988. Designed to take off like a helicopter, but offering the speed and range of a turboprop airplane, the V-22 was conceived to serve the needs of all four U.S. armed services.

In spite of new technology firsts on military and space frontiers, major focus remained on commercial airplanes. However, the next generation promised to be facing a more severe gestation period than ever before.

Scarcely three months after the Boeing-Japanese agreement was announced, Pan American ordered twenty-eight Airbus planes, including the new A320s, for more than one billion dollars.

It appeared that Airbus would run away with the future medium-range market, as Boeing continued to study the options.

Almost a year later, Boeing announced its market strategy—essentially to battle Airbus for the early market opportunities with derivatives of the 737, while taking several giant strides in technology for a future machine.

Boeing visualized major technology developments in aerodynamics, flight systems, structural materials, and propulsion, the latter promising a 60 percent improvement over the existing engines. The new darling was called the UDF, or UnDucted Fan, a design with aft-facing engines, and multiple, counter-rotating blades.

The question of whether derivatives could stop the A320 challenge began to be answered in 1986. It seemed to be no. In September, Northwest Airlines, long an exclusive customer of Boeing, surprised the commercial airplane community—signing an agreement to purchase up to 100 A320s. That decision was taken in the face of Boeing's offer of the 737-400, with comparable capacity.

To round out its stable of commercial airplanes, in January 1986, Boeing purchased de Havilland Aircraft of Canada, Ltd., from the government of Canada. Of its major products, the DHC-6 Twin Otter, the DHC-7 short takeoff and landing aircraft, and the DHC-8 commuter aircraft, the DHC-8 offered the most potential for commercial sales.

The arrangement with Japan went far beyond the subcontracting mode of the 767, involving an equity share and participation in all phases. The airplane was designated the Model 7J7 in recognition of the new partnership. A separate division in the company was formed, headed by James "Jim" Johnson, a 1965 graduate from Iowa State with a masters degree in aeronautical engineering.

Selected for the Sloan Fellowship program, he received an MBA from MIT in 1977, and was appointed to vice-president in 1987.

There were major problems to solve in the development of the UDF engine, however unbridled enthusiasm prevailed on all fronts.

The General Electric GE36 aft-mounted engine was chosen, and rigorously tested on a 727. Detailed performance documents were prepared, looking to a kickoff by several major customers by early 1988. First flight was scheduled for 1991, with certification to be completed in January 1992.

However, with key airlines unable to agree on passenger capacity, and engine growth requiring additional development, Boeing announced in mid-1987 that there would be a fifteen-month delay. Soon, engineers began to be transferred off the program. By year end the projected $3 billion program had moved back into the new project development category.

When Jim Johnson summarized the operational factors which drove the 7J7 decision, he emphasized three major items: fuel costs, capital costs, and maintenance costs.

Fuel costs—30 to 35 percent of total direct costs in 1978—had fallen to 18 percent by 1987, voiding the engine efficiency advantage. Capital costs per pound of thrust had gone up by 15 percent. Maintenance costs doubled during the nine-year period, representing almost one-third of the total direct costs in 1987.[3]

On December 31, 1987, T. Wilson retired, and Frank Shrontz succeeded him as chairman of the board. Mal Stamper remained as vice-chairman, but had not been passed over for lack of confidence. He was simply the victim of Father Time, having reached the invisible barrier of 62 years of age. Perhaps by conventional standards, Stamper also fell somewhat outside the mold of what chief executives were supposed to be. Foregoing the expected emphasis on the social set, Stamper conducted a constant crusade for conditioning, even to mountain climbing and marathon running.

As vice-chairman, he did not go on the shelf—contributing mightily to the new challenges of change.

Looking back from 1987, the banner year of 1978 paled in comparison. Sales were over $15 billion, triple that of 1978, and the backlog stood at $33 billion. The company was sitting on $3.4 billion in cash and short term investments, the 747 joined the 737 as a "cash cow," and Boeing was designing the 747-400.

In naming Boeing as the country's third most admired corporation in 1987, *Fortune* editor, Kenneth Labich, wrote:

"Boeing has always been known as a company where all the employees, no matter the color of their collar, take a serious interest and genuine pride in their work. In many ways, the loyalty and dedication of the Boeing work force has been instrumental in building the company's legendary excellence. Most people at the company with some gray in their hair turn out to have been Boeing employees for at least 30 years."[4]

Shrontz inherited a company that was the most prosperous in history. Nevertheless, earnings on sales had fallen to a worrisome 3.1 percent, down from the 1980 high of 6.4 percent. Employment had ballooned again—to 136,000 at the end of 1987.

The signs of a self-satisfied complacency were all too obvious to top management: increased absenteeism, customer complaints on quality, defective parts, missed deadlines, and a general laissez-faire feeling that prosperity was finally guaranteed. It was the kind of climate that was more difficult to address than bona fide adversity.

"You look at companies that have disappeared," said Phil Condit, executive vice-president of the Commercial Airplane Company. "What they did, they did well, but they failed to change."[5] Condit, a new star in the company, graduated from the University of California with a B.S. in mechanical engineering, and received an M.S. in aeronautical engineering from Princeton. He was an MIT Sloan fellow in 1974.

In 1985, to get the adrenaline flowing again, Stamper had hatched a new program called Operation Eagle. Its goal was no less than to change the culture of the company from the more authoritative top-down type to a more participative type.[6]

Thus, even while enjoying the most prosperous period in its history, Boeing developed a blueprint for massive change.

A company-wide program to more fully inform employees as to the company's standards of business conduct was formalized in 1985 when government contractors were subjected to intense criticism from the media and some members of Congress. Allegations of mischarging and overcharging produced legislation which increased the complexity of defense procurement. The standards were updated in 1987, after two years of working with them. Central to those standards was the company's basic ethics creed: "All Boeing employees are expected to conduct their business with the highest ethical standards and treat with fairness and integrity all employees, customers, suppliers, and associates to earn and maintain their trust."[7]

In 1988, sales exploded. Completing a fourth consecutive record year, announced orders were made for 636 commercial jet transports and 54 commuter aircraft, worth $30.1 billion. At year end, the commercial backlog stood at $46.7 billion.

There seemed to be no end to the sales tide as it rolled on into 1989. In February, All Nippon Airways placed a $3.15 billion order for twenty 747-400s—the largest order for the new queen of the air—which logged sales of 192 planes to twenty-two customers less than two months after completion of certification.

In March, the 757/767 twins began to confound the naysayers about the viability of those programs, with American Airlines announcing a $2 billion order.

Competition intensified. McDonnell Douglas, nearly written off as a producer of commercial airplanes in 1978, breathed new life. In February, American Airlines placed what was the largest single order in history—estimated at $7 billion for up to 150 airplanes, including eight firm orders and forty-two options for its MD-11, newest challenger to the 747.

Airbus landed a $3.6 billion order in March for the A320. Significantly, the order was from a U.S. carrier, Trans World Airlines.

When the GPA Group, Ltd., of Shannon, an Irish leasing firm, placed orders for 308 planes worth $17 billion in April, 59 percent—182 planes—were Boeing models. McDonnell Douglas was second with 72, and Airbus captured 54.

Only eight days after the Irish leasing order, United Airlines blasted all previous Boeing sales records into the dustbin with a $15.7 order for 370 airplanes, including options.

Success was compounded with problems. Quality began to suffer as thousands of employees worked extensive overtime.

Billed as a derivative, the -400 was in many ways a new airplane, challenging Boeing and its subcontractors all along the line. Most troublesome was the electronics system. In the face of working out the "bugs," the delivery schedule that Boeing had set for itself, proved to be unrealistic. By mid-year, deliveries were lagging almost three months, and the preponderance of the year's planned total were still ahead. The uphill battle continued to worsen.

In 1989, too, fallout accelerated from an April 1988 Aloha Airlines accident wherein the upper half of a forward fuselage section departed from a 737 airplane in flight. The subject of aging airplanes was brought dramatically to the front pages of the world's newspapers. After that accident, members of the press, who appointed themselves as instant experts, began decrying the safety of airplane structures.

With more than 5,000 Boeing jets crisscrossing the world's skies—making a landing or takeoff about a million times a month, exposure was intense. The media began trumpeting findings regarding even the smallest cracks.

Reporting reached the height of triviality in a September 1989 account of the finding by Alaska Airlines of a small crack in a door frame of a 727.[8] The principal result of the eight-inch column on the front page of the business section was to needlessly frighten the traveling public. In fact, such fatigue cracks are expected as airplanes age, and can be found by routine inspection, allowing early repair.

The Aloha accident was studied in great detail by the National Transportation Safety Board (NTSB). Thirteen months later, in May 1989, the board voted four-to-one that the accident's "probable cause" was the failure of Aloha's maintenance workers to detect the presence of significant disbonding and fatigue damage along the aluminum alloy skin of the nineteen-year-old airplane. The FAA was criticized for insufficient rigor in the enforcement of the emergency "alert" service bulletin which Boeing directed to all operators several months before.

The hearings following in the wake of the Aloha accident resulted in an FAA directive to modify older airplanes rather than to merely inspect and repair them. This development weighed heavily in accelerating the wave of orders for domestic carrier fleet modernization.

The decades-long discussion as to what was the correct lifetime for an airplane seemed to be settled. Boeing held the position that there was no structural age limit, as long as proper inspection and repair procedures were rigorously followed. Thus, the life question was thrown into the economic arena—and back to the operators— where it belonged. In the final analysis, it is the airline which must weigh the complex factors of higher maintenance costs, more extensive repairs, decreased utilization, and possible decline in image by travelers—against the cost of a newer fleet.

In the face of press criticism, Boeing's market share—rather than falling—increased. Customers appreciated the integrity which Boeing consistently built into its airplanes. Delivery positions filled rapidly—some of the firm orders for 737s in the latest United Airlines purchase were scheduled for delivery in 1995, with options extending into 1998.

The maverick year of 1989 held other surprises. An increasingly restive labor force, eyeing the billions cascading into Boeing's coffers, could scarcely wait until October 3, when their contract would expire.

In commercial airplanes, by far the largest product volume, work had become compartmentalized and routine. The *Outplant Crew* of Minuteman days, and the *Incredibles* of the early 747 program were history. Those larger-than-life challenges had been replaced by the humdrum of the production line. Wages and fringe benefits had become more sharply focused than the historic dedication to excellence of performance.

Hardly bothering to read—much less understand the company's new contract offer—more than 40,000 machinists gathered at Seattle's Kingdome, where by an 85 percent majority, they gleefully voted to strike. The holiday atmosphere was described as "controlled hysteria" in the local press.[9] At midnight, 57,000 employees, represented by Lodge 751 of the IAM, hit the bricks.

The work stoppage was the first since October 1977, and only the fourth in the history of the company. Where the 1977 strike had heavy undertones of the desire for a union shop—lost in the 1948 walkout—the 1989 strike was solely about money and mandatory overtime. Members had only received cost-of-living adjustments (COLAS), but no general raise since 1983, when they accepted one-time bonuses that did not increase base wages. They settled for bonuses again in 1986.

The strike was also a showdown for organized labor in Washington State, where Boeing was the largest private employer, setting the pace for other union contracts.

Boeing was caught by surprise at the new militance of the IAM, believing their offer of wage increases of 4, 3, and 3 percent for the three-year contract; bonuses of 8, 3, and 0 percent; COLAS of 99 percent of inflation; a reduction in mandatory overtime from 200 hours a quarter to 160; plus improved medical retirement benefits would be handily approved.

Frank Shrontz was firm. "We're not going to pay more money," was his blunt reaction.[10] The lines were drawn for a protracted strike. Boeing supervisors and non-strikers—it was estimated that only about five percent crossed the picket lines—took on the task of completing and delivering airplanes as best they could. However, delays that were attributable to the strike carried no penalties.

The union did not reveal its bottom line. Tom Baker, union president, would only say it had to be more.

Both sides settled down for a long wait. On November 4, Boeing improved its offer—which union officials promptly rejected—declining to submit it to a vote by the membership.

Shrontz indicated the strike had already caused irreparable losses to the company, after it was only three weeks old. Nevertheless, customers maintained their trust in the company and its products. On November 15, with no end in sight to the forty-three-day-old strike, Delta Airlines placed an order for 100 737-300 airplanes valued at up to $4 billion.

By mid-November, as the last of the dry leaves skittered past the pickets' feet, anxieties began to mount. Bills were piling up, and the $100 per week from the union's strike fund, which began in the third week, did not go far.

After earlier unsuccessful attempts to bring an agreement, federal mediator Doug Hammond called the parties together again on November 13. A few hours later, sensing no movement on either side, he took the unusual step of laying his own proposal on the table. After a marathon fifteen-hour session, his compromise became the basis for agreement.

On November 21, the membership voted by a 81 percent majority to go back to work, and the forty-eight-day strike, longest since 1948, came to an end.

On December 18, 1989, the day of reckoning for the SPEEA negotiations arrived, when the engineers responded with an emphatic *No!* to the company's offer for a new three-year contract. At the same time they declined to vote to strike.

In reality, not even the hungriest SPEEA engineer expected a strike vote. Engineers by nature find the idea of a union repugnant. Moreover, SPEEA, a voluntary union, had never achieved more than about a 60 percent membership level. Further, in spite of cries of low pay, they were well off, averaging $40,000 a year. Most of the problem seemed to be personal pride. With starting salaries rising in a never ending spiral, a three-year Boeing engineer would be making about the same as a new hire. Nevertheless, the relative success of the IAM in gaining wage concessions continued to draw them toward unionization.

Two months after the December *no*, the membership voted *yes* to a new contract which included larger bonuses than originally offered.

The company had been built by engineers—and management was laced with engineering graduates. Thus, although SPEEA represented some 15,000 engineers and scientists in the 28,000 bargaining unit, the company total of *degreed* engineers stood at over 19,000 in late 1989, about 12 percent of the Company's labor force.

In a thorny year, there seemed to be no respite for Boeing officials. On November 13, lawyers for the company entered a guilty plea in Federal Court in Arlington, Virginia, to two counts of conveying government property without authority. The plea bargain marked the end of a three-year federal probe into Boeing's role in what prosecutors described as widespread security violations to obtain secret Pentagon and National Security Council spending plans. Boeing agreed to pay $4 million restitution, $1 million for the cost of the investigation, and $20,000 in fines. The government property covered by the plea consisted of two documents—a Department of Defense Five-Year Defense Program Summary and Program Element Detail, and a Program Decision Memorandum.

The documents, which were used to plan funding and priority of defense programs, were brought into the Boeing Rosslyn, Virginia, office by Richard L. Fowler. Fowler was a Boeing employee from 1978 to 1986, previously a career civilian budget official for the air force.

In acknowledging that the practice was widespread, the prosecution appeared to have targeted giant Boeing to focus industry attention.

As in the mid-seventies case of illegal payments for commercial airplane sales overseas, the document activities were the province of a few less thoughtful men in middle management—in complete violation of corporate policies and practices.

When asked about the episode, Vice-Chairman Mal Stamper, in charge of the company's ethics committee, had a ready reply. "What happened here is quite simple. We have 160,000 employees. We hired one fellow a number of years back, from the air force, and when he came, he kept his connection with the air force and brought documents with him, that he said everybody does. They were secret documents, of value to him, and he thought they would be of value to the company. It was, of course, illegal, immoral, and unethical. When we found out he was doing it, we fired him."[11]

Stamper, noting that about 30 percent of Boeing's revenues came from defense business, summed the company's approach to that business:

"As one of the nation's leading aerospace contractors, we have an obligation—a moral imperative—to be above reproach. We can neither hide behind statistics nor make excuses about only a few untrustworthy people out of tens of thousands of good employees—or isolated breaches of trust out of countless legitimate actions. Our goal is to be without fault. If that takes forever, then we will work at it forever."[12]

1. *Seattle Times*, 20 March, 1984, Section D.
2. *Boeing News*, 9 June, 1983, 1.
3. Private Communication.
4. *Fortune*, 28 September, 1987, 64.
5. Private Communication.
6. M.T. Stamper interview by Donald S. Schmechel, 1 November, 1986.
7. *Annual Report*, The Boeing Company, 1985, 3.
8. *Seattle Times*, 2 September, 1989, B8.
9. Ibid., 4 October, 1989, A8.
10. Ibid., 24 October, 1989, 1.
11. M.T. Stamper interview by E. E. Bauer, 13 November, 1989.
12. M.T. Stamper, *If We Are Smart*, Speech before the National Contract Management Assn., Los Angeles, 22 July, 1988.

30

The Future

As 1989 drew to a close, the decade of the nineties appeared to be already on the books for Boeing. The factory was producing twenty-eight airplanes a month and airlines were placing orders as far in the future as the year 2001. The rate was increased to thirty-four in 1990 and plans were in place to increase again—to thirty-eight airplanes a month by mid-1991—the company's seventy-fifth anniversary year. Projections of the future market indicated that the 1990–2005 period would demand 9,935 jetliners worth $626 billion. Historically Boeing had enjoyed a 54 percent share.

"We hope to continue that trend."[1], said John Hayhurst, vice president of marketing. He was probably correct.

Yet, in an increasingly volatile world, it would be corporate suicide to consider coasting into the future. In the event of a severe economic downdraft, options would disappear overnight, and firm orders could be canceled with a modest financial penalty. Witness February 1982, when American Airlines terminated an order for fifteen 757 twinjets valued at $600 million, because of "inadequate profits and a discouraging outlook."[2]

Witness too, the consistent growth in market share for Airbus Industries. Over its corporate life, that company amortized most of the costs of developing new airplanes through government subsidies.

History has demonstrated that the only predictable aspect of the aerospace business is its unpredictability. In one of the most dramatic events of this century, on the 10th of November 1989—as the Eastern Bloc began to shed the shackles of Communism—the entire face of Europe was changed in a single day. Three months later, Aeroflot, the Soviet Union's airline giant, announced the purchase of the Airbus Industrie A310 twinjet.

At home, action quickly crystallized toward major reductions in defense spending. Boeing's complete restructuring of its non-commercial organizations only six months before were already obsolete. It was conceivable, indeed probable, that defense-oriented work could be cut in half from the 30 percent achieved in the late eighties. Making a profit on defense work was also becoming increasingly difficult—1989 showed a loss of $474 million—due to "technical, cost, and schedule problems."[3]

Boeing held the subcontracting role with Northrup for the avionics package of the Stealth (B-2) bomber, a program which was being restructured under a more critical eye in the Congress.

Selection by the air force of a prime contractor for an advanced tactical fighter, on which Boeing was teamed with Lockheed and General Dynamics—one of the two finalists—kept sliding into the future. The result of four years of intense effort, the YF-22 will enter a fly-off competition with the YF-23, developed by McDonnell Douglas and Northrup, before facing a hostile Congress for further funding. The air force and the navy,

Advanced Tactical Fighter—YF-22

Boeing teams with old rivals, General Dynamics and Lockheed, to design an
advanced fighter for the twenty-first century.

with "wish lists" of 750 and 546 machines, respectively, suddenly
found themselves searching for a mission.

Even the most promising new military airplane, the tilt-rotor,
Bell-Boeing, V-22 *Osprey*, was riding a rocky course, following a
recommendation by the Secretary of Defense for cancellation.

Tilt-Rotor V-22 *Osprey*
The Bell-Boeing vertical takeoff airplane, showing both modes of flight.

The next step for land based ICBMs, which represented one of the largest programs in Boeing's history, was more uncertain than ever.

Facing those imposing obstacles, Boeing will doubtless respond in the manner of Marshall Foch in World War I. When his armies were being pushed back by superior German forces at the second battle of Verdun, he commanded. "The situation is excellent, we attack!" History recorded the battle to be the turning point of the war.

Boeing has been taking new initiatives for seventy-five years—shrugging off program cancellations and economic downturns—always determined to produce something new. The excellence of its products is sufficient testimonial to the quality of its work force—determined to *get it right*. Consider only some of the major ones since World War II:

—*The B-52* would soon complete its fourth decade as the backbone of the nation's strategic bomber force—a primary instrument of both peace and war.

—*The 707*, with Pan American making its inaugural commercial flight in October 1958,—was still being manufactured in the nineties as the airframe for the AWACS electronic surveillance system.

—*The Minuteman*, from contract award in 1958, until the last missile was produced in 1978, consistently beat schedule and cost targets, providing the nation one of the best managed, mission-capable strategic systems in its history.

—*The 727 trijet*, kicked off in 1960—with a production run of twenty-four years—is expected to still be in service in the twenty-first century.

—*The Lunar Orbiter*,—an obedient robot, contracted to take 200 photographs of the moon—promptly sent back 400.

—*The Saturn V*—after Chrysler had won the contract for the 1,500,000-pound-thrust C-1—utilized Boeing's 7,500,000 pound-thrust-first stage, which launched the Apollo astronauts to the moon.

—*The 737*—with only a single customer, Lufthansa, in December 1967—grew into a family of airplanes. In the early nineties, the Boeing factory was building twenty-one airplanes a month, having sold nearly 3,000 machines, working against a backlog stretching into the next century.

—*The 747*—undisputed queen of the world's skies for more than twenty years—was Boeing's resolute response to defense secretary McNamara's award of the C-5 military transport to Lockheed. It would not be presumptuous to expect its derivatives to be flying for another twenty-five years.

—*The 767/757 twins* were beginning to take command of the medium-range commercial market in the face of extensive government subsidies for its Airbus Industries competitor.

Model 777—The Jumbo Twin

Artist's rendition of the Model 777, Boeing's response to the challenge of the McDonnell Douglas MD-11 and the Airbus A330.

The early sales strength of the McDonnell Douglas MD-ll was a harbinger of another round of fierce competition, which had become the hallmark of the United States commercial airplane business. In 1990, the three major engine producers; General Electric, Pratt & Whitney and Rolls Royce, offered new "superengines" with ten-foot-diameter bypass fans, capable of producing 70,000 to 95,000 pounds of thrust—a giant leap from the 45,000-to-55,000 pound thrust level of the seventies. With these new jet engines, the McDonnell Douglas strategy was simple—attack the four-engine 747 market dominance with a three-engine machine.

Boeing's response was to design an advanced twin—a completely new airplane costing $2 billion to $3 billion to develop, to exceed the performance and capacity of the MD-11. Evolving from studies of 767 derivatives, the new design became the Model 777.

The high aspect-ratio wing of the 777, increasing cruise efficiency dramatically, required innovation of another sort—how to park the wide-winged machines at the gates of existing airports. To accommodate, the Boeing design provides for the outboard twenty-one feet of the wing to fold upward. Airlines may choose this option at extra cost and weight, as an alternative to modifying or rebuilding the terminals.

The cabin size of the giant twinjet is comparable to the 747-200, accommodating 350 to 375 passengers. With the MD-11 already in production, Boeing seized the opportunity for an additional competitive advantage by designing the fuselage five inches wider—allowing ten abreast seating. Perhaps it will become known as the five-inch decision.

On October 15, 1990, United Airlines placed an order for thirty-four Model 777 airplanes, with options for an additional thirty-four and Boeing officially committed the airplane to production. The new machine will fly in 1994, with first deliveries scheduled for the following year.

Of special significance in the 777 "kickoff" order was its exclusivity—100 percent Boeing. Once again, despite a late start, the market responded to demonstrated product quality and unequalled service support. United, a market leader, saw no reason to hedge its bet.

Further in the future—to maintain control of the top of the sky—Boeing will offer an even larger 747, possibly extending the upper deck all the way back to the tail and designing a new wing—increasing capacity to 600 or more.

To improve productivity, increase capacity, and shorten flow times, Boeing invested about $1.4 billion in new equipment and facilities in 1989 alone.[4]

In spite of a McDonnell Douglas financial crunch—17,000 jobs were cut in 1990 to conserve cash—the company must go forward—or abandon the commercial airplane business. On the drawing boards is a still larger trijet, with a new wing—the MD-12X.

Airbus Industries was also hatching some new birds. Late in 1989, the consortium announced the A321—an elongated version of the successful A320 twinjet—to compete head-to-head with Boeing's 757. Airbus envisions the manufacture of 1,300 of the A321s, with first deliveries in 1994. Another new model, the 335-seat A330 twinjet was also committed to production—competing with the MD-11 and the 777. In January 1990, the backlog for all Airbus models stood at 923 airplanes, worth $51 billion.

Finance appeared to be the final arbiter in the competitive battle, with government subsidies providing Airbus the advantage in both global and U.S. domestic markets. The U.S. Commerce Department has indicated that Airbus Industries has received more than $16 billion in subsidies since its formation in 1969—to cover its consistent losses. According to one source, "The estimated $500 million loss at Airbus (1989), would be the 21st annual deficit in its 21-year history."[5]

It appears probable that some version of the unducted fan (UDF)—postponed by both Boeing and McDonnell Douglas in the eighties—will return to center stage, if not in the nineties, then soon after the turn of the century. Another oil crisis—a future economic certainty, with only the date in question—will trigger both Boeing and McDonnell Douglas to bring their UDFs out of the mothballs. Airbus will respond with their own design, and perhaps Lockheed will reenter commercial competition.

A commercial version of the tilt-rotor Osprey may very well bring the most surprises. With a current capacity of forty-to-fifty passengers, it could easily become the vehicle linking satellite *vertiports* to a series of giant airports, yet to be conceived.

A supersonic airplane, currently referred to as the HSCT—for high-speed civil transport—seems destined to become economically viable. Technological advances along many fronts, notably propulsion and materials of construction—augur well for a machine with speeds in the Mach 2.0 to Mach 2.5 range.

High Speed Civil Transport—HSCT

Artist's rendition of the Mach 2 to Mach 2.5 commercial transport, expected to be operational in 2005.

Boeing continues to study such a plane, both independently and as part of an international group. The 300-passenger plane, which could be built early in the twenty-first century, would be utilized predominantly over water, primarily the Pacific.

The 1983 production contract for Inertial Upper Stages (IUS) heralded a continuing future for Boeing in trans-space propulsion. In October 1989, an IUS, orbiting aboard the shuttle *Atlantis* launched the Galileo probe on its six-year journey to Jupiter.

The Lunar Orbiter, Lunar Rover, Saturn V, and Apollo TIE programs, all preceding the IUS, provided Boeing with a solid base for its contract to build major elements of the manned space station. Further, Boeing visualizes a space transportation system, to be operative in the next century. Although it is currently difficult to imagine how such a system would be economical, who could have predicted in 1900—the year when the zeppelin made its first flight near Friedrichshafen—that heavier-than-air machines would become one of the principal means of world transportation and commerce before the century was out?

Or, that man would have set foot on the moon and returned safely to earth?

Or, that journeys to near space would have become commonplace, and unmanned satellites would escape the solar system?

Chairman Frank Shrontz, reiterating the convictions of his predecessors, went back to basics in a special message to all Boeing employees in September 1989.

> *"The key to the future," he said, "also lies in our past. Throughout our Company's history, we have achieved success by designing and building quality products with quality service. Our plan for the future is to build on those traditional principles, not replace them."*[6]

A worthy goal—which will call to the heart of every employee—present and future—for dedication, determination and persistence—is to be chosen as the most admired corporation in the United States.

Why not?

1. *Boeing News*, 16 March, 1990, 1.
2. International Herald Tribune, 27–28 February, 1982.
3. *Annual Report*, The Boeing Company, 1989, 2.
4. Ibid.
5. *Business Week*, 18 December, 1989 47.
6. *Boeing News*, 29 September, 1989, 1.

BIBLIOGRAPHY

BOOKS

Allen, S.A. *Revolution in the Sky*. Brattleboro, Vt.: The Stephen Greene Press, 1964.

Bauer, Eugene E. *China Takes Off*. Seattle: University of Washington Press, 1986.

Boulton, David. *The Grease Machine*. New York: Harper and Row, 1978.

Bureau of Aeronautics. *Aircraft Recognition Manual*. Washington, D.C.: Departments of the Army, the Navy and the Air Force, 1959.

Cohn, E.J. Jr. *Industry in the Pacific Northwest and the Location Theory*. New York: King's Crown Press, 1954.

Collison, Thomas. *The Superfortress is Born*. New York: Sloan and Pearce. 1945.

Crouch, Tom D. *The Eagle Aloft*. Washington, D.C.: Smithsonian Institution Press. 1983.

Cunningham, Frank. *Sky Master*. Philadelphia: Dorrance and Company, 1943.

Daley, Robert. *An American Saga*. New York: Random House, 1980.

Dillon, Mary Earhart. *Wendell Willkie*. Philadelphia: J.B. Lippincott & Company, 1952.

Emme, Eugene M. *Two Hundred Years of Flight in America*. San Diego: American Astronautical Society, Univelt, Inc., 1977.

Franz, Anselm and Others. *The Jet Age*. Washington, D.C.: Smithsonian Institution Press, 1979.

General Dynamics Corporation, *Dynamic America*, New York: Doubleday.

Gibbs-Smith, C.H. *A History of Flying*. London: B.T. Batsford, 1953.

Gilbert, James. *The World's Worst Aircraft*. New York: St. Martin's Press, 1975.

Godson, John. *The Rise and Fall of the DC-10*. New York: David McKay, 1975.

Halberstam, David. *The Reckoning*. New York: Avon Books, 1987.

Hardy, M.J. *The Lockheed Constellation.* New York: Arco Publishing Company, 1973.

Hart, Ivor B. *Mechanical Investigations of Leonardo Da Vinci.* London: Chapman & Hall, 1925.

Holmes, Donald B. *Air Mail: An Illustrated History.* New York: Crown Publishers, 1981.

Horwitch, Mel. *Clipped Wings.* Cambridge: The MIT Press, 1982.

Jacoby, N.H., P. Nehemkis, and R. Eells. *Bribery and Extortion in World Business.* New York: MacMillan, 1977.

Khayyam, Omar. *Rubaiyat of Omar Khayyam.* London: George G. Harrap and Company, 1940.

Knight, Geoffrey. *Concorde: The Real Story.* New York: Stein and Day, 1978.

Mansfield, Harold. *Vision.* New York: Popular Library, 1966.

Mansfield, Harold. *Billion Dollar Battle.* New York: Arno Press, 1980.

Maynard, Crosby. *Flight Plan For Tomorrow.* Santa Monica: Douglas Aircraft Company, 1962.

McArthur, Warren. *Four Miles South of Kitty Hawk.* New York: Warren McArthur Corporation, 1943.

Monteith, Charles N. *Simple Aerodynamics and the Airplane.* Washington D.C.: Office of the Army Air Corps, 1925.

Newell, Gordon. *Ready All!* Seattle: University of Washington Press, 1987.

Rice, Berkely. *The C-5A Scandal.* Boston: Houghton Mifflin Company, 1971.

Rosen, Milton W. *The Viking Rocket Story.* New York: Harper and Brothers, 1955.

Schon, Donald A. *Technology and Change.* New York: Delacorte Press, 1967.

Schreiber, Servan, J.J. *The American Challenge.* New York: Atheneum, 1968.

Shakespeare, William. *Five Great Tragedies.* New York: Pocket Books, 1939.

Sikorsky, Igor. *The Story Of The Winged-S.* New York: Dodd, Mead, and Company, 1938.

Wagner, William. *Reuben Fleet and the Story of Consolidated Aircraft.* Falbrook, CA: Aero Publishers, 1976.

Willkie, Wendell L. *One World.* New York: Simon and Schuster, 1943.

THESES

Bauer, E.E. "Spin-Off Utilization in Research and Development," MBA Thesis, University of Washington, 1971.

Calkins, K.L. "An Analysis of Labor Relations News Coverage in the Boeing Company Paper and the Union Paper During the Strike of 1948," Master's Thesis, University of Washington, 1968.

MacDonald, A.N. "Seattle's Economic Development 1880–1910," Ph.D. Thesis, University of Washington, 1959.

REFERENCE BOOKS

Chronicle of the 20th Century. New York: Chronicle Publications, New York, 1987.

Flight: A Pictorial History of Aviation. 1953.

PERIODICALS

AVIATION WEEK & SPACE TECHNOLOGY
February 9, 1959, Page 39; December 8, 1975, Page 15; December 18, 1978, Page 18; January 8, 1979, Page 25; August 4, 1980, Page 21; November 17, 1986, Page 29; February 13, 1989, Page 16.

BOEING NEWS, THE BOEING AIRPLANE COMPANY/THE BOEING COMPANY
January 1930, Page 1; February 1933, Pages 4 and 5; April 1936, Page 12; September, 1936, Page 6; June 1937, Page 4; July 1942, Page 1; April 26, 1945, Page 5; January 24, 1946, Page 1; March 21, 1946, Page 1; April 24, 1947, Page 1; July 17, 1947, Page 1; May 6, 1948, Page 1; June 10, 1948, Page 2; June 2, 1949, Page 1; May 25, 1950, Page 1; August 11, 1960, Page 4; August 25, 1966, Page 2; November 26, 1969, Page 1; October 5, 1978, Page 3; August 26, 1982, Page 1; June 9, 1983, Page 1; April 18, 1985, Page 1; December 19, 1986, Page 1; August 7, 1987, Pages 1 and 2; September 30, 1988, Page 1; September 29, 1989, Page 1; January 6, 1989, Page D; March 16, 1990, Page 1.

BUSINESS WEEK
December 1, 1980, Page 81; December 18, 1989, Page 47.

DUN'S REVIEW
December, 1978, Page 36.

FORBES
November 26, 1979, Page 42.

FORTUNE
January, 1962, Page 65; September 25, 1978, Page 46; September 28, 1987, Page 64.

INTERNATIONAL HERALD TRIBUNE
December 21, 1981, Page 7; September 12, 1985, Page 20.

NEW YORK TIMES
February 23, 1977, Page A22; February 15, 1979, Page A1; February 16, 1979, Page D5; June 2, 1979, Page 29.

SEATTLE POST INTELLIGENCER
January 1, 1980, Page D11.

SEATTLE TIMES
May 30, 1949, Page 1; May 27, 1979, Page A7; March 11, 1984, Section D; March 20, 1984, Section D; June 3, 1984, Pacific Section, Page 12; October 20, 1987, Page D6; January 9, 1989, Page 1; September 2, 1989, Page B8; October 4, 1989, Page A8; October 24, 1989, Page 1.

TIME
March 15, 1937, Centerfold; January 18, 1943, Page 72; March 1, 1943, Page 56; July 19, 1954, Page 68; April 7, 1980, Pages 54 and 57.

WALL STREET JOURNAL
December 4, 1975, Page 1; May 7, 1976, Page 1; February 10, 1979, Page 13; October 9, 1980; September 11, 1981, Page 12; July 1, 1982, Page 40.

WASHINGTON The Evergreen State Magazine
November, 1988, Page 117.

SPECIAL REPORTS

ALIGNMENT CHECK—AIRPLANE N712PA, Internal Boeing Communication, CSPR-18, February 10, 1959.

BOEING ARCHIVES, Numerous Historical Details.

CORPORATE STATISTICS, The Boeing Company, 10-00-10, Page 1.

DC-3 DAKOTA NEWSLETTER, McDonnell Douglas, Douglas Aircraft Company, December 17, 1985.

DC-3 FEATS—FACT OR FANCY, McDonnell Douglas NEWS, December 17, 1985.

Charles E. Simon and Company Study, 1977.

M. T. Stamper Speech Before the National Contract Management Assn., Los Angeles, California, July 22, 1988.

FIRST ANNUAL REPORT TO THE STOCKHOLDERS, United Aircraft and Transport Corporation, December, 1929.

REPORT TO THE STOCKHOLDERS, The Boeing Airplane Company, 1934, Pages 5 and 6.

REPORT TO THE STOCKHOLDERS, The Boeing Airplane Company, 1942, Pages 6 and 7.

REPORT TO THE STOCKHOLDERS, The Boeing Airplane Company, 1957, Page 19.

REPORT TO THE STOCKHOLDERS, The Boeing Company, 1965, Page 25.

REPORT TO THE STOCKHOLDERS, The Boeing Company, 1975, Page 5.

REPORT TO THE STOCKHOLDERS, The Boeing Company, 1976, Page 4.

REPORTS TO THE STOCKHOLDERS, The Boeing Airplane Company/The Boeing Company, 1941-1989.

LETTERS

Boeing Letter, J.C. Foley, to Helen Holcombe, August 6, 1917.

INTERVIEWS

Bauer, E.E., with M.T. Stamper, November 13, 1989.

Schmechel, Donald S., with E.C. Wells, June 1986.

Schmechel, Donald S., with M.T. Stamper, October 17, 1986.

Schmechel, Donald S., with M.T. Stamper, November 1, 1986.

Spitzer, Paul, Boeing Archives, with Charlie Thompson.

PRIVATE COMMUNICATIONS

Countless conversations between the author and other Boeing employees, managers, and executives.

INDEX

E.E. BAUER

E.E. "Gene" Bauer joined Boeing in 1941. A two-year engineer from the University of Washington, he started as a blueprint clerk, but was soon transferred to the B-29 project. With time out for World War II, he was appointed to management in 1956, and was involved in many major military, space, and commercial programs. He sold airplanes in eleven countries, and headed the customer support offices in Brazil and China. A microcosm of the company—intertwined in his long career—he learned two foreign languages, earned two engineering degrees, and an MBA in international business, retiring in 1988.

The author's 1986 book, *China Takes Off*, received the Grand Prize in the Pacific Northwest Writer's Contest and enjoyed many favorable reviews. David Whitten, editor of the *Wall Street Review of Books*, had this to say: "The Bauer book is a work of history: social, economic, business, cultural, political, technological."

Boeing In Peace and War is all of these—with an added attribute—it bares the heart of a great American company.